Michael Kirst

The Power of Competency-Based Teacher Education

Report of the Committee on National Program Priorities in Teacher Education

Benjamin Rosner, Chairman
CITY UNIVERSITY OF NEW YORK

Saul B. Cohen
CLARK UNIVERSITY

M. Vere DeVault
UNIVERSITY OF WISCONSIN

H. Del Schalock
OREGON STATE SYSTEM OF HIGHER EDUCATION

Charles E. Stewart
DETROIT PUBLIC SCHOOLS

Richard L. Turner
INDIANA UNIVERSITY

Carol K. Tittle,
Research Associate
CITY UNIVERSITY OF NEW YORK

Allyn and Bacon, Inc.
Boston

Final Report
Project No. 1-0475
Grant No. OOEG-0-71-2849

This work has developed under a contract with/or grant from the U.S. Office of Education, Department of Health, Education and Welfare. However, the content does not necessarily reflect the position or policy of that Agency, and no official endorsement of these materials should be inferred.

Library of Congress Catalog Card Number: 72-88785

Second Printing

Contents

Preface to the First Printing v
Preface to the Amended, Second Printing ix

PART I | *Report of the Committee*

1. Rationale for Competency-Based Teacher Education and Certification 3
2. Recommendations for Competency-Based Teacher Education and Certification 23

PART II | *Papers Prepared by the Committee*

3. A Five-Year Goal for Training Complexes
   SAUL B. COHEN, *Clark University* 37
4. An Operational Plan for Program Development in Teacher Education
   M. VERE DEVAULT, *Program Design*
   MARY GOLLADAY, *Economics Analysis* 45
5. Notes on a School-University Consortium for Teacher Education
   BENJAMIN ROSNER, *City University of New York* 89
6. BEPD, NCERD, and Teacher Education that Makes a Demonstrable Difference
   H. DEL SCHALOCK, *Oregon State System of Higher Education* 100
7. Facilitating Local Options and Coordination of Programs
   CHARLES E. STEWART, *Detroit Public Schools* 170

8. Relationships Between *Teachers for the Real World* and the Elementary Models, Programmatic Themes and Mechanisms, Payoffs, Mechanisms, and Costs
RICHARD L. TURNER, *Indiana University* **174**

APPENDIX A Description of the Five Programs **211**

APPENDIX B Educational Specialty Boards
MYRON LIEBERMAN, *City University of New York* **216**

APPENDIX C The Role of the Disciplines in the Training of Teachers in the 1970s
ALAN C. PURVES, *University of Illinois* **220**

APPENDIX D Summary of the Review of Committee Papers
CAROL K. TITTLE, *City University of New York* **227**

APPENDIX E A Review of *The Power of Competency-Based Teacher Education*
STEPHEN M. BARRO, *Rand Corporation* **249**

APPENDIX F Comments on the Final Report
IVAR BERG, *Columbia University* **260**

APPENDIX G Some Remarks on the Report of the Committee on National Program Priorities in Teacher Education
ROBERT E. HERRIOTT, *Abt Associates* **265**

APPENDIX H The Power of Competency-Based Teacher Education: A Critique
MICHAEL W. KIRST, *Stanford University* **270**

APPENDIX I The Power of Competency-Based Teacher Education: Views of a Civil Rights Lawyer
WILLIAM L. ROBINSON, NAACP, *Legal Defense and Education Fund* **276**

Preface

to the First Printing

The Committee on National Program Priorities in Teacher Education was formed during March and April, 1971. The Committee included persons knowledgeable about the programs under consideration, as well as representatives from a large city school system and an urban teacher-education institution.[1]

The procedures followed by the Committee included preparation and discussion of papers by Committee members, meetings to discuss papers with Task Force '72 and Bureau of Educational Personnel Development personnel, and the circulation of abstracts of Committee papers to external critics and individuals within the Office of Education. In addition, papers on special topics were commissioned for Committee consideration.

One of the Committee's first tasks was the clarification of definitions of Protocol Materials, Training Materials, Training Complexes, Performance-Based Certification, and the Models for Elementary Teacher Education. Although major papers had been prepared for BEPD and USOE on each of these five programs,[2] the Committee

[1] M. Vere DeVault and H. Del Schalock, the Models for Elementary Teacher Education; Richard L. Turner, Protocol and Training Materials; Saul B. Cohen, Training Complexes; Charles Stewart, Detroit Public Schools; and Benjamin Rosner, City University of New York.

[2] Training Complexes: Ad Hoc National Advisory Committee on Training Complexes, *Final Report* (Clark University: Training Complex Administrative Center, July 1, 1970).

Protocol and Training Materials: B. Othanel Smith, *Teachers for the Real World* (Washington, D.C.: AACTE, 1969).

Models for Elementary Teacher Education: J. Burdin and K. Lanzillotti, eds., *A Reader's Guide to the Comprehensive Models for Preparing Elementary Teachers* (Washington, D.C.: ERIC Clearinghouse on Teacher Education and AACTE, 1969).

prepared brief working descriptions which are presented in Appendix A.

In an effort to define possible relationships among the five programs, and to present an integrated program for development in teacher education, Committee members prepared papers which were discussed at a series of meetings (March 23–24, April 15, April 26–27, and June 1–2). Revisions and additions were made by the authors based on Committee discussions. These papers appear as Chapters 3 through 8.

Critical comments were solicited from a number of individuals knowledgeable about and concerned with the problems of teacher education. This group of critics was assembled from names suggested by Committee members, as well as by BEPD staff. The individuals who commented on abstracts of the papers represented community groups, school administrators and teachers, critics of teacher education, associations for professional groups in education, and university faculty and administrators—both in education and the liberal arts. These comments were used to guide individual members of the Committee in revising their proposals and to provide a context within which to evaluate the recommendations of the Committee as a whole. The abstracts and a summary of the comments received are presented in Appendix D.

The special papers commissioned by the Committee are presented in Appendices B and C. These papers dealt with the idea of Educational Specialty Boards (Myron Lieberman) and the role of the disciplines in the training of teachers (Alan C. Purves).

The initial planning of the Committee's activities provided for the development of a cost analysis; however, time did not permit the anticipated analysis and, as a result, individual authors prepared some cost data. The main recommendations in the body of the report are accompanied by tentative cost estimates.

The Committee wishes to express its appreciation for the assistance and encouragement given by William L. Smith, Acting Associate Commissioner of the Bureau of Educational Personnel Development; and to Don Davies, Acting Deputy Commissioner for Development, who initiated Task Force '72 within BEPD and whose interest was critical to the establishment of the Committee and definition of its purpose.

The helpful criticism of B. Othanel Smith and Donald Orlosky is also appreciated, as well as the comments received from the many individuals who read and reviewed the committee program proposals.

The Committee also wishes to acknowledge the services of staff

---

Performance-Based Certification and Teacher Education: K. Massanari, "Performance-Based Teacher Education: An Annotated Bibliography." Inquiries to Dr. Karl Massanari, AACTE Associate Director, Suite 610, One Dupont Circle, Washington, D.C. 20036.

members of Educational Testing Service, who assisted the Committee by ensuring the competent administration of the project: Mrs. Peggy Bates, who initially coordinated the project; Mrs. Charlotte Farley, who was responsible for contract negotiation; and Mrs. Carol McKnight, who was responsible for exercising fiscal control for the project and who served as liaison between ETS and the Committee.

Preface
to the Amended, Second Printing

This amended second printing of the Report of the Committee on National Program Priorities in Teacher Education incorporates a series of critic papers commissioned by the Committee (Appendices E through I). On June 19, 1972, the Committee met with a number of individuals in the social sciences who were able to critique the Report and interact with the Committee in a one-day meeting to clarify both the position of the Committee and that of the critics. The critics represented major social science areas such as economics, manpower development, sociology, political science and law, as well as significant academic, research, and civil rights organizations. Discussion centered on the following papers:

A Review of "The Power of Competency-Based Teacher Education." Stephen M. Barro, Rand Corporation

Comments on the Final Report. Ivar Berg, Columbia University

Some Remarks on the Report of the Committee on National Program Priorities in Teacher Education. Robert E. Herriott, Abt Associates.

The Power of Competency-Based Teacher Education: A Critique. Michael W. Kirst, Stanford University.

The Power of Competency-Based Teacher Education: Views of a Civil Rights Lawyer. William L. Robinson, NAACP, Legal Defense and Education Fund.

The members of the Committee found the papers and discussion both informative and stimulating. In publishing the critic papers in this second printing, it is the intent of the Committee to further the level of understanding of Competency-Based Teacher Education and its relationship to systems and manpower planning, professional and legal issues affecting teacher certification, and the role of the federal government in promoting developments in Competency-Based Teacher Education and Certification.

BR
CT

PART I

Report of the Committee

CHAPTER 1

Rationale for Competency-Based Teacher Education and Certification

This section of the report presents a number of questions on the design of teacher-education programs which arose during the course of committee discussions. The answers to the questions provide a rationale for Competency-Based Teacher Education leading to the recommendations presented in the final section.

1. What criteria can be used to assess the effectiveness of teacher-education programs?

One of the most complex problems confronting teacher education is the identification of criteria by which to assess the effectiveness of trainees and teacher training programs. This complexity derives in part from philosophic considerations about the appropriateness of specific criteria for objectives of the teacher-education program, and in part from technical issues bearing on the feasibility of collecting, analyzing, and interpreting data pertinent to criteria of program effectiveness.

LEVELS OF CRITERIA

Richard L. Turner

The levels of criteria presented here are intended to make clear the points at which feedback to teacher-education programs could be generated and the points at which Performance-Based Certification could occur. These levels are applicable to all teacher-education programs which are performance and data based, such as the Elementary Models, as well as those which are oriented toward pupil outcomes.

Criterion Level 1

At the highest level, the criterion against which teachers (or teaching) might be appraised consists of two parts. The first part is observation of the acts or behaviors in which the teacher engages in the classroom. The observations must be conducted with a set of instruments which permit classification of teacher behaviors in both the cognitive and affective domains. The second part is systematic analysis of the level of outcomes achieved by the teacher with the pupils he teaches. Outcomes in both the cognitive and affective domains must be included. Because of variation in the entry behaviors of students and variations in teaching contexts, the residual outcomes in pupil behavior (the terminal behaviors corrected for entry behaviors and moderating variables) should be used as the criterion measures. To be placed at Criterion Level 1, the above two-part appraisal of teacher performance must be conducted over a relatively long period of time, probably at least two years (on a time-sampling basis), with both the observational and residual pupil behavior components assessed during each of the years. The reason for the two-year period is that both teacher and pupil behavior are open to some random fluctuation and care must be taken to obtain a sufficient sample of behavior from both sources to assure fair conclusions.

There are two principal uses to be made of the data obtained at Criterion Level 1. First, if the data are obtained during the teacher's first three years of teaching experience, they might be used to certify that the performance of the teacher is at a level to warrant relatively permanent certification. How permanent the certification might be depends on whether a cyclical pattern of certification (e.g., recertification once every ten years) becomes a socially acceptable policy or whether life certification remains as the socially acceptable policy. Second, if observational data on teachers as well as pupil performance data are included in the criterion, the *relationships* between the observed behavior of teachers and pupil performances can be utilized as general feedback to teacher-education programs. These relationships will indicate which types of teacher behavior are most likely to be influential in bringing about particular changes in pupil behavior. Teacher-education programs would thus be able to increase the amount of confidence they have in intermediate performance criteria which involve only the actions of the teacher.

Criterion Level 2

This criterion level is identical to Criterion Level 1 except that a shorter performance period is involved. Some current thinking about Performance-Based Certification, such as that in the Comfield Model,[1] appears to assume a teacher performance period of one year or less, after which initial certification might be awarded. Although a performance criterion involving the latter period of time is at a high criterial level, it is sufficiently open to error attributable to fluctuations in teacher behavior, pupil behavior, and the teaching context that it inspires considerably less confidence than does criterion performance based on wider sampling over a longer period of time.

Criterion Level 3

This criterion level differs from Criterion Levels 1 and 2 in that pupil performance data are eliminated from the criterion. Judgments about competence or proficiency are thus based on the observable behaviors of the teacher rather than on the pupil outcomes associated with these behaviors. Nonetheless, this criterion level is still performance based in the sense that the teacher actually does engage in teaching and is gauged on the quality of his professional actions. How "good" or valid this criterion level is depends almost wholly on whether empirical relationships between teacher actions and pupil performance have been established through research or through data obtained by use of Criterion Levels 1 and 2.

The degree of confidence in Criterion Level 3 lies in the upper-intermediate range. This criterion seems to yield sufficient confidence to be useful in the provisional certification of teachers. It is also highly useful in teacher-education programs since one may observe teachers to determine explicitly whether they evidence the behaviors which a particular teacher-preparatory program claims to be producing. Observation data at this criterion level provide evidence about the efficacy of the teacher-education program.

Criterion Level 4

This criterion level differs from Criterion Level 3 in that both the teaching context and the range of teacher behavior observed are restricted. The context might be a typical microteaching context involving a few pupils or even peers acting as

[1] H. D. Schalock and R. Hale, Jr., eds., *A Competency Based, Field Centered Systems Approach to Elementary Teacher Education, Vol. II.* Final Report for Project No. 89022, Bureau of Research, Office of Education, U.S. Department of Health, Education and Welfare, 1968.

students. The teacher behavior observed would be restricted to a few categories in the cognitive or in the affective domain.

This criterion lies in the intermediate range, but it inspires very modest confidence and cannot be construed as an adequate basis for Performance-Based Certification. Rather, its utility lies in providing feedback about the efficacy of particular segments of the teacher-education program and in providing diagnostic feedback to students about their own progress. It tells whether a student has acquired certain behaviors or skills and whether he can integrate these skills under specially arranged teaching conditions.

Criterion Level 5

This criterion level differs from Criterion Level 4 in that the teacher need not perform before live students (simulated students would be satisfactory). He must, however, be able to produce or show in his behavior at least one teaching skill, e.g., probing.

This criterion inspires virtually no confidence as a criterion for Performance-Based Certification, but it is very useful for providing information about the efficacy of Training Materials or subcomponents of instructional modules or of courses. Its "goodness" as a criterion depends in substantial part on the extent to which the skill being assessed can be shown to be a skill associated with pupil performance outcomes as established either by research or by use of data obtained in using the higher order criteria noted above.

Criterion Level 6

Criterion Level 6 differs from Criterion Level 5 in that the teacher need not engage in producing a performance, but rather, only show that he understands some behavior, concept, or principle germane to teaching. Within this criterion several levels of "understanding" can undoubtedly be identified. These levels of understanding can be operationalized by varying the kinds of problems the teacher is asked to respond to in accord with some type of taxonomy, such as Bloom's.[2] Like Criterion Level 5, the utility of this criterion is primarily to provide data about the efficacy of particular program components within teacher education. Similarly, its "goodness" as a criterion level depends largely on the extent to which knowledge of particular behaviors, concepts, or principles may ultimately be shown to be useful in predicting attainment of one or more of the higher criterion levels.

[2] B. S. Bloom, ed., *Taxonomy of Educational Objectives, Handbook I: Cognitive Domain* (New York: David McKay Company, 1956).

Criterion Level 6 is concerned with the effects of a training program on improvements in teacher knowledges and understandings. *Criterion Levels 5 and 4* are concerned with the effects of teacher training on improvement in pedagogic skills under laboratory or simplified training conditions. *Criterion Level 3* addresses itself to the effects of training on a teacher's behavior under actual classroom conditions. The concept of pupil change as a criterion of teacher effectiveness is introduced at *Criterion Levels 2 and 1. Criterion Level 2* is concerned with changes in pupil behavior that can be effected in a relatively short time period (one or two weeks) and under actual classroom conditions. *Criterion Level 1* is concerned with the long-range effects of teacher behavior on changes in pupil achievement and well-being.

There are fundamental differences between Criterion Levels 6 through 3, and Criterion Levels 2 and 1. Criterion Levels 6 through 3 focus directly on the impact of training on teacher behavior. Criterion Levels 2 and 1 are concerned with both the effects of training programs on teacher behavior and with the effects of teacher behavior on pupil performance.

Because teacher educators accept responsibility for the preparation of educational personnel whose performance under actual classroom conditions results in desired changes in pupil behavior, some teacher educators argue that Criterion Levels 1 and 2 are the most appropriate levels for assessing the effectiveness of training programs. (See, for example, Chapter 6 for a discussion by Schalock of the use of pupil change as the criterion for assessing the effectiveness of trainees and teacher-training programs.) The emphasis on pupil change in Criterion Levels 1 and 2, therefore, equates accountability in teacher education with school accountability. Teacher education, however, does not address itself directly to the modification of pupil behavior. It is uncertain, therefore, whether measures of school accountability are appropriate measures of the effectiveness of teacher-education programs. On the other hand, teacher education does accept responsibility for the modification of teacher behavior. Training programs should, therefore, be held accountable for changing teacher behavior.

The most appropriate criterion level for accountability in teacher education is Criterion Level 3, i.e., demonstrations of change in teacher competency under actual classroom conditions. Moreover, the evaluation of individual trainees at Criterion Level 3 provides the evidence for Competency-Based Certification at the entry and permanent certification levels.[3] The use of Criterion Level 3 to eval-

[3] See also M. V. DeVault, in Chapter 4, for a statement identifying three competency levels for certification and Turner, Chapter 8, for an extension of Performance-Based Certification to Master-Supervisory teachers.

uate the effectiveness of teacher-education programs and to evaluate the competencies of individual trainees for certification integrates the objectives of the teacher-education programs with the requirements for professional service in the classroom. It is important, therefore, that teacher education introduce evaluation procedures at Criterion Level 3 to measure the degree of mastery attained by personnel in the program. Unfortunately, few in-service or preservice programs have carefully articulated the competencies to be acquired, nor does teacher education possess the necessary instruments to measure change in specific competencies. For these reasons, evaluations of the effectiveness of programs have relied almost exclusively upon subjective appraisals of quality by students (teachers) participating in the programs. Clearly, teacher education must adopt a more rigorous approach to the definition and evaluation of its training curricula.

Although Criterion Level 3 carries the major weight in Competency-Based Teacher Education and Certification, Criterion Level 1 is the major criterion for assessing the *validity* of the competencies which comprise the teacher-education curriculum. Assessing the validity of the curriculum is a research function. In this sense, the research criterion (Criterion Level 1) monitoring the selection of teacher competencies is distinct from the accountability criterion (Criterion Level 3) monitoring the effectiveness of the training program.

2. What steps must be taken to assure the validity of teacher-education curricula?

A valid teacher-education curriculum provides for the acquisition of teacher competencies with demonstrated capacity to effect changes in pupil behavior. The validity of the teacher-education curriculum can only be established through research which relates teacher behavior to pupil behavior.

Three conditions must be present before the content of a teacher-education curriculum can be validated: (a) the training program must provide evidence of teacher growth in specified competencies; (b) the school system must provide evidence of pupil progress in the attainment of specific educational objectives; and (c) a research design must be developed to study the relationship between the two sets of measures. If either set of measures is missing, it is impossible to carry out the research essential to establish the validity of the teacher-education curriculum.

At the present time the lack of specificity about the competencies included in the teacher-education curriculum and the lack of measures to establish degrees of teacher competency preclude consideration of the relationship between the effects of teacher training and change in pupil behavior. It is essential, therefore, that teacher educators concentrate on the development of measures of teacher competency and contribute to the development of measures of school effectiveness. Unless such measures are developed, the validity of teacher-education curricula will remain unknown.

3. In the absence of studies relating teacher behavior to school effectiveness, how are the competencies that comprise teacher-education curricula to be identified?

Although the number of studies examining the relationship between teacher behavior and school effectiveness is small, some studies have been conducted and these offer a useful starting point.[4] In addition, specific concepts and skills may be identified by examining the research and theory of the behavioral and social sciences, by examining the content and skill emphases of specific school curricula, and by conducting inquiries of master teachers and teacher trainers. The important point here is that the knowledges and skills identified must be made explicit. In addition, mastery of the curriculum to a specified level of expertise must also be made explicit and confirmed with appropriate instruments.

4. Assuming the identification of a competency-based teacher-education curriculum, what conditions are necessary in order to facilitate its mastery?

Four conditions must be met in order to facilitate the acquisition of specified teacher competencies: (a) the development of measures to ascertain the degree of mastery acquired; (b) the development of instructional or training materials to guide the study and practice of particular competencies; (c) the development of opportunities to study and practice with little delay in the evaluation of performance; and (d) the development of incentives to motivate the acquisition of knowledges and skills. Each of these conditions is discussed below.

a. Measures of competency

The significance of measures of competency in the evaluation of teacher-education programs has already been discussed. In addition, the role of measures of teacher behavior in studies relating

[4] See, for example, B. Rosenshine and N. Furst, "Research on Teacher Performance Criteria," in B. O. Smith, ed., *Research in Teacher Education* (Englewood Cliffs, N.J.: Prentice-Hall, 1971).

teacher competencies to pupil performance has also been discussed. It is important to note here that measures of specific competencies must establish degrees of expertise in order to serve as standards of attainment for teachers in the program. These standards would enable both teachers and teacher trainers to determine the need for additional study or practice in order to attain specified levels of mastery. By establishing levels of expertise, measures of competency tend to motivate higher levels of performance. As incentives, as yardsticks for training, and as tools for research, measures of teacher competency are indispensable elements of the teacher-education program.

b. Instructional materials

The efficiency with which specific knowledges and skills can be acquired is a function of the effective integration of both human and material instructional resources. Teacher trainers are handicapped without instructional materials. Instructional materials can give concepts concrete meanings, they can display skills in different settings at various levels of expertise, they may be independent of the level of knowledge or level of skill of the teacher trainer, and they can be field tested to assure their utility. The development of instructional materials to facilitate the acquisition of teacher competencies is essential to an effective program of teacher education.

c. Opportunities for practice

A third condition for the development of competencies is provision for study and practice under supervision. In this regard the teacher trainer has a number of critical functions: (1) to participate with other teacher trainers in designing the teacher-education curriculum; (2) to acquire and maintain an adequate supply of instructional or training materials; (3) to acquire and maintain instructional equipment, e.g., audio-visual equipment; (4) to direct trainees to appropriate materials and equipment for the study or practice of specific knowledges and skills; (5) to provide a model for behavior; (6) to administer measures of competency in order to determine the need for additional study or practice; (7) to report to the trainee the results of systematic assessment in order to recommend additional study and practice or to recommend the acquisition of new knowledges or skills; and (8) to participate in the evaluation of teacher-education programs and the field testing of instructional materials or equipment.

The various roles of the teacher trainer clearly establish the need for a highly trained clinical instructor. Although each of the roles is important, the training and evaluation functions implied by items

4, 6, and 7 are probably the most critical for effective instruction. The need to maintain instructional materials and equipment suggests the desirability of a teacher-education laboratory. In addition, opportunities to practice at Criterion Level 3 will require access to live pupils. Obviously the teacher-training program will need to develop organizational structures and facilities to coordinate trainers, materials, equipment, pupils, and trainees. It seems reasonable to suggest that these organizational structures and facilities will have to take into account the opportunities and limitations unique to each local situation.

d. Incentives for learning

The major difference in the design of training programs for in-service and preservice teachers is the matter of incentives. Preservice teachers are motivated by the need to acquire certification in order to seek employment. In-service teachers are employed, although large numbers of in-service teachers are motivated by the need to obtain continuing or permanent certification in order to maintain their positions. The problem of motivating staff development is most acute for the majority of the nation's two million experienced teachers who require no further certification to hold their jobs. An effort must be made, therefore, to develop incentive systems for experienced educational personnel. Unless these incentive systems are developed, it is unlikely that fully certified teachers will seriously engage themselves in programs of in-service training.

5. If certification requirements are the major incentives for preservice and relatively inexperienced in-service personnel, is it possible to introduce additional certification requirements for more experienced personnel?

It is doubtful whether additional certification requirements can be introduced for senior educational personnel. Teacher unions are unlikely to agree to the introduction of additional certification procedures which would threaten the job security of the majority of their members. It is possible, however, to introduce certification which would not affect job security but which would have direct impact on senior educational personnel. Such certification would need to identify the bearer with a special expertise and entitle him to special salary increments. If experienced personnel can acquire new status and additional income through special certification as "master-level teachers" or teacher trainers, such certification would be an effective incentive for staff development.

For several reasons, new certification for master-level teachers or teacher trainers is best introduced on a national scale outside the legal framework of state certification. First, establishing special certification on a national level could be initiated immediately without modification in each state's legal certification procedures. Second, special "extralegal" status permits experimentation with Competency-Based Certification without tampering with legal certification procedures. Finally, special national certification could assure uniform standards of excellence by establishing Educational Specialty Boards to govern the certification process. These boards would consist of distinguished scholars, educators, school board members, representatives of professional teacher associations, representatives of civil rights organizations, and other prominent citizens. The development of Educational Specialty Boards would exercise great influence on the establishment of high standards of teacher competence in the public interest.[5]

6. What other incentives might be introduced?

Other incentives are clearly necessary for certified personnel who are not at the "master-level teacher" or teacher trainer level. Some effective incentives for fully certified personnel include: (a) staff development programs to meet immediate teacher needs; (b) released time for in-service training; (c) elimination or reduction of other direct training costs; (d) salary increments associated with postcertification training; and (e) introduction of group "profit sharing" for efficient or highly effective school performance, that is, "performance contracting" with in-service personnel. The elimination of pay raises, threatened salary reduction, or threatened job loss are unlikely to prove useful incentives. In periods of teacher shortage such threats are idle; in periods of teacher surplus such threats invite union protest and defensive action, weaken staff morale, and create tense school-community, management-labor relationships.

7. Are incentives the only factor differentiating in-service from preservice teacher education?

Although the need to introduce incentives for fully certified personnel appears to be the major factor differentiating in-service from preservice teacher education, it is not the only factor. In a given period of time, only a specified level of expertise in a limited range of knowledge and skill can be developed. The objective of in-service education is to build upon existing knowledges and skills and to

[5] For additional discussion of Educational Specialty Boards, see M. Lieberman, Appendix B; and also *The Future of Public Education* (Chicago: University of Chicago Press, 1960).

encourage the development of new knowledges and skills. In-service education, therefore, differs from preservice education in the range of knowledges and skills encompassed by the training program and in the levels of mastery anticipated. Accordingly, the scope of instructional materials and measures of competency will also differ.

8. What program development priorities are implied by the preceding discussion?

The major need of preservice and in-service teacher education is the identification of teacher competencies associated with the attainment of educational goals. Unless teacher education can determine which teacher competencies are related to which instructional objectives (and under what conditions), investment in teacher training is speculative. It is imperative, therefore, that a major research effort be undertaken to identify the competencies associated with criteria of school effectiveness.

Although teacher education cannot be postponed until the requisite research has been conducted, new program development in teacher education should emphasize procedures and products that are compatible with research needs. The primary requirement for both training and research is the definition of teacher competencies. Accordingly, program development in teacher education must be directed towards the operational definition of the training curriculum.

Operationally, teacher-education curricula are defined by measuring instruments and instructional materials. Despite their limitations, tests and textbooks—measurements and materials—have traditionally served to make concrete the objectives and procedures of educational programs. Teacher education is no exception. The development of instruments to identify beginning, experienced, and master levels of teacher competency and the development of compatible instructional materials to define the elements of teacher-education curricula are the highest priorities for teacher-education training and research.

In addition to rigorous operational definition of the teacher-education program, in-service teacher education must develop incentives for experienced teachers who no longer require certification to maintain their jobs. The development of special Competency-Based Certification for master-level teachers or teacher trainers is, therefore, a high priority for in-service teacher education. Such "extra-legal" Competency-Based Certification for master-level teachers not only establishes career incentives for teacher training, but also serves the instrumentation needs of teacher behavior research at superior levels of knowledge and skill.

An additional need for both preservice and in-service training is the provision of opportunities to practice under supervision, with little delay in the evaluation of performance. Opportunities to practice will require access to instructional materials and, frequently, pupils. The evaluation of performance would be facilitated by audio- and video-tape recordings. A training laboratory to house instructional materials and equipment would seem desirable.

As noted earlier, there are several criterion levels to guide observation of the trainee's performance. During training, assessments of performance could be made under simulated conditions (Criterion Levels 5 and 4). At the conclusion of a training period, assessment of competencies should be made in actual classroom settings (Criterion Level 3). The location of the laboratory in a university setting would be compatible with the observational requirements of Criterion Levels 5 and 4, but would not easily accommodate the need for assessment at Criterion Level 3. (Universities would need to make additional provision for the observation and recording of student performance in the actual classroom setting.) Conversely, the location of an observational facility in a school setting would easily accommodate Criterion Level 3, but the cost of the laboratory facility would have to be justified in terms of the number of students under observation at Criterion Levels 5 and 4.

The decision to locate a laboratory in a university or school, therefore, needs to take into account at least two factors: maximizing the number of preservice and in-service students having access to the facility, thereby reducing laboratory costs per trainee; and maximizing opportunities for practice under actual conditions, thereby minimizing the discontinuity between performance assessed at Criterion Level 4 and performance assessed at Criterion Level 3. It would be useful to encourage schools and universities to develop prototypes for laboratory installations to reflect a number of solutions to this cost/effectiveness problem.

9. In what ways can the elements of an effective Competency-Based Teacher-Education Program be organized to reflect the strengths of local settings?

The major elements of a Competency-Based Teacher-Education Program include trainers, trainees, pupils, instructional materials, measures of competency, and evaluation procedures. Specifically, the training program will need to provide for:

1. Installation of audiotape and videotape facilities to record demonstrations of pedagogic skills under simulated and real-instruction settings (a training laboratory).
2. Use of materials for training teachers in the diagnosis and interpretation of pupil behavior.

3. Use of materials for skill training.
4. Access to, and involvement of, teacher trainers skilled in observing and evaluating teacher competencies.
5. Access to school pupils.
6. Access to advanced work in subject or specialized fields.
7. Development of evaluation procedures, relating assessments of laboratory-based knowledges and skills to measures of competency in the classroom (Criterion Level 3).
8. Access to and use of instruments and devices for Competency-Based Certification at Criterion Level 3.

The organization of these elements must reflect the opportunities and constraints—the strengths and limitations of the local situation. Accordingly, the particular structure or facility for "housing" the essential elements of the teacher-education program should be left to local discretion. This is not to suggest the desirability or expectation of hundreds of variations in structure nor is it to suggest that federally funded programs ignore federal guidelines.[6] It is, rather, to suggest that administrative or organizational structures must be valid for the setting and population served. In this sense, organizational structures should be "contextually valid." In addition, laboratory facilities for training must be justified by the development of competent educational personnel as defined by Criterion Levels 5, 4, and 3. The location and installation of laboratory facilities, therefore, must be cost/effective.

In all likelihood several major organizational structures will emerge to reflect the strengths of local organizations and satisfy cost/effectiveness criteria. These structures will draw upon the personnel and material resources of state education departments, universities, school systems, community agencies, and industrial organizations in local areas. In addition, the structures will necessarily take into account the number of trainees to be served, trainee costs associated with access to the program, and institutional costs associated with program maintenance.

Four types of organizations which seem sensitive to considerations of cost/effectiveness and local resources are identified below.[7] The first three are described in greater detail in committee papers.

[6] Federal guidelines, however, might be written to encourage the pooling of federal resources in order to facilitate program development more responsive to local needs. This issue is discussed in more detail by C. Stewart in Chapter 7.

[7] Additional descriptions of organizational structures are contained in the Models for Elementary Teacher Education. See in J. Burdin and K. Lanzillotti, *op. cit.*, for example, Florida State University's *portal school;* Michigan State University's *clinical school network;* Syracuse University's *teaching centers,* located in the public schools; Teachers College's *inquiry school;* University of Pittsburgh's *clinical settings;* and University of Toledo's *multi-unit elementary school.*

Organization 1: State-wide consortium of centers. This type of organization has been described in detail by Schalock (Chapter 6). It is characterized by a central coordinating agency, typically a state department of education or agency of the state department. The agency coordinates a number of regional centers, involving public schools and one or more universities, supported on a cost-sharing basis. Under this type of organization, instruction and certification procedures would occur in regional centers, while support services would be coordinated by the central agency. A substantial strength of the organizational scheme is that the state department, the certifying agency, plays an intrinsic and important role. By assuming a statewide focus, the model both recognizes the state as the primary political entity in the financing, preparation, and certification of teachers and attempts to deal directly and realistically at a state- and individual-program level with matters such as program development and implementation, coordination, certification, and resource management. Although the structure is applicable to all states, it is probably best suited to states in predominantly rural regions which have universities located around the state in small urban areas. In any circumstances, a strong, active state department is required.

Of special significance in the proposed plan is the commitment to level 2 criteria for purposes of initial certification (demonstrated ability to bring about desired short-term learning outcomes in children under regular teaching conditions) and level 1 criteria for permanent certification (demonstrated ability to bring about desired long-term learning outcomes in children under regular teaching conditions). In addition, the model strongly emphasizes the need to establish teacher education on a sound empirical base. The model also attempts to incorporate the ideals of a program that is student oriented, personalized, and open to input from a broad, representational decision-making base.

Organization 2: The university center. This type of center has been described by DeVault (Chapter 4). It is characterized by the presence of a university which coalesces with a number of school systems. Although the center resulting from this coalition is not necessarily based directly in the university, the university is the dominant agency and would be expected to play the key leadership role in the development and support of the center. This organization is best suited to universities which have by tradition held a strong service orientation to the state and to their locales, e.g., the mixed urban-rural areas of the Midwest.

DeVault describes the Competency-Based Program Center as a context for the implementation of teacher education in both the university and the public schools. The coordination of interinstitutional cooperation is the responsibility of an administrative unit called a "Training Complex." The development, coordination, and implementation of instructional aspects of the teacher-education program is a function of the university.

The heart of the university-based center is the organizational structure of an Elementary Teacher Education Model. This structure is hypothesized to serve equally well for secondary- and elementary-education programs. The structure requires the broad support of interinstitutional cooperation. The Model is predicated on the feasibility of a heavily mediated instructional program and requires staff in both the university and the public schools willing to explore and implement new roles.

DeVault refers to the need for coordination of material development through a systems approach. This approach emphasizes a careful study of needs and development strategies, including cost/effectiveness and cost/benefit data, and careful attention to assessment of the continued effectiveness of materials within the Competency-Based Program and Centers.

Organization 3: The school training center. This type of organization has been described by Rosner (Chapter 5). It is characterized by a set of exemplary public schools, each of which has extended capability for training personnel and conducting in-service programs. In this organizational framework the schools are committed to a training function and share with the university responsibility for the preservice- and in-service-education program.

The governance of the program is the responsibility of a parity board including representatives of the university, the schools, professional teacher association, and community agencies.[8] The location of laboratory training centers in both the school and the university facilitates the acquisition of teacher competencies at Criterion Level 3.[9]

The emphasis on developing schools with exemplary curricula is intended to relate the resources of teacher training institutions to the instructional needs of pupils in inner-city schools. This organization is probably best suited to major urban areas in which there are many large schools easily accessible to both preservice and in-service teachers.

Organization 4: The technology-based individual study center. This type of organization has not been described in committee papers. The committee has discussed the key features of such centers and believes that the technological capability to support them exists.

[8] See S. Cohen, Chapter 3, for a discussion of the governance of a Training Complex.

[9] See also R. Turner, Chapter 8, for a discussion of university- and field-based laboratories in preservice and in-service programs.

There would be a need for a special study and planning group involving personnel from the electronics and communications industries as well as school and university personnel to further develop the technology center idea.

The technology-based center should serve two functions. First, it should make quality training programs available to individual teachers and small groups in areas with remote schools, such as the Mountain States and the Great Plains. Second, it should serve as an important shared resource for other types of centers in more heavily populated areas. Although each such center would be expected to vary somewhat, several key features would appear in each with greater or lesser emphasis according to circumstances.

A. A telecommunications network. The network would consist of a closed circuit or microwave television system together with telephone connections so that both transmission and feedback could occur. Such a network would probably work best as a shared resource of several centers so that each could transmit or receive special instructional programs according to its own resources. As a device to aid in the instruction of individual teachers, the network would probably focus on transmission with limited telephone feedback since the cost of line rentals for extended sender-receiver interactions may be prohibitive.

B. Instruction by correspondence. The use of correspondence for instructional purposes is probably far below full potential in teacher-education programs. A major advantage of appropriately developed and packaged instructional materials is that they can form the core of a program for individual teachers through correspondence. Correspondence study coupled with television transmission capabilities from the center may enhance the potential of each type of medium while preserving relatively low costs. In most instances, the costs of television receiving equipment and the videotape recording and playback equipment required for training are within the capabilities of individual school systems and, indeed, already exist in many.

C. Shared-time computer-assisted instruction. The feasibility of CAI for instruction and training teachers depends on individual schools and systems being able to use terminals regularly with pupils as well as with teachers. For example, the capability of the Plato system at the University of Illinois extends both to teachers and to pupils. By participating in a larger system on a shared-time basis, a technological training center would be responsible primarily for assuring the presence on the computer of needed instructional materials and for managing communications and instructional costs. The cost of capital investment in computer hardware could be largely avoided by the center, which would rent the hardware on a shared-time basis.

D. On-line, real-time computer monitoring of instruction. A forthcoming development in computer utilization lies in the use of small, inexpensive real-time computers which are connected on-line to classrooms. One method of using this type of system is to code the behavior of the teacher in the classroom as it occurs, transmit it to the computer for virtually instant analysis, and transmit the analyzed behavior back to the teacher so that he or she has continuous feedback about his own instruction. A second method is to transmit the events in the classroom by television or by telephone (audio only) to the center, where they are coded and, after immediate computer analysis, returned to the teacher where they may be continuously displayed by oscilloscope. Either of these methods permits precise training of teachers since feedback can be delivered on an almost instantaneous basis. The second method has the advantage of being able to employ coders in a central location from which many classrooms can be observed on a time-sampling basis.

The central advantage to a system of this type is that it has the capability to eliminate the direct supervision of teachers in training and replace it with a more effective method of changing teacher classroom behavior at Criterion Level 3. Its disadvantage is that the classrooms in which supervision is to occur must be properly equipped for transmitting behavior data and transmission lines to these rooms must be rented.[10]

10. In what ways do the program development priorities identified above relate to the purpose of Task Force '72 and CNPPTE?

As indicated in the introductory section, the committee and Task Force '72 were asked to make recommendations concerning the future development of Protocol and Training Materials, Training Complexes, Performance-Based Certification, and the Elementary Models. The program development priorities discussed above include instrument development, instructional materials development, contextually valid organizational structures, cost/effective laboratory facilities for training, and incentives for in-service personnel. The discussion also notes that program development for training must be compatible with requirements for research. Accordingly, the priority assigned to in-

[10] Although the overall costs of establishing a technology-based individual study center cannot be determined without a special planning study, the cost data developed in conjunction with the Wisconsin Elementary Teacher Education Project suggests that the development and maintenance of a single center might require between $1M and $2M per year over a five-year period. See *Wisconsin Elementary Teacher Education Project Feasibility Study: Pricing and Economic Analysis, vol. VI* (Madison, Wisconsin: University of Wisconsin, January, 1970).

strument development at Criterion Level 3 is compatible with Competency-Based Certification. Similarly, the emphasis on instructional materials is congruent with the development of Protocol and Training Materials. The requirement that program development for instructional materials be consistent with instrument development establishes the necessary articulation between Competency-Based Teacher Education and Competency-Based Teacher Certification. Establishing incentives for experienced in-service personnel is an operational extension of Competency-Based Certification to emphasize the highest levels of knowledge and skill available to the field.

Although the Committee's emphasis on instruments, materials, and incentives is completely compatible with the concept of the performance base and Protocol and Training Materials, the Committee regards the "Training Complex" as a generic term for a contextually valid organizational structure with cost/effective laboratory facilities for Competency-Based Teacher Education and Certification. Accordingly, the committee tends to de-emphasize the concept of "neutral ground" and emphasizes instead the concept of "contextual validity"—organizational structures to reflect the opportunities and strengths of the local setting. Finally, the emphasis in the Elementary Models on modular instructional units, the evaluation of student performance against specific mastery criteria, and the systematic integration of training and research for continuous curriculum renewal is reflected in the committee's stress on teacher behavior research, the emphasis on program development to facilitate both training and research, and the priority accorded operational definitions of teacher competencies for training and certification. The Elementary Models also provide descriptions of organizational structures which may be "contextually valid" for teacher training.

11. What program development sequence is implied by these priorities?

It is clear from the preceding discussion that the immediate needs of both training and research are served best by the development of instruments and instructional materials. Because Competency-Based Certification is completely dependent upon instruments to assess knowledges and skills at both the preservice and in-service levels, instrument development for certification purposes must be initiated immediately. Moreover, because the development of Educational Specialty Boards for highly skilled and experienced teachers or teacher trainers offers an essential incentive for in-service teacher education, instrument development for Competency-Based Certification at the highest level of knowledge and skill should also be initiated immediately.

As much as Competency-Based Certification is dependent upon instruments, competency-based training is dependent upon instructional materials. Efficient and effective training cannot be instituted until the knowledges and skills that comprise the training program are defined. It is essential, therefore, that the Protocol and Training Materials Programs already underway be maintained. However, instructional materials development must be closely related to the development of instruments. They should, in fact, be developed simultaneously or at least derive from the same set of knowledge and skill specifications. In this manner training and certification reinforce and support one another.

The development of a modest supply of field-tested instructional materials will probably require a period of two to three years. For this reason the installation of training laboratories should proceed slowly, with more time allotted to planning and development than is usually available. The immediate need in establishing training laboratories is not for full-scale training operations but for the design of cost/effective laboratory prototypes and the development of a variety of contextually valid organizational structures. These laboratory prototypes and structures would serve as models for other institutions in similar settings. In addition, they would serve as field testing centers for materials and instrument development, for pilot projects in Competency-Based Certification, and for development as examining centers for the Educational Specialty Boards.

12. In what ways do the program development priorities relate to priorities established in the Office of Education and the Bureau of Educational Personnel Development?

The program priorities established by the Office of Education for the Bureau of Educational Personnel Development include: (a) the improvement of the quality of educational personnel available to children and youth from low-income, racially and culturally isolated populations; (b) the improvement of educational personnel serving the needs of handicapped children; and (c) the improvement of educational personnel serving the needs of children between the ages of three and nine.

In addition to these general program priorities, specific BEPD program objectives include: (a) the development of a career ladder in teaching which includes paraprofessional personnel; (b) the introduction of an undergraduate teacher preparation program with emphasis on the integration of the liberal arts and professional education; (c) the improvement of in-service education through the establishment of teacher centers; and (d) the development of alternative training programs with the emphasis on innovation.

CNPPTE program development priorities appear to be compatible with the program objectives and priorities of the Office of Education and BEPD. CNPPTE strongly advocates program development to establish the conditions essential to Competency-Based Teacher Education and Certification. The development of instruments, instructional materials, laboratory facilities for training, and incentives for in-service teachers offers an opportunity for a major test of the hypothesis that Competency-Based Teacher Education and Certification will improve the preparation of educational personnel at the paraprofessional, preservice, and in-service levels. Further, within the framework of the general program development strategy, specific program development priorities are established addressed to the needs of low income, racially and culturally isolated preschool, elementary, and secondary school pupils. These priorities include establishing laboratory training facilities in depressed areas, proposing instrument and material development for bilingual teachers, and encouraging the location of master-level teachers or teacher trainers in ghetto schools by salary incentives for board certified personnel. Other instances of compatibility with OE and BEPD priorities are included in the five-year program development plan presented in the next chapter.

CHAPTER 2

Recommendations for Competency-Based Teacher Education and Certification

The Committee on National Program Priorities in Teacher Education recommends a major test of the power of Competency-Based Teacher Education to improve the performance of educational personnel in the nation's schools. To implement this recommendation, an integrated program development effort must be undertaken. The elements of this program include:

1. A committee for program planning and coordination.
2. Training laboratories for educational personnel.
3. Instructional materials for concept and skill attainment.
4. Instruments to define competencies in actual classroom settings.
5. Career development for master-level teachers and teacher trainers.

The elements of the program are described in greater detail in the following sections. Tables 2–1 through 2–5 present costs associated with the five-year development plan.[1]

[1] The committee wishes to be on record as recommending a full-scale research effort to investigate the relationships between teacher competencies and the attainment of school objectives. The recommendations contained in this report provide essential elements for this research program and underscore the interdependence of training and research. No attempt has been made, however, to define the scope of research or to estimate the research budget.

PROGRAM PLANNING

The creation of a committee on program planning and coordination is essential to the development and maintenance of general program integrity. The committee believes that Competency-Based Teacher Education and Certification are critical to the revitalization of educational personnel development and strongly advocates a coordinated program development strategy to test the power inherent in the concept. As indicated in Table 2–1, the planning and coordination committee could design an evaluative research study to test the Competency-Based Program on a broad scale; would recommend or carry out special studies; and would disseminate information and, in general, assist BEPD to establish the conditions vital to the program's success. The committee recommends the allocation of $.3M per year for five years, or $1.5M for program planning and coordination.

TRAINING LABORATORIES

A fundamental component of Competency-Based Teacher Education and Certification is the development of training laboratories to facilitate practice under real and simulated instructional conditions. These laboratories would be part of an organizational structure for teacher education and would contain the equipment and materials for the evaluation of trainee performance. In addition, the training laboratories would collect and transmit data pertinent to Competency-Based Certification, would participate in the field testing of instructional materials, would evaluate the success of preservice and in-service training against the criteria of classroom performance, and would participate as examination centers for the Educational Specialty Boards.

The committee recommends the establishment of 100 training laboratories (TLs) with a training capacity of at least 20,000 educational personnel per year at an average cost of $.75M per laboratory. The distribution of training laboratories should be flexible. Individual laboratories might be located in universities or schools; school-university consortia might make application for the installation of TLs in both schools and universities; and state or city education agencies might plan for the distribution of clusters of TLs on a statewide or citywide basis. It is anticipated that a number of these TLs would be distributed across the four organizational structures described on pages 16–19. This distribution should provide for several replications of each of the state, university, school, and technology-based organizational structures. Accordingly, the support base for each organiza-

TABLE 2–1. Five-year program development plan: Competency-Based Teacher Education and Certification*

Year	*Program Planning and Coordination*	*Training Laboratories*	*Instructional Materials*	*Instruments*	*Career Development*	*Total*
1	.3†	4.5	1.0	.75	.3	6.85
2	.3	23.0	2.0	1.00	1.3	27.60
3	.3	22.5	4.5	1.00	1.6	29.90
4	.3	14.5	5.5	2.00	3.3	25.60
5	.3	10.5	6.0	.75	6.5	24.05
Total	1.5	75.0	19.0	5.50	13.0	114.00

* The budget estimates included in Tables 2–1 through 2–5 do not reflect a rigorous cost analysis and should be regarded as general guidelines. In particular, it should be noted that the estimates do not provide for indirect costs.

† Dollars in millions.

To establish a program planning and coordination committee to assure the unification of the Competency-Based Teacher-Education Program development effort (provides for special studies and reports—e.g., in Year 1 a survey of existing laboratory designs and development of specifications/cost estimates for alternative designs; recommends funding for special projects; disseminates information on the program; etc.).

To establish 100 training laboratories with minimal training capacity of 20,000 educational personnel per year.

To develop, field-test, package, and distribute 1000 units of instructional material for concept and skill attainment.

To develop approximately 250 school-based criterion measures leading to Competency-Based Certification at the paraprofessional, provisional, and permanent certification levels.

To develop a career line in teaching by establishing Educational Specialty Boards offering professional Competency-Based Certification to master-level teachers and teacher trainers.

tional prototype would be obtained by multiplying the per laboratory cost by the number of laboratory units required to establish the organizational structure.

The development of 100 TLs would occur over a five-year period as indicated in Table 2–2. During Year 1, for example fiscal 1973, *up to* 100 school-university or school-university-state department consortia would be funded for planning "contextually valid" organizational structures, including the location of TLs on a cost/effective basis. Approximately $4.5M would be required to support the planning activities.

During the second year, consortia would complete TL specifications and install equipment. Approximately $23M would be required to install 100 TLs during Year 2, fiscal 1974. Year 3, fiscal 1975, has been allocated to staff development, pilot projects, and field testing. The committee estimates $22.5M as necessary for these functions. Finally, during Years 4 and 5, fiscal 1976 and 1977, the TLs would be approaching optimal operating efficiency; that is, training at least 200 educational personnel each, engaging in recording and reporting services for certification, evaluating the training program, and examining master-level teachers and teacher trainers for board certification.

TABLE 2–2. Training laboratories for educational personnel

Year	*Planning*	*Installation Field Testing Materials Maintenance*	*Staff Development*	*Records Reports*	*Evaluation*	*Total*
1	2.5*	—	—	1.0	1.0	4.5
2	—	20.0	—	2.0	1.0	23.0
3	—	10.0	7.5	3.0	2.0	22.5
4	—	5.0	2.5	4.0	3.0	14.5
5	—	2.5	—	5.0	3.0	10.5
Total	2.5	37.5	10.0	15.0	10.0	75.0

* Dollars in millions.

Purpose: To establish approximately 100 training laboratories with a minimal training capacity of 20,000 educational personnel per year

Functions: Training, certification (Criterion Level 3), field testing of materials and instruments, evaluation, and record keeping

Individual laboratory development and operations:

Year 1 Plan, coordinate school-university operations, design preliminary specifications for laboratory facilities—$25,000.

Year 2 Complete specifications and install laboratory—$200,000.

Year 3 Train staff, conduct pilot projects, participate in field testing of materials and instruments—$175,000.

Year 4 Operate laboratory and continue field testing activities—$75,000.

Year 5 Maintain equipment and materials and continue field testing activities—$25,000.

Evaluation ($100,000): includes staffing, planning, computer programing and analysis, and program evaluation at Criterion Level 3.

Records and Reports ($150,000): includes collecting and summarizing data for competency profiles and reporting for certification.

Approximately $25M has been allocated to TL operations during the fourth and fifth years.

Overall, $75M appears to be the minimal level of funding essential to the development of 100 training laboratories for Competency-Based Teacher Education and Certification over a five-year period. It should also be noted that the program development schedule outlined above takes cognizance of the two to three years' lead time required for the preparation of instructional materials and instruments. If Competency-Based Teacher Education and Certification is to succeed, BEPD cannot anticipate full competency-based operational services until the requisite materials and criterion measures have been developed.

INSTRUCTIONAL MATERIALS

The rationale for Competency-Based Teacher Education and Certification has clearly underscored the importance of developing instructional materials for concept and skill attainment. The committee recommends that $20M be allocated for the development, field testing, packaging, and distribution of approximately 1000 units of instructional material over a five-year period. The committee further recommends that the development of these instructional materials be guided by committees of school and college personnel responsible for the development of Competency-Based Teacher Education in the training laboratories. The formation of these committees will serve to sensitize school and college faculty to their use and prepare them for the necessary field testing operations. Finally, the committee recommends that priorities for material development take into account the training needs of paraprofessionals, the needs of elementary school teachers in the teaching of reading and mathematics, and the needs of bilingual teachers working with children who speak English as a second language.

Table 2–3 suggests a materials development program which provides approximately 200 units of instructional material for field testing, packaging, and distribution to 100 TLs during the third year of development—a schedule compatible with the field testing capability of TLs during their third year of developmental operations—and approximately 700–750 field-tested units for distribution to TLs during full competency-based operations. By the termination of the five-year materials development program, 1000 units will have been in use in Competency-Based Teacher-Education Programs across the country. Regardless of the number of TLs installed, the availability of 1000 units to facilitate the development of understandings and skills will have a marked impact on the design of teacher-education programs throughout the nation, and may stimulate the private sector to develop additional instructional materials. The development of instructional materials by the private sector is particularly important, given the need for periodic revision of materials.

TABLE 2–3. Instructional materials development

Year	*Develop and Field-test*	*Package and Distribute*	*Total*
1	1.0*	—	1.0
2	2.0	—	2.0
3	4.0	.5	4.5
4	4.0	1.5	5.5
5	4.0	2.0	6.0
Total	15.0	4.0	19.0

* Dollars in millions.

Purpose: To develop, field-test, package, and distribute approximately 1000 units of instructional material for concept and skill attainment.

Budget provides for field testing and distribution of materials to approximately 100 training laboratories.

INSTRUMENT DEVELOPMENT

No factor is more crucial to the success of Competency-Based Teacher Education than the method of assessing the mastery of concepts and skills. The preparation of instruments to define performance criteria is the sine qua non of Competency-Based Certification. The committee cannot emphasize too strongly the needed development of measures of teacher performance in the classroom.[2] If BEPD had to support a single effort to establish Competency-Based Teacher Education, it should invest in the development of instruments to assess teacher competencies.

Table 2–4 presents an instrument development schedule to prepare approximately 250 competency measures over a five-year period. All the measures are to be developed for use in actual classroom situa-

[2] For further discussion of school-based measures of teacher competency, see B. Rosner, Chapter 5.

TABLE 2–4. Instrument development

Year	*Project Adminis-tration*	*Plan-ning*	*Develop-ment*	*Train-ing and Dissem-ination*	*Installa-tion and Utiliza-tion*	*Total*
1	.2*	.5	—	.05	—	.75
2	.25	—	.6	.15	—	1
3	.25	—	.6	.15	—	1
4	.25	—	1	.5	.25	2
5	.25	—	—	—	.5	.75
Total	1.2	.5	2.2	.85	.75	5.5

* Dollars in millions.

Purpose: To develop approximately 250 school-based criterion measures leading to Competency-Based Certification at the paraprofessional, provisional, and permanent certification levels.

tions; i.e., assessments of teacher competency are to be made in the presence of pupils, at Criterion Level 3. The cost of instrument development at Criterion Level 3 is estimated as $5.5M.[3] No other investment in teacher education would yield the same dollar benefit.

During the five-year period, the development of approximately 250 instruments might be distributed among certification levels as follows: paraprofessional personnel (30); provisionally certified personnel (160); and permanently certified personnel (60). Areas of competency to be assessed would probably include: general elementary (reading, mathematics, etc.); early childhood; bilingual; and high school English and mathematics. The specific allocation of instruments across levels of certification and areas of competency would be made by committees of teacher educators—both school and university personnel—who would also participate in the identification of classroom instructional skills. (It should be noted that the design of the instrument blueprint should closely follow the design of the instructional materials blueprint, or vice versa. There is little point in generating instructional materials and standards of attainment that do not address the same set of competencies.)

The preparation of instruments at the high school level, and the specific subject fields at the elementary level, would also involve university faculty from the liberal arts. The instrumentation part of

[3] This budget does not provide for instrument development appropriate for Criterion Levels 6, 5, and 4. An additional $10M could be projected to assess knowledges and skills at these levels.

the program thus offers the opportunity to involve the disciplines in the definition of competencies needed by teachers. The blueprint to develop the instruments would need to take into account a diversity of curricula in schools and universities and thus provide for the development of tasks representing various points of view of the competencies important for teachers. This would yield a set from which schools, universities, and state education agency consortia could select the instruments related to their objectives.

The need to coordinate all phases of instrument development—to assure the efficient allocation of resources, to maintain uniformly high standards of quality, and to facilitate liaison with training laboratories and BEPD—clearly underscores the importance of vesting responsibility for instrument development in the hands of a program planning and coordination committee empowered to sub-contract with a consortium of instrument developers. Regardless of the form of project direction, the overall instrument development effort must be tightly controlled.

CAREER DEVELOPMENT

The specific recommendations identified above establish the conditions essential to Competency-Based Teacher Education for personnel aspiring to provisional or permanent Competency-Based Certification. In order to assure the impact of competency-based staff development for fully certified teachers, the committee recommends the establishment of Educational Specialty Boards. The Educational Specialty Boards would offer a competency-based certificate to highly skilled master-level teachers or teacher trainers. These certificates would be awarded by the board operating outside the legal framework for state certification. Individuals acquiring board certificates would be recognized as among the most competent teachers or teacher trainers in the nation and would be entitled to special salary increments. The status of board certification and the right to special salary increments would offer experienced teachers considerable incentive for career development.

The committee recommends, therefore, that BEPD allocate $13M over five years to establish the Educational Specialty Boards as indicated in Table 2–5. The program would provide for a national policy board consisting of approximately twenty distinguished educators, scholars, and lay citizens to assure the establishment of board certification at a high level and in the public interest.

During the first year the board, acting as a special commission, would investigate the feasibility of developing special certification for master-level teachers and teacher trainers. The commission's studies

TABLE 2–5. Career development (educational specialty boards)

Year	*National Board*	*Board Adminis-tration*	*Research and Devel-opment*	*Board Exami-nation*	*Federal Total*	*Dis-trict* Share*
1	.10†	.20	—	—	.3	—
2	.10	.20	.50	.50	1.3	—
3	.10	.25	.75	.50	1.6	—
4	.10	.40	.80	2.00	3.3	(1.5)
5	.10	.50	.90	5.00	6.5	(3.75)
Total	.50	1.55	2.95	8.00	13.0	(5.25)

* Local district matching of salary increments for board certification salary increment estimated at $3000 per year.

† Dollars in millions.

Purpose: To develop a career line in teaching by establishing Educational Specialty Boards offering professional Competency-Based Certification to master-level teachers and teacher trainers.

Provides for board headquarters, National Commission (20 members) and administrative staff.

Establishes 25 Board Examination Centers with capacity for assessing 2500 candidates per year.

Provides career development program in 12 master-level teacher and teacher trainer specialty fields; e.g., General Elementary; Early Childhood; Reading; Bilingual, Elementary Mathematics; Special Education; High School Mathematics; High School English; High School Biology; and High School Social Studies.

Provides salary increment of $1,500 for 3,500 board-certified teachers for one year; assumes matching salary increment by local districts.

Provides board examination fee ($500) for 3,000 candidates.

would require consultation with school board associations, civil rights organizations, state education agencies, and other professional specialty boards in order to determine the conditions under which the board certification procedures might be implemented. In addition, the commission would request position papers on a variety of issues affecting the public interest. Approximately $.3M is allocated for the commission during the first year.

Assuming the feasibility of the Educational Specialty Board concept, the full program would establish 25 examination centers with capacity for testing 2500 candidates per year. Costs for establishing these centers would include a $500 examination fee for 3,000 candidates. It is anticipated that individual candidates would bear the examination fee once the boards were instituted. In addition, the program would provide a salary incentive of $3,000 per year for 3,500 board certified personnel. The salary incentive of $3,000 would consist of two parts—a $1,500 grant from the Office of Education and a matching grant from a local school district or state. In order to place large numbers of board certified personnel at the service of low-income, racially or culturally isolated children and youth, OE-BEPD incentive grants could be made available to school districts eligible for Title I funds or in Model Cities communities. In effect, OE-BEPD salary incentives would be available to board certified personnel upon their acceptance of assignment in schools located in legally designated poverty areas.

As Table 2–5 suggests, the program provides the developmental funds for twelve board examinations at the early childhood elementary, and secondary school levels. The development of instruments for board certification at the secondary level will, once again, require the active participation of the most knowledgeable liberal arts faculty. In this manner, the Educational Specialty Boards may help to integrate the liberal arts with professional education at the highest levels of expertise in the field.

In summary, CNPPTE recommends the establishment of conditions necessary to test the power of Competency-Based Teacher Education to improve the performance of educational personnel in the nation's schools. The cost of the program is estimated at $114M. Investment in the program would require an allocation of approximately $7M the first year in order to carry out major planning activities and initiate preliminary development. Assessment of the results of the first year will help to determine needed changes in program development strategy for the second year. Assuming reasonable results during the first year, the program would require approximately $28M to install 100 training laboratories, engage in materials and instrument development, and initiate the development of the Educational Specialty Boards. During the third year, additional funding in the amount of $30M would maintain developmental operations at the training laboratories, contribute significantly to materials and instrument development, and introduce board examination procedures. The fourth and fifth years, funded at $25M, would maintain the program of Competency-Based Teacher Education at 100 training laboratories with a capacity to train at least 20,000 educational personnel annually.

The committee is convinced that these recommendations should be implemented. The recommendations offer an integrated program development plan to introduce Competency-Based Teacher Education on a broad scale.

The concept of Competency-Based Teacher Education has great power. The power of the idea resides in the clear expression of the objectives of the teacher-education program and the ability to assess teacher competencies. Both are critical to the introduction of accountability in teacher education.

SUMMARY

The Bureau of Educational Personnel Development established Task Force '72 in November, 1970, to study the utility of five developmental programs in USOE: Protocol Materials, Training Materials, Training Complexes, Performance-Based Certification, and the Models for Elementary Teacher Education. In March, 1971, the Committee on National Program Priorities in Teacher Education was formed to represent the nonfederal sector of the teacher education community and to make recommendations for needed program development.

The procedures of the committee included the preparation and discussion of papers prepared by members, meetings with Task Force '72 and BEPD personnel, circulation of abstracts of the committee papers to external critics, and commissioning of papers on special topics for committee consideration. As a result of these activities and deliberations, program recommendations were developed. The rationale underlying the program evolved during the course of discussions among committee members, and as a result of the ideas presented in various papers prepared by and for the committee.

The recommendations of the committee are summarized in Table 2–6 for a five-year program development plan. The program development effort has these objectives.

1. To establish a program planning and coordination committee to assure the unification of the Competency-Based Teacher Education Program development effort.
2. To establish 100 training laboratories with a minimal training capacity of 20,000 educational personnel per year.
3. To develop, field test, package, and distribute 1000 units of instructional materials for concept and skill attainment.
4. To develop approximately 250 school-based criterion measures leading to Competency-Based Certification at the paraprofessional, provisional, and permanent certification levels.
5. To develop a career line in teaching by establishing Educational Specialty Boards offering professional Competency-Based Certification to master-level teachers and teacher trainers.

The program development effort recommended by the committee emphasizes specific activities which serve the function of defining and making explicit the competencies required by educational personnel within the career line of paraprofessional, provisional and permanently certified teachers, and master-level teachers or teacher trainers. These activities are intended to assist in the development and improvement of training programs funded by BEPD through the development of instructional materials, the construction of instruments to assess competencies in the classroom, the provision of opportunities to practice specific skills with evaluation of performance in the facilities provided in the training laboratories, and by extending careers for teachers through Competency-Based Certification by Educational Specialty Boards as master-level teachers or teacher trainers.

TABLE 2–6 Five-year program development plan: Competency-Based Teacher Education and Certification*

Year	*Program Planning and Coordination*	*Training Laboratories*	*Instructional Materials*	*Instruments*	*Career Development*	*Total*
1	.3†	4.5	1.0	.75	.3	6.85
2	.3	22.0	2.0	1.00	1.3	27.60
3	.3	22.5	4.5	1.00	1.6	29.90
4	.3	14.5	5.5	2.00	3.3	25.60
5	.3	10.5	6.0	.75	6.5	24.05
Total	1.5	75.0	19.0	5.50	13.0	114.00

* The budget estimates do not reflect a rigorous cost analysis and should be regarded as general guidelines. In particular, it should be noted that the estimates do not provide for indirect costs.

† Dollars in millions.

The program recommended by the Committee on National Program Priorities in Teacher Education represents an effort to implement several major ideas which have developed during the past decade. The idea of making explicit the competencies of educational personnel has power to become a major force to improve teacher education. The clear expression of the objectives of teacher education and the ability to assess teacher competencies are critical to the introduction of accountability in the preparation of educational personnel.

PART II

Papers Prepared by the Committee

CHAPTER 3

A Five-year Goal for Training Complexes

Saul B. Cohen

The Training Complex is conceived as a new kind of mechanism within which teachers will be trained with the assistance of Protocol and Training Materials. The guiding spirit behind this mechanism is to provide the teacher with an experience which will sharpen his sense of professionalism and which will put in the forefront Performance-Based Criteria as the indices for achieving and verifying long-range competence in the field. The concept of a Training Complex has for its objective at one and the same time development of an entity sufficiently independent of existing institutions to take responsibility for the training of the classroom teacher, and establishment of a system that will interact and be interrelated with those institutions that are concerned with teacher preparation on a continuing, long-term basis. The training regimen offered by the Training Complex follows the sequence of teacher preparation in higher education, either undergraduate or the combination of undergraduate and graduate, and precedes the in-service preparation that the schools continually provide the teacher upon entry into the system. "Neutral ground," as a concept upon which the Training Complex is built, therefore, does not mean isolation but rather interdependence. "Neutral ground" is suggested as a functional technique for involving both higher education and the schools, and to a certain extent the community and industry, rather than as a means of ignoring them or allowing them to disengage from the teacher training process. Perhaps the analogy of the medical residency training process is stretching the point, but we see the Training Complex as providing the prospective teacher with an ingredient of *professional training and on a saturation basis* that neither college teacher preparation nor school in-service reeducation can offer.

We see the Training Complex being operated by a consortium which would be built upon existing structures, such as universities and schools, and yet have an independent life of its own. This means not scrapping existing networks but gaining their support to create something new. To make the distinction sharper, the Training Complex would not try to displace existing institutions but rather undertake to do what such institutions currently are not doing. At no time in a prospective teacher's current training does the teacher serve as the focus. Instead, the teacher is either a student intern under the wing of a university supervisor who has many other duties to perform or a starting teacher in a school under the wing of a master teacher who is also preoccupied with day-to-day teaching. In the Training Complex, responsibility would be solely to the trainee, providing both teaching and learning experiences and evaluation of those experiences in a clinical setting.

In addition to its linkage and dependence upon the aforementioned institution, we see the Complex serving as the core for another kind of an institutional framework, also linked to the existing educational and educationally oriented institutions. This framework has been referred to in *Teachers for the Real World* (ed. by Smith et al., A.A.C.T.E., Washington, 1968), as the "Educational Service District" (p. 104). Such districts are conceived as bold and comprehensive agencies which would include the country's more than 20,000 public school districts and its over 3,000 higher educational institutions. These districts would serve as structured arrangements, linked to the schools, the universities, the community, and industry. As systems they need not be organized in traditional geographical regions. They could, for example, cut across the county and state lines. Their cores, i.e., higher education institutions or key schools, might be located physically outside of the geographical area which contains the remaining elements of the system. Broadly speaking, these educational service districts might number as many as 3,000 each including ten school systems, a college or university, an industry or groups of industry, and lay community representation. Very large cities, on the other hand, might be subdivided into five to ten such Educational Service Districts.

If the role of the Training Complex is to train teachers, then the role of the Districts in which they are located would include placement, paraprofessional recruitment and programing, diffusion of Protocol and Training Materials, curriculum innovation, serving as a locus for community social action programs, and research services. Again, to stretch an analogy, the Educational Service District might be likened to the Soil Conservation District, manned by a very small group of specialists whose operations serve a varied clientele. Educational Service officers would hold roles in the Districts similar to those of County Agents (or, for the United Kingdom, Her Majesty's Educational Inspectors). The Training Complex would serve, as has been suggested, as nucleus for the Education Service District.

Staffed by school teachers and college faculties (some part-time, and some on two-year leaves from their systems) and supplemented by part-time faculty from industry and from the community, the Training Complex would use as pupils youngsters from the schoolroom and school dropouts (after hours and summers), adults without schooling, and, for specialized purposes, other trainees. Starting with small groups, eventually, the trainee would take on full school classes, upon which his training needs would be further diagnosed. At the end of from half a year to a year in the Training Complex, the trainee would enter the school system as an intern—the internship to cover the first year as a teacher and under direct control of the school. The training milieu of the Complex would be the real world and teaching problems of the real world that teachers must face. This is why the students in the Training Complex with whom the teacher trainee would work would be "problem" people—the dropout, the handicapped, the adults without schooling, the bored suburban housewife. The prospective teacher should be sensitive to the individual needs of such individuals, and only through exposure to them in a clinical setup for a relatively long, intensive period can successful training be undertaken. The training period in the Complex is quite distinct from the period in which the starting teacher enters the school as an intern. During the internship period, the starting teacher could have experience with the typical middle-class student or the inner-city or rurally disadvantaged student depending upon the character of the school. The teacher would be sharpening the experiences gained in the Training Complex in a further extension of the real world.

College teacher preparation would abandon student internship and would concentrate on the theoretical aspects of learning, on subject-matter specialization, and on career development. The Training Complex could perform a direct function in this preservice phase by conducting "Career Interest Workshops" for college students interested in teaching. These could take place during the academic year and in summers, first serving to identify those college students most interested in and suited to teaching careers, then, sequentially, exposing the student to the world of elementary education, secondary education, education of the handicapped, etc. These short-term workshops would be held at an early stage (freshman and sophomore years). Then, during the junior and senior college years, Career Interest Workshops would be developed along specialized interest lines and would include "reality" exposure (perhaps through work as teaching aides and tutors).

As the Training Complex focuses upon *training of teachers,* so college teacher preparation can focus upon teacher education in its broader context which is essentially a liberal arts–philosophical-psychological framework. It is possible to suggest that the best form of teacher preparation is a solid undergraduate, general educational–liberal arts foundation. From such a foundation, independent and sensitive teachers can emerge. The courses that would specifically be characterized as teacher-education courses would deal with theoretical aspects of the learning process, an understanding of social systems, of personality and role, etc.

The number of individuals to be trained in a Training Complex would include the 225,000 beginning teachers who enter the school lists each year, half again as many teacher aides and other paraprofessionals (with perhaps two-to-three-month training periods), and about one-quarter as many in-service personnel who would go through the training process to become part of a rotating or part-time Complex staff or who would take on supervision of the trainee's internship period. A total of approximately 400,000 individuals should be accommodated by the Training Complexes each year. Ideally, there would be 3,000 Training Complexes nested within 3,000 Educational Service Districts, each Complex handling between 100 and 175 trainees.

The 400,000 trainees would be the target number to be handled by the Complexes. Some of the larger higher educational institutions and big-city systems would have the capacity to be involved in several Training Complexes, but keeping the number of individuals at any one Complex to an average of about 150 would appear to represent the best way for individualizing the training needs. The rationale for having 3,000 Training Complexes is that nearly every higher educational institution (and not merely the 1,000 institutions engaged in formal teacher preparation) could have some spearhead role in development of the Complexes (and the Districts). Aiming for 400,000 trainees would put the nation on a crash program for improving teacher education. All new personnel, and a significant number of key experienced personnel (60,000 per year, or over one-fourth of all experienced personnel in the schools over a ten-year period), would undergo the training. It is significant to involve a critical mass of experienced personnel either through retraining or through operational tasks in the Training Complex so as to minimize the tensions between the prospective teachers who have gone through the Training Complex and existing school personnel.

Such a major effort, coming today, as part of a major effort to reshape the nation's economy to peace-time efforts would make economic as well as educational sense. To meet the crisis in the schools through an effort that provides a major boost to quaternary industry is not only necessary but eminently practical.

To develop the networks of Training Complexes over a five-year period, we would opt for the following program:

1. First year—Total 100 Training Complexes, linked essentially to the 10 largest metropolitan areas which require almost one-fifth

of all beginning teachers. By and large, these first Complexes would be built around large higher educational institutions with strong teacher preparation capacities, and combinations of major big-city and adjoining suburban systems.

2. Second year—Total rises to 400 Training Complexes, 300 in the 10 largest metropolitan areas (to build about half the necessary networks there), and 100 Training Complexes, spread for pilot purposes, over rural, small- and medium-sized city population areas.
3. Third year—Total rises to 900 Training Complexes including 600 in the 10 largest metropolitan areas (completing the network there), and adding 200 more Training Complexes in rural, small- and medium-sized population areas.
4. Fourth year—Total rises to 2,000 Training Complexes doubling the previous year's number.
5. Fifth year—Total rises to 3,000 Training Complexes or adds approximately 1,000 more to complete the national network.

It is assumed that *the cost* of each Training Complex (150 trainees and 30 staff) *would be $1,500,000* ($750,000 for the 30 instructional personnel, administration, materials, rents and $750,000 for the trainees at $5,000 each). First-year costs would therefore amount to $150 million. This would increase to $450 million for the second year, $1.35 billion for the third year, $3 billion for the fourth year, and $4.5 billion for the fifth year. Thus, with the program in full gear, annual costs for the Training Complexes would be $4.5 billion, exclusive of the 1.5 billion expended for the 3 to 4 year college preparation of the beginning teacher. The annual teacher "crop" (including paraprofessionals and in-service) emerging from the Training Complex would then represent a cumulative cost of $6 billion. Of this, approximately $3.5 billion would be spent on beginning teachers as against the $1 billion that is currently spent on this group. As a percentage of the Gross National Defense Budget, $6 billion is a small price to pay for the "professionalization" of the nation's teachers and for the lifting of public education to a new plateau of achievement. For if the schools are to be saved, they will be saved first and foremost by the quality of the educational personnel who must lead the educational process. Unless we are prepared to invest in the professional training of the teacher, school reform will continue to be a mirage.

To speak of jumping the number of Training Complexes from 150 to 3,000 in a five-year period might appear wishful and naïve. But without a *crash program* trainees would become isolated and lost. *Our aim is to change the system, not merely individuals.* To do so, a mass impact must be made. The numbers of instructional staff needed (at 30 per Complex) would be 3,000 for the first year; 12,000 for the second; 27,000, the third; 60,000, the fourth; and 90,000, the fifth. Not all would be required on a full-time basis but to start with the first year, the 3,000 number seems attainable. Each of the 100 higher educational institutions directly involved might be asked to contribute 4 faculty, and each of the major school systems involved, 4, for a total of 800. The remainder would be recruited nationally through a program that eventually (within 3 years) would draw 1 recruit from every higher educational institution and 1 from every school district to develop a national cadre that would then be available for the National Network of Training Complexes.

Prior to the start of the five-year program, two years would be necessary to recruit and do advanced training of instructional staff, to experiment with materials (an interim measure while full-blown Protocol and Training Materials are being prepared at national centers), and to develop the organizational framework. During this period, a handful of Training Complexes, say twelve, would be established to experiment with structure and with the functional aspects of the training. We would urge opening of such Complexes immediately as centers of experimentation and feedback. The aim of such centers would include contact with *all* beginning teachers entering a particular system (through summer workshops) prior to the start of employment, and on a part-time basis during the first year, as a way of easing into the full-scale operation. The cost of twelve such Complexes would be $12 million the first year and $18 million the second.

The *scope and cost of a Training Complex effort is not beyond the capacities of this nation.* What is required is an organizational effort of unprecedented proportions for educators, parallel to, although hardly on the same scale as, what has been done in industry and in the military. The educational bureaucracy, federal and state especially, would be fully enlisted in the effort. For perhaps the first time, this bureaucracy would become a "field" bureaucracy, bending most of its efforts to helping the training process. For federal government, especially, this would be a challenging role. But if federal funding is to be used to spearhead the program, the bureaucracy must become directly and operationally involved in its implementation. The problem is national and the initiative for its solution should be national, regardless of whether the Complex and Educational Service District funding mechanisms operate directly through the states. The current drive for revenue sharing may make the funding of the Training Complexes as a combination federal/state operation more feasible.

In considering the problems of developing the Training Complex, the effect of such an institution upon a variety of different groups, sometimes in conflict, must be assessed. Tables 3–1 and 3–2 attempt to summarize the positive and negative effects from both the short- and long-term perspectives.

TABLE 3–1.

Groups	*POSITIVE EFFECTS* *Short-term*	*Long-term*	*NEGATIVE EFFECTS* *Short-term*	*Long-term*
Minority Groups	1. Recruitment of more talented teaching personnel. 2. Direct links to universities in operation of Training Complexes. 3. Retraining of displaced teachers.	1. Better teaching in the schools. 2. Improvement of black teacher training institutions through questioning of the current educational process. 3. Broadening of paraprofessional training opportunities.	Strengthening of position of teacher in community-controlled schools, vis-à-vis community control interests.	None.
Colleges of Education Faculty	Recruitment of more talented preservice trainees at university.	Improvement of teacher-education program, by differentiation from teacher training—more time at universities to emphasize the theoretical and to link with liberal arts.	Loss of in-service training links with schools.	Increase of gap between universities and schools.
Liberal Arts Faculty	1. Closer links with college educators, as latter have more time to emphasize the theoretical. 2. Opportunity to be involved in use of materials, especially curricular, at the teacher training level.	1. More competent teachers to disseminate content and knowledge in the schools. 2. Opportunity to be involved with master teachers in supervision of schools internships after Training Complex experience.	None.	None.

TABLE 3–2.

	POSITIVE EFFECTS		*NEGATIVE EFFECTS*	
Groups	*Short-term*	*Long-term*	*Short-term*	*Long-term*
Undergraduate Student	1. Excitement of a new mechanism. 2. Improved first-year in-service internship conditions. 3. More optimal job recruitment situation.	1. Sense of professionalization is heightened. 2. Less turnover: better screening processes and greater success factor.	Increased length of pre-service training.	Increased cost of professional training.
Professional Associations	More school personnel (especially paraprofessionals)	1. Stronger, more stable, more professional constituency. 2. Greater public fiscal support.	Harder to enter profession.	None.
Boards of Education	Less personnel turnover.	Better teaching.	Less control over teacher training.	Greater costs.
School Administrators	1. Prescreening of potential staff. 2. Involvement with university personnel in operating Training Complexes.	1. Better teaching. 2. A more professional teacher.	Teacher as a more confident adversary, in day-to-day relationships.	None.

CHAPTER 4

An Operational Plan for Program Development in Teacher Education

M. Vere DeVault
Program Design

Mary Golladay
Economic Analysis

ABSTRACT

Introduction and Rationale. The purpose of the Operational Plan for Program Development in Teacher Education is to create a climate and a context which will encourage change in the nature of schools and schooling in this country. The creation of a corps of teachers and other school personnel competent to perform new roles is the first order of business if schools are to change. Such reform requires the integrative efforts of a wide variety of cooperating institutions. The complexity of any undertaking designed to reform teacher education and the schools imposes a demand for maximum efficiency. It is hypothesized that systems designs provide the most viable alternative presently available for the management of this complexity. The presently emerging Competency-Based Teacher-Education movement contains the essence of initial steps in the reform which is to be given continuous direction and encouragement through the Operational Plan. The Operational Plan is a context in which research can be generated to provide a flow of information necessary to direct continuing reform of teacher education. Widespread reform will result from the Operational Plan through both product and process demonstration and dissemination. Existing Office of Education programs provide the essential elements required to give direction and impetus to the realization of the Operational Plan.

Teacher-education program requirements. Reform implied by the Operational Plan clearly dictates that essential program requirements will be set in new contexts facilitated by new relationships and characterized by new instructional modes. Improved interinstitutional cooperation, new expectations of faculty roles, and adequate assessment and research facilities provide appropriate contexts for evolving teacher-education programs. Management of facilities among and within institutions will create an even flow of human and material resources available to students from recruitment to certification and beyond. The new teacher education is predicated on the accessibility of new and varied learning modes made possible through the continuous generation of a wide variety of mediated materials.

Confirmatory mechanisms of the Operational Plan. To identify specific objectives of the Operational Plan for Program Development is not enough. Mechanisms must exist to make it possible to assess the functioning of the Operational Plan. The Operational Plan—a system of subsystems—accommodate to such mechanisms throughout its structure. Not only must we assess the success of the Operational Plan in reaching its objectives, we must be sure the Operational Plan does not become closed to innovation, persistent in error, or isolated from society's changing emphases. Multilevel Confirmatory Mechanisms represent the most reliable and accurate means of monitoring the Operational Plan and insuring its continuous regeneration.

Resources for realizing the Operational Plan. The effectiveness of the Operational Plan will be realized through the coordination of resources at the federal, state, and local levels. Three specific activities must be continuously maintained if the Operational Plan is to function effectively. These include (1) policy and coordination, (2) implementation of operating instructional programs, and (3) the development and regeneration of Protocols and Training Materials. As complementary elements in the Operational Plan, present programs underway in the Office of Education can maintain these requirements for reform in teacher education. The expectation that the Operational Plan for Program Development in Teacher Education can bring about needed next developments in American education carries a parallel expectation that adequate funding sources can be coordinated and directed toward essential elements charged with the responsibility to initiate and sustain the Operational Plan over a long-term period.

Benefit analysis of the Operational Plan for Program Development. Benefits arising from the Operational Plan may be viewed as direct, interactive, and intertemporal. Direct benefits accrue immediately from specific components to specific audiences. Interactive benefits arise from the interaction of direct benefits from various components upon various audiences. Intertemporal benefits flow from one point in time to another, from one set of receivers to another. We concentrate, in this analysis, primarily on direct benefits of the experimental models to various audiences within the university, the schools, the community, and the profession.

Cost analysis for the Operational Plan. Policy decisions regarding the development of the Operational Plan must be based on a study of the relationships between the costs and the benefits of alternative development strategies. Estimates of the costs of one CBP Center provide the basis for determining costs of development strategies which vary the number of participating institutions and the variety of instructional programs. These estimates of alternatives, together with a discussion of their expected effects, illuminate the nature of the choices which must be made.

A five-year plan for the development and implementation of the Operational Plan. A five-year development strategy for the Operational Plan involves considering not only the nature and magnitude of the impact which the total program will have on teacher education, but also the interrelationships among aspects of the overall Operational Plan and their effect on development strategies over time.

PREFACE

The Operational Plan for Program Development in Teacher Education has evolved over a period of several months and has drawn on experience and discussions extending over a much longer period of time. Colleagues on campus at the University of Wisconsin, those working on the Committee on National Priorities in Teacher Education, others working in various capacities within the National Center for Educational Research and Development, and the Bureau of Educational Personnel Development, as well as the Directors of the Elementary Teacher-Education Models have either directly or indirectly contributed significantly to the nature of the present paper.

We wish to mention specifically the thoughtful assistance provided at particular points by Michael Appel, Ted Czajkowski, and Ron Cohen at the University of Wisconsin. John M. Kean, codirector of the Wisconsin Elementary Teacher Education Project, provided continuous criticism of the manuscript as it progressed through a number of editions. Special appreciation is also expressed to Miss Dixie Carney whose editorial assistance made the completion of this assignment possible during heavily committed spring and summer months.

July 15, 1971 M.V.D.
M.A.G.

INTRODUCTION AND RATIONALE

The purpose of the Operational Plan for Program Development in Teacher Education is to create a climate and a context which will encourage change in the nature of schools and schooling in this country.

There is widespread agreement that the schools of this country have improved substantially as a result of the educational revolution which has been underway during the past fifteen years. Nonetheless, there is also widespread agreement that the gap continues to widen between what the schools are and what they must be if they are to meet the changing requirements of society. As the pace of change in society increases, schools and schooling must be able to adapt appropriately. The protests registered daily by students in colleges and universities and by parents in the inner city are only part of the evidence that attests to the need for creating educational alternatives which more nearly meet the needs of all youth.

The creation of a corps of teachers and other school personnel competent to perform effectively in new roles is the first order of business if schools are to function in a climate of change.

The purpose of the Operational Plan for Program Development in Teacher Education is to create a heightened possibility of necessary change in schools through changes in the nature of teachers and teaching. The model is designed not to serve preconceived notions of what the schools should be but to encourage, direct, and control evolutionary change. Viable national alternatives evolving simultaneously may be tested at the same time. A system which monitors progress by providing knowledge about the nature of change and its impact on learners delivers a continual flow of information useful in determining the utility of various alternatives.

Major reform in teacher education requires the cooperative efforts of a wide variety of cooperating institutions.

If reform in teacher education is to result in changing schools and in teachers who are competent in new roles, the importance of contributions which can be made by each individual faculty member and by specific institutions cannot be overestimated. The major hypothesis of the Operational Plan is that these variable resources, faculty, and institutions can be organized to focus the uniqueness of each on the task to which all are committed.

The complexity of any undertaking designed to reform teacher education imposes a demand for maximum efficiency. It is hypothesized that systems designs provide a management alternative to assure the efficiency.

It is hypothesized that the uniqueness of the audiences to which the plan is addressed, the learners or would-be teachers and the schools they serve, can be served most effectively through an efficiently operating systems design. These diverse demands of persons and institutions coupled with the varied contributions which can be made by other persons and institutions pose both the threat to and the hope for improvement in teacher education. The hope stems from the rich potential of innovative thrusts in many directions; the threat stems from the danger of losing contact, understanding, and control of innovation so that necessary resources can no longer be applied effectively at appropriate points.

The presently emerging Competency-Based Teacher-Education movement provides the initial essence of improvement which is to be given continuous direction and encouragement through the Operational Plan.

The Competency-Based Teacher-Education movement has developed along with management by objectives and accountability emphases. Criteria of teacher competency have been identified at three levels. In the past and presently, certification has been based largely on knowledge demonstration. We have had substantial evidence that the certified teacher possessed given sets of knowledge. A second level requires assessment of the performance of the teacher. This is the focus of the Operational Plan. Certification, at this level, is based on assurances that the teacher can perform in stated and specified ways. The third level involves product criteria. Evidence is given that the teacher can, in whatever way, obtain specified results with learners in the classroom. The Operational Plan based primarily on performance criteria assumes that all three levels will be considered in establishing the evidence on which a given teacher can be certified although major emphasis will be at the performance level.

The Operational Plan is the context through which research can provide a flow of information necessary to direct continuing improvement in teacher education.

Through the operating systems design, the Operational Plan for Teacher Education serves as a major research instrumentality. Working with a set of hypotheses about what teaching is, what teaching should become, and how we can move in the directions indicated, the Operational Plan serves as a testing ground through the utilization of a wide variability of resources and responsiveness to the demands of variable audiences. These audiences include both prospective teachers and their respective employees. Needed is a plan which can respond to the desire of one student to prepare for teaching in a "free" school while at the same time responding to needs of other students who choose to prepare for any of several other patterns of schooling.

Three descending orders of phenomena are inherent in the research potential of the Operational Plan. The first of these is the concept of systems and its implications and applications in education. The first order of business for the educational research community in the seventies may well be determining the viability of using systems designs for both management and instruction in education. At the second order the Plan provides a setting for research in a variety of related areas: systems designs and academic freedom; technological systems and human values; competency-based instrumental systems; interinstitutional cooperation; and economics and educational efficiency. Further, the Plan provides an opportunity to test a wide range of specific hypotheses related to instructional and management techniques with wide applicability throughout the educational community and special relevance within systems contexts.

Extensive improvement in teacher education will result from the Operational Plan through the dissemination of both its product and process.

Generalizability of findings within the context of the Operational Plan can be made both for product and for process. Many of the products developed, tested, and refined can be transferred to other institutions as parts of other programs or as collections of parts which make up a new system with special adaptive mechanisms appropriate to the setting. On the other hand, the processes (e.g., the use of systems management, procedures for faculty training) by which the plan has been developed and implemented can be shared with other institutions. Exchange of faculty members and other technical specialists would make it possible to duplicate a process which has resulted in the successful implementation of a program at one set of institutions for implementation at another.

The Operational Plan will ultimately be judged a success only if it demonstrates the capacity to respond to students with diverse needs, who can leave the program with diverse talents, and who serve effectively in diverse schools. In this context the Operational Plan is expected to lead to substantial diversity within the competency-based movement through implementation in a large consortium of institutions, each testing hypotheses in a different model. There are common bases from which such models may be initiated and common patterns of organization which may be expected to generate the anticipated model program. To these common beginnings, the identification of essential tasks and the organizational patterns designed to facilitate the implementation of these tasks, we now turn our attention.

Existing Office of Education programs provide the essential elements required to give direction and impetus to the realization of the Operational Plan.

TEACHER-EDUCATION PROGRAM REQUIREMENTS

The major functions of the Operational Plan for teacher education are (1) the preparation of educational personnel for the schools and (2) research designed to contribute to reform in education. The central theme of the Operational Plan is the potential of systems in education. Because the use of systems is central to the Plan, the two functions are integral to each other. Models and modeling imply the generation of new knowledge even as the preparation of personnel is under way. The Operational Plan then, is concerned with the demonstration of an operating model, with basic and applied research endeavors, while continuously utilizing information to improve the model, either as a total entity or as the educational system meeting specific requirements for specific learners.

Teaching/learning

The Operational Plan provides a teaching/learning facility which derives its focus from carefully defined and publicly displayed sets of performance criteria. The environment in which learning is to take place is carefully contrived so that learners may move efficiently to perform at criterion level. In its fullest operation the teaching/learning facility is extensive enough, both in quantity and in variety, to provide for a vast array of individual differences in goals (the kind of teacher I want to be), sequence (I'm really more interested right now in creativity, whatever the content area), instructional mode (I'm on an independent study kick right now), rate (political activities are taking much of my time this month), and personal involvement (I have this one instructor who helps me make sense of all this). Without this variety potential, a model is static and modeling is impossible. Only as students are able to design for themselves instructional programs which result in the competencies they deem essential may we expect the system to reflect the needs of individuals or the changing needs of schools. Within the Operational Plan the evolution of schools to new forms depends upon parallel evolution of educational personnel in preparation.

Management

Essential to the most fruitful use of the teaching/learning environment is the management of both students and resources. In the first instance, the problem is one of providing enough information about the student and about the potential teaching/learning opportunities for appropriate decisions. In the second instance, it is essential that both human and material resources are available when a learner needs them.

Monitoring student progress. From the student's entry into the program, information is generated for an extensive individual profile. Throughout the preparation program the student's progress is closely monitored and information is continuously made available to him and his counselor/instructor/advisors so that choices are made on the fullest possible information. Although the student may have preferences for a given instructional mode, abundant evidence may be available indicating that some other mode for the learner is more efficient. On the basis of this information the student may or may not wish to make a specific choice on the basis of an earlier preference.

Managing resources. The most difficult and essential resource to manage—by making certain it is available when required by the student—is the human resource. Human resources include those who would provide instructional guidance by helping the student interpret and understand data about himself and the program opportunities, instructors who help students through individual conferences or group seminars, or other learners who are ready for the common seminar or other small-group learning experiences.

Materials development and regeneration

Both Protocol and Training Materials are essential ingredients of the Operational Plan for teacher education. Although it is anticipated that for most students heavy emphasis in the program will center on experiences in the schools, Protocol Materials are essential for at least two reasons. In the first place, most students derive the greatest benefit from classroom observation or participation when they have been conceptually prepared for the experience. Protocol Materials provide visual images of learner activities organized as a base of experience for the development of psychological, philosophical, and sociological concepts. They prepare the learner to organize what he sees and experiences in the classroom. The experience of interpreting in simulated settings is expected to contribute much to the student's ability to interpret in the live classroom setting.

Training Materials of a wide variety are required of the Operational Plan Materials of instruction, drawn from many media including films, computerized instructional sequences, and slidetapes, are all potential sources of effective units in the integrated instructional system.

By design, the use of both Protocol and Training Materials has been anticipated in the Operational Plan and can be tested for effectiveness only in the crux of an operating system. Regeneration of materials is essential as data on effectiveness and use become increasingly available and concepts of the nature of schooling are altered. The Operational Plan has the potential for creating a context for continually changing schools. If the renewal of schools and school personnel is to be expected, then every element of the system must be viewed with this in mind: The potential to create must be held open and the response to the needs of all learners must be highly valued.

Faculty training

New programs in new schools require new teachers. Both at the university level and in the schools retraining is essential. The Operational Plan is designed on the assumption that teachers will play roles either in addition to or completely other than those which are presently exhibited in the lecture halls and classrooms throughout the country. No reform in teacher education will succeed without a comparable reform in the faculty member's concept of his own role. Much has been written about these roles; by and large these statements have been mildly reformational and have been received by the profession with little recognition of their significance. Not only must vigorous efforts be made to initiate the needed reform in faculty roles, both in the universities and in the schools; comparable study and effort must be made to assure that the nature of faculty roles for the future can be designed and redesigned as the nature of schooling takes on new dimensions reflecting the variety envisioned in earlier segments of this document.

Interinstitutional cooperation

Education is the responsibility of all society. For too long the responsibility for the education of youth has been delegated. The failure of the schools so delegated is not so much in what they are, but rather in problems associated with their isolation from society and from our demands which deny youth choice in the nature of their schooling. Interinstitutional cooperation as envisioned in the Operational Plan is but an opening wedge designed to make teacher education, the schools and schooling, responsive to and a part of a larger society. Teacher education in the universities has been separated too much from the schools it serves, and schools have been separated too much from the communities they serve. Interinstitution cooperation is required if the schools are to become a part of the whole again. Not only must schools respond to institutions in society, but those institutions must soon come to serve the educational requirements of all youth. Business, government, and the arts all have a stake in the schools and a responsibility to become actively involved, not only in helping schools but in actually providing schooling for youth everywhere.

The educational enterprise as it presently functions is fragmented and frequently at odds with itself. Schools and universities function on differing philosophies; state departments of public instruction too often are ineffective either because they lack direction or because they move to institutionalize a monolithic design for education throughout the state; and the dichotomy between preservice and inservice education provides a watershed in the professional career of each teacher. Initially progress must be made in clarifying these enormously distracting discrepancies before we can move on to the more essential cooperative efforts which lie outside the presently conceived educational establishment.

Student recruitment and placement

Recruitment and placement procedures which are integrated with the total teacher preparation program are essential ingredients of the Operational Plan. If reform in teacher education and thus in schooling is to take place, mutable initiates are required. Although our definitions of education typically imply that learners are mutable, we here imply that initiates have potential to become the innovators now and in the future. Of equal importance is the placement of these initiates in mutable schools. There are few of these in existence today, and those schools that are thought to be innovative are usually only mildly so. The Operational Plan must make possible the recruitment and placement of teachers whose qualities commend them to a philosophy of the changing nature of schooling.

Certification

Perhaps in no facet of teacher education of the past have we been more Procrustean than in our certification practices. The entire structure of certification needs careful reexamination in the light of the essential demands of reform in teacher education and education. If individual teacher education programs are to be generated and if extensive variety is to be fostered in the schools, new flexible concepts of certification are essential. Through the Operational Plan the option is presented to teachers in preparation, or at points in mid-career, to identify the sets of criteria by which their own performance is to be judged and ultimately certified. Schools then will be in a position to identify the kinds of performance they want in the teacher they seek. Certification is then a verification of the fact that the teacher can perform as indicated in the records available. With such a system, variability is possible in two dimensions. The first is the variability associated with the nature of the performance itself, and the second is variability in the extent (amount) of performance which can be verified at any given time. Thus, teacher aide, teacher, master teacher are not discrete entities but exist along a continuum on which a given teacher can be specifically placed on his own terms.

Assessment and research

Although assessment and research are closely related concerns in the Operational Plan each serves a unique function. Assessment data, continually collected make possible the essential monitoring of student progress, provide feedback on the effectiveness of specific instructional activities, and suggest the appropriateness of a given teacher's associated personal goals, instructional program, and ultimate career expectations.

The Operational Plan as a research facility functions at a variety of levels. At the highest level, the Plan provides a facility for the investigation of the utility of systems in education. The Operational Plan is a system. It functions as an evolving system, and its success is as a system open to change, creating teachers of diverse characteristics for service in schools of diverse nature.

At a second level, the Plan provides for research in a number of areas essential to the continued improvement of schooling in the decade ahead as the utility of systems in education is investigated in a variety of settings. Competency-based instructional systems, systems and academic freedom, systems and personalization, technology and human values, systems as means of implementing interinstitutional cooperation, and systems as vehicles to increase economical efficiency of education are some of the major areas needing research throughout the seventies if we are to meet our educational obligations in the eighties.

At a third level, research within the Operational Plan focuses on the relative effectiveness of various instructional modes; on the viability of specific modes for learners of identified characteristics; on the impact of specific faculty roles on college instruction; on the impact of learner choice in program plan and implementation; on the need for the amount of in-school experience which is required; on the effectiveness of Protocol Materials in the development of concepts about learning, learners, teachers, and schools; on the effectiveness of units of the interinstitutional cooperative; and on the impact of changing teacher-education programs on changing concepts and practices in schooling.

CONFIRMATORY MECHANISMS OF THE OPERATIONAL PLAN

Each of the Elementary Models projects has emphasized the importance of feedback at points on a variety of levels. Throughout the development and implementation of those programs some kind of Confirmatory Mechanism is the *sine qua non* of Competency-Based Education. To identify specific objectives is not enough without a mechanism to serve as a check on the extent to which those objectives have been achieved. In the Models projects many such mechanisms have been designed to ask and seek answers to questions relating to viability, consistency, or efficiency. Such mechanisms are integrated elements within the Operational Plan; they are empowered not only to analyze but to apply the resultant findings to future operations.

Integrating Confirmatory Mechanisms

A generalized model of a Confirmatory Mechanism is shown in Figure 4–1.

Purpose:

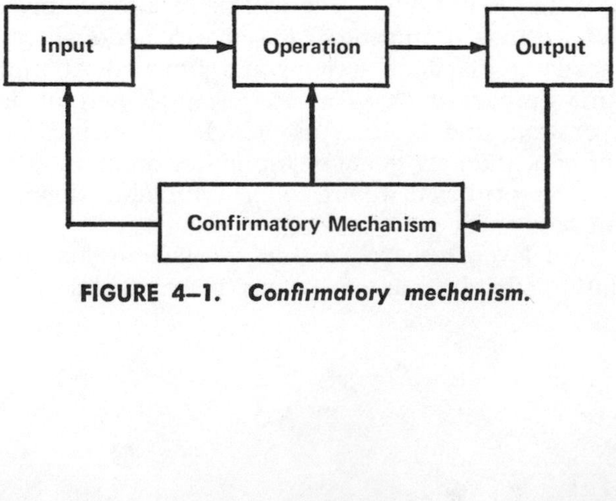

FIGURE 4–1. ***Confirmatory mechanism.***

This Model assumes the system has been designed to achieve a specific purpose, already clearly identified. In relation to that purpose, the system has an input, operation, and an output. Through the Confirmatory Mechanism, staff members consider the extent the output of the system is congruent with the stated purpose of the system. The review of the output may, indeed, indicate that the system fulfilled its objectives in any given instance. In this case, achievement of purpose is confirmed.

Often, however, an analysis of output will indicate the purpose has not been achieved. Now the disposition of the case is not quite so simple. It is not enough to indicate simply that the purpose is not confirmed. Essential to the continued operation and improvement of the system is some evidence as to why the purpose was not achieved; so the Confirmatory Mechanism seeks additional evidence. Failure to confirm achievement of purpose is usually, at first, cause for scrutiny of the operation. What was done within the operational component of the system has been inadequate or misdirected. Were the operation the only place for error to exist, the focus of Confirmatory Mechanisms would be relatively simple, but such is not the case. There are at least two other points at which the system may be at fault. One of these is the nature of the input. The operation may be appropriate for the purpose if, and only if, the input does adequately meet certain prerequisites. Perhaps those prerequisites have been improperly identified or emphasized. At still another point, the purpose itself may be inappropriate either in intent or in statement. The purpose may be impossible to achieve; it may be stated in such a way that it is difficult to determine which operation to use or what standards to apply to the output. Additional complications grow from the interaction of these components. These interactions exist in almost every system. The purpose may be right for some inputs but not for others. Perhaps the operation, as in an instructional system, is appropriate for some inputs (learners) but not as appropriate for others. Perhaps the assessment devices used to measure the output or the prerequisites of the input (learners) may be inappropriate (not reliable, e.g., not culture free). These complexities indicate both the difficulties involved and how essential an effectively operating Confirmatory Mechanism is as an aspect of any system.

The Operational Plan for Program Development in Teacher Education is itself a system. As such, it contains Confirmatory Mechanisms at a number of points and throughout the interrelated network of system and subsystem. The network of system and subsystems ranges from the macrolevel of the Operational Plan for Program Development to the smallest microlevel system which can be identified as a single learning experience. Macrolevel systems include the Operational Plan as shown in Figure 4–2, the State Model (not diagrammed), and the Local Teacher-Education Program Model depicted in Figure 4–3. At the Microlevel I is the Program Element or interrelated Set of Modules; at Microlevel II is the Instructional Module shown in Figure 4–4. Microlevel III, not shown, is the single instructional activity.

Purpose:

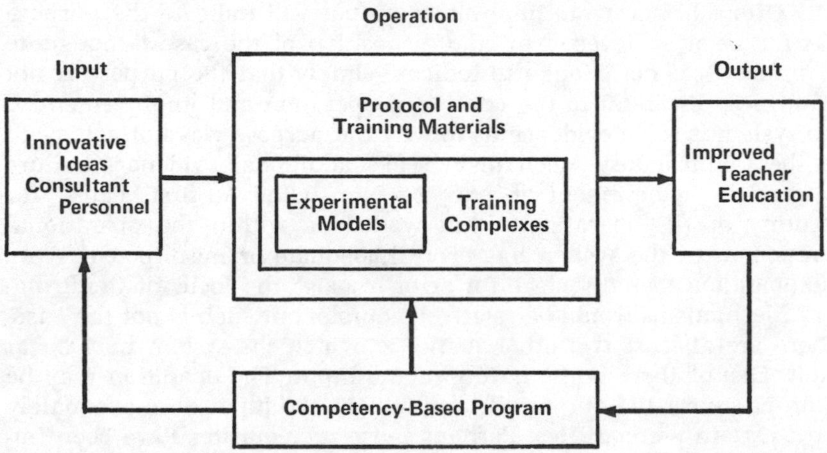

FIGURE 4–2. ***Confirming mechanism at Macrolevel 1: Operational Plan.***

Purpose:

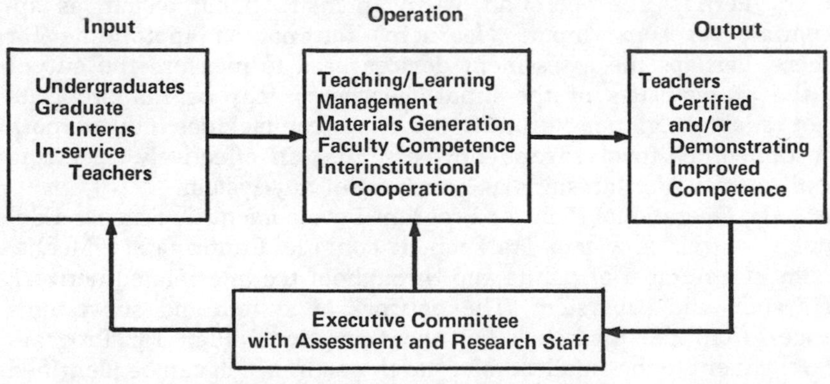

FIGURE 4–3. ***Confirming mechanism or Microlevel III: Local Teacher-Education Program.***

Purpose:

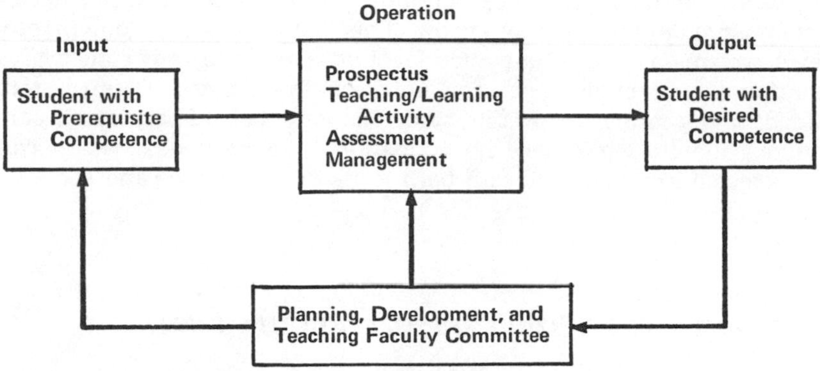

FIGURE 4–4. ***Confirmatory mechanism or Microlevel II: Instructional Module.***

All of these subsystems, those pictured, those mentioned, and perhaps others still to be identified or designed depend for their success on many things; none is more crucial than the confirming mechanism. Within each of these subsystems the confirming mechanism by design and function has much in common with the others. Each depends upon carefully identified and administered measuring devices which directly reflect the intent stated or implied in the purpose. These measuring devices provide a flow of data which must be processed. The processing provides a continuing analysis of the output of the system. If this analysis does not confirm the achievement of the purpose, a series of hypotheses must be made about where the fault lies. Methodical investigations must be made to determine at what specific point the system has failed. Ultimately corrections are made on the recommendation or at the direction of staff members responsible for the confirming mechanism. Data are continually collected again at the output to determine the nature of the improvement which has resulted from the change made in the system.

Because instructional systems are sensitive to a variety of changes outside themselves, one would not expect a satisfactorily operating system to remain so over time. Students who enter educational institutions each year differ from those who entered the year before. Materials which are effective one year may be quite ineffective later for any number of reasons. The impact of a McLuhanesque treatment five years ago would have resulted in different responses from those it would cause today. Martial music accompanying an instructional film would have a very different impact on many students today from that on their counterparts ten years ago. Even changes in clothing styles can at times alter student response to visual materials. We can readily see that a well-adjusted, well-balanced, and finely tuned instructional system serving our purposes today will not necessarily serve our purposes tomorrow. This is as true within our macrolevel systems as within our microlevel systems. The importance of a continually functioning complement of interrelated Confirmatory Mechanisms cannot be overstressed. Without their effective and continuous monitoring service no educational/instructional system can be expected to remain relevant both to its own purposes and society's demands.

RESOURCES FOR REALIZING THE OPERATIONAL PLAN

Realization of the Operational Plan will require human and financial resources of considerable diversity. Only through the coordination of these resources at the federal, state, and local levels can the Plan be effectively realized. The role of the federal government through the Office of Education will be that of initiating and coordinating a long-term well-planned change effort.

Present programs under way in the Office of Education can contribute significantly as complementary elements in the Operational Plan for Program Development in Teacher Education. Three specific kinds of activities are required if the Operational Plan is to function effectively. These include (1) policy making and coordination, (2) implementation of operating instructional programs, and (3) the development and regeneration of Protocols and Training Materials.

The development and maintenance of policy which gives direction to the Operational Plan and is supported widely within the professional community is of utmost importance. It is recommended that policy leadership be provided through the Competency-Based Program presently supported at the national level by the Office of Education. A strong national committee, not unlike that presently funded through AACTE, should assume the responsibility (1) to identify continuing national needs, (2) to monitor and disseminate information concerning the effectiveness of Competency-Based Programs as they evolve, (3) to coordinate through subcommittees, local level OE partially funded Competency-Based Program (CBP) Centers, and (4) to make regular reports, including recommendations, to the Office of Education. In a sense, the Competency-Based Program will serve as the feedback system serving the Operational Plan for Program Development in Teacher Education (Figure 4–5).

The operating instructional programs of the Operational Plan take place within the CBP Centers. These centers include the oper-

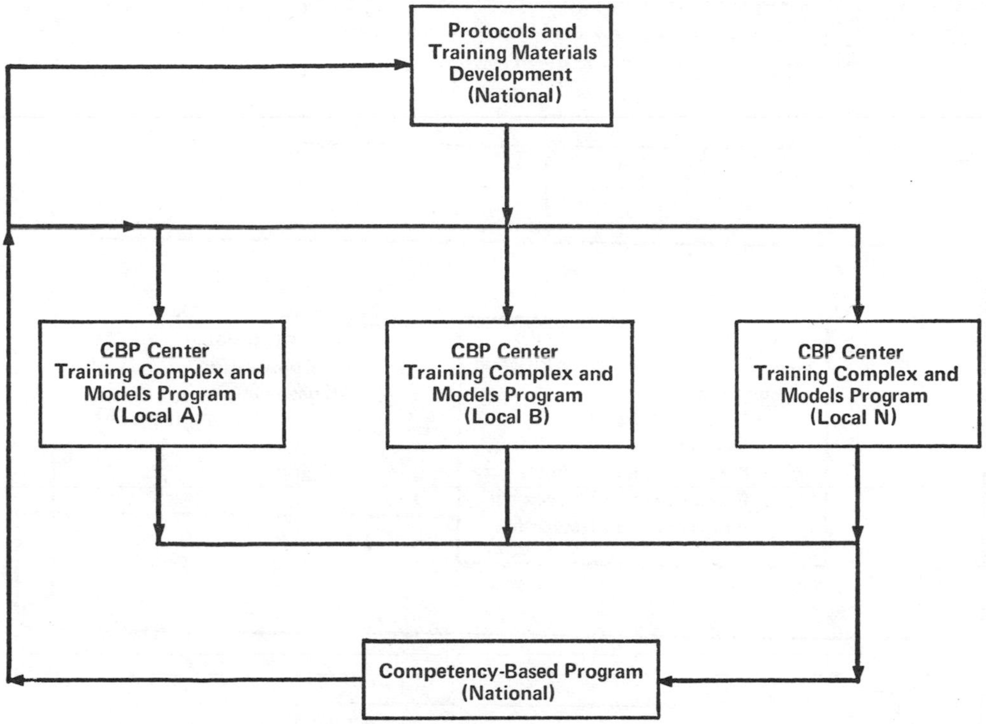

FIGURE 4–5. ***Relation of the present BEPD programs within the Operational Plan.***

ating elements of both the Training Complex and the Experimental[1] Models Program. The Operational Plan function of each of several present OE programs are identified in Figure 4–6 which details the interdependence of these programs within the Competency-Based Program Center at the local level. The Experimental Models Program functions within the Training Complex in that the latter is responsible for the interinstitutional cooperation which gives major impetus to operating instructional programs. The Training Complex assumes certain management functions, faculty training within the schools, and final certification of teachers. On the other hand, within each CBP Center the Models Program assumes responsibility for teaching/learning activities, management of resources and learners,

[1] The term *experimental* rather than *elementary* is used throughout this paper to imply the need for including both elementary and secondary education in the design and implementation of the Operational Plan for Program Development in Teacher Education.

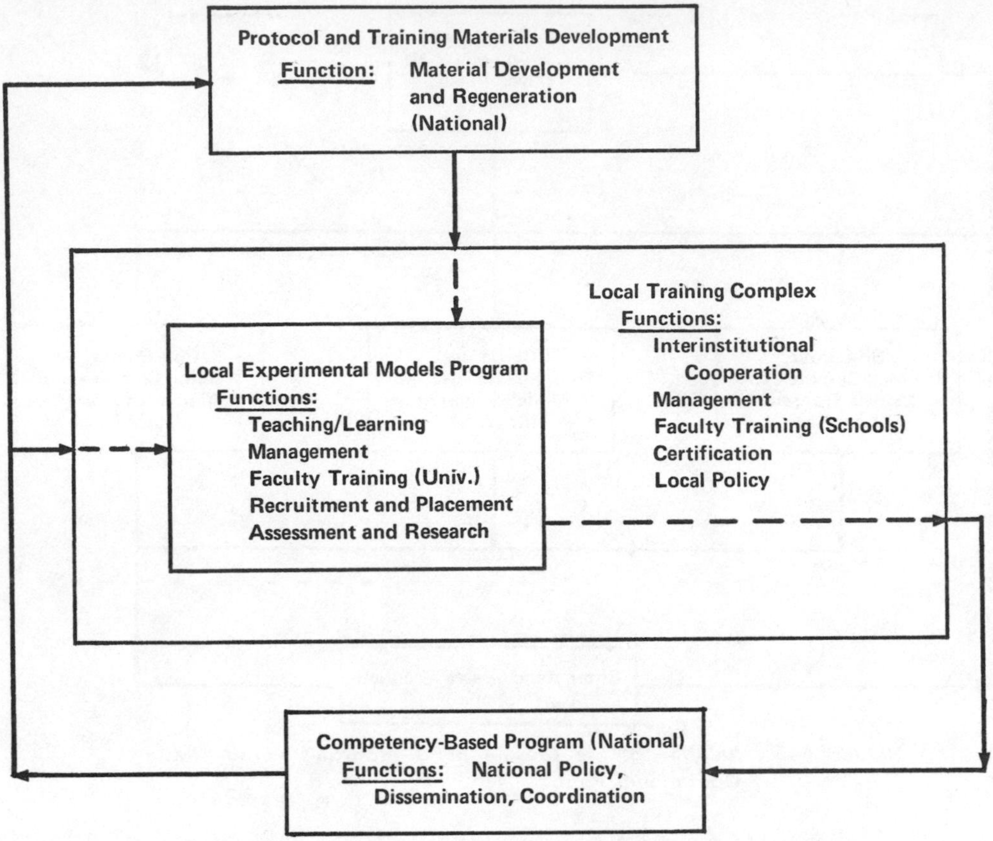

FIGURE 4–6. ***Functions of the present BEPD programs within a Competency-Based Program Center.***

faculty training on campus, student recruitment and placement, and assessment and research activities.

Each of the CBP Centers is served by the National Program for Protocols and Training Materials. It is recommended that these instructional materials be developed with balance between the need for program variety among CBP Centers and the need to reduce to a minimum duplication of materials which could be equally effective for instructional programs in more than a single center.

The expectation that the Operational Plan for Program Development in Teacher Education will create the reform so necessary for next developments in American education carries a parallel expectation that funding sources must be coordinated and directed specifically to essential elements charged with the responsibility to initiate and to sustain the Operational Plan over a long-term period.

Benefit analysis of the Operational Plan for Program Development

Any analysis of the benefits of educational innovation first must clarify the nature of these benefits. Benefits may be viewed as direct, interactive, and intertemporal. Direct benefits are those that accrue immediately to specific audiences. Since both audiences and innovations are multifaceted, a second class of benefits are interactive. That is, they arise from the interaction of direct benefits of various innovations upon various audiences. Third, benefits flow from one point in time to another and from one set of receivers to another. In this sense, benefits of the Experimental Models accrue to students at the precertification level; in following years additional benefits accrue to their pupils; in turn these pupils return benefits to society. This flow of benefits from college students, to public school pupils, and to society is an example of intertemporal benefits.

Comprehensive benefit analysis, then, must deal with these three benefit streams: direct, interactive, and intertemporal. First, direct benefits will be considered for each of the major components of the Operational Plan. These will include the Experimental Models, the Training Complexes, the Protocol and Training Materials, and the Competency-Based Program identified as the Confirmatory Mechanism. Although the Training Complexes, the Protocol and Training Materials, the Competency-Based Program, and the Experimental Models exist as an integrated system, in this analysis, the focus is primarily on the benefits resulting from the implementation of the Experimental Models. The Models are emphasized for two reasons. First, they have been more extensively defined than other components; second, the authors have been closely associated with the Experimental Models Program.

Benefits of the Experimental Models

Benefited audiences are easily identified by location. These we shall order to include the university, the schools, the community, and the profession.

The university

Audiences within the university to be considered here include precertification students, teacher-education faculty, and graduate students and faculty throughout the university.

Precertification students. The Experimental Models Programs emphasize the individualization of instruction in four ways: rate, sequencing, mode, and goals.

An instructional program which allows each student to progress at his own rate assures an optimum use of student time only if students are capable of judging wisely; to do this, they need information and counseling. The Models' designs encourage students' progress at individual rates while progress data are made continuously available for student and instructional staff review. This benefit (rate) makes it possible for students to continue their teacher educational study twelve months of the year or any segment of that twelve months. It is possible for students to drop out of the program

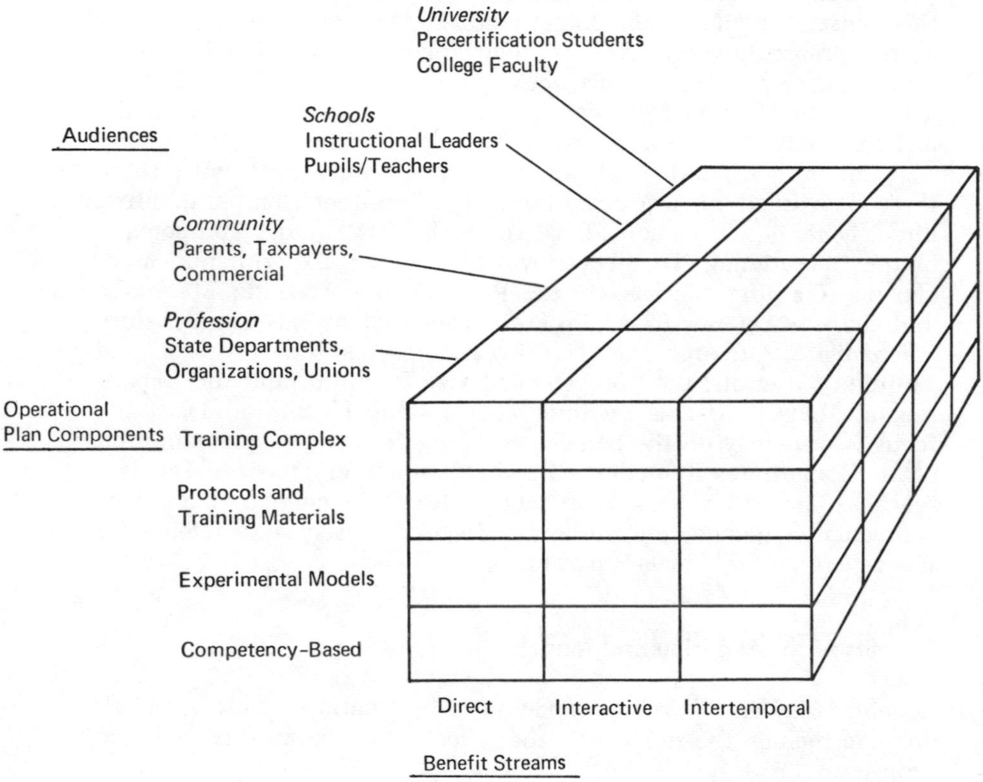

Benefit Analysis Framework: Components X Audiences X Benefit Streams

FIGURE 4–7. *Benefit analysis framework.*

temporarily for whatever reason and return again at their personal and professional convenience. Students enjoy the benefit of moving easily to and from their education and noneducation work elsewhere on campus. This same characteristic makes it possible for students to move in and out of public school experience or other work experiences. Each student develops a rate of progression most efficient for himself.

In typical educational programs the class structure is such that sequence freedom is limited to two or three credit units. Usually there is an additional constraint: Certain courses may be taken only after other prerequisite courses have been completed. The Models, on the other hand, are designed to enable students to choose frequently among sequence alternatives. Minimal sequence requirements are established; beyond that, personal choice dictates the student's next topic for study. Not only can a student pursue topics of personal interest, he can delay other topics until he feels he is ready—or until he can pursue such a topic in close association with related topics; students enjoy the benefits of many possible variations. Of special benefit is the opportunity to study topics in association with immediate problems in the clinical setting. For instance, a student may find, in working with elementary children, that he is lacking in his understanding of language. This student can turn at that time to the study of linguistics; should he become interested in that topic, he can pursue it in depth. The student is able to put his program together according to his own sense of coherence.

Instructional mode choices as a function of individualization are of special significance in the Experimental Models Program. Students do not learn equally well from instruction in any given mode. Choice of mode throughout the Experimental Models is of double benefit. First, the student is enabled increasingly to decide (both intuitively and from data feedback sources) which modes serve him best. Further, that he can make a choice is a substantial benefit; a student is a better motivated learner if he has helped choose his learning resources.

Within the Experimental Models, each learner has an opportunity to determine to a considerable extent the kind of teacher he wishes to become. His area of specialization, his level of competence (aide, teacher, master teacher) and the manner in which his professional program is related to his education in the arts and sciences are determined by the individual learner in cooperation with his advisors. We have recognized that no one learning theory describes all teaching or all teachers. The Models permit individual students to determine the theory or theories they wish to use to design their teaching styles. This will result in teachers who differ substantially from each other but understand the bases on which they make their individual decisions.

Personalization is emphasized in each of the Models. Two personalizing functions are significant in terms of student benefits. The first is that personalization derived from faculty/student conferences and small-group seminars; from peer-group relations, both in advisory sessions and in planning and decision making in (simulated and actual) team teaching experiences. There seems to be an increasing evidence that individualization alone, through independent study, is not enough. Apparently, in the schools as well as higher education, independent study must be associated with personal interaction. Through interaction the social aspect of ideas developed through independent study is made clear to individual learners. Thus, learners are able to identify points of application for their new understanding of other learners and teaching.

Another important dimension of personalization designed as part of the Models Program is program negotiation. Negotiation between students and faculty advisors enables students to identify and develop programs appropriate both to their own interests and to the needs of the schools they will serve.

Finally, the benefits to precertification students are clear in relation to the Competency-Based Programs within the Models. A crucial advantage to the learner is the knowledge of those competencies he must master to progress within his program to meet the objectives he has set for himself, and to understand fully the implications of his study for his image of himself as teacher.

The competency-based nature of the program makes it possible for the student to obtain continuous information on his progress in developing the desired competence. Specific and immediate information on results is a particularly strong motivational source; the Models Program, through its competency-based nature, provides the student with such information.

We expect schools to move increasingly toward instructional systems, behavioral objectives, and accountability. Many students will work during their precertification program in schools where such emphases exist. The Competency-Based Programs inherent in the Models benefit the student by providing him with experiences relevant to such concepts. Through such experiences the student not only sees examples of practices and attitudes comparable to those unfolding in many schools now, and through the seventies; also, the student can become familiar with both the advantages and the problems he will typically confront in such an orientation.

Professional education faculty. The professional education faculty responsible for teacher-education benefits from the implementation of the Experimental Models in a number of ways. Specifically, benefits can be classified as (1) resource support, (2) faculty retraining, (3) administration, and (4) scholarship.

Instructional staff associated with the Models are recipients of continuous feedback data concerning their own (and their students') effectiveness. This flow of data will make it possible for faculty to improve the quality of their own learning and instruction decisions. Just as the effectiveness of instructional mode and strategy varies with the individual learner (ATI), it can be expected that something like Instructor/Strategy Interaction (ISI) is also operating. If ISI is to be understood, and if actions are to be based on the realities of ISI, pertinent information to the instructor is essential. The variety of mediated materials which will be readily available to instructors will improve their effectiveness. The need for continuous updating of instructional materials and strategies will keep instructors up-to-date. The demand of the Models for new faculty roles and increased competence can be met through extensive in-service training activities; such training can be continuously provided to faculty, both prior to and throughout implementation of the Models' operation.

The concept of the Models can do much to benefit faculty by keeping schools of education in the vanguard of educational/technological/humanistic integration. Presently we believe there is a division among those who would individualize; this division exists as a tendency to humanistic/technological polarity. The free school movement and American technological society at large both generally support the drive to find appropriate ways to individualize instruction at all levels. The humanistic/technological polarity, therefore, reflects disagreement on means, not ends. The challenge of the seventies is to find ways of bringing together these divergent views, projections, and practices into a coherent approach to humane education. Technological expertise will contribute to our success in this venture. To be part of this unifying vanguard throughout the seventies and eighties is the major benefit we expect to accrue to an involved faculty.

Faculty involvement in part-time administration of professional education programs consumes too much of the time of a large proportion of the faculty. The systematic design inherent in the Models provides for administrative support that is more specific and more clearly defined; it is separate from the instructional responsibilities assumed by the professional education faculty. The separation of these tasks and the resulting efficiency (in the use of both time and energy) represents a major benefit in faculty. Administration, scholarship, and teaching—each will benefit from the systematic approach implementing the Models will entail.

The benefits of the Models to faculty scholarship appear to be unlimited. The developing Model represents the best we can project concerning the future of education both in the schools and in colleges and universities. Curriculum developments in the schools and in teacher education will be constantly evolving under the direction of a faculty and staff committed to maximal quality in the teacher-education programs. The research potential in the Models Program is extensive. The operating Experimental Model system is a major research vehicle; a wide range of variables can be independently manipulated and a continuous flow of data can be derived. These data may be expected in such quantity as to make present data sources for educational research seem miniscule in comparison. The faculty association with such an ongoing curriculum and research development facility will substantially benefit those faculty members who are primarily interested in research.

The service opportunities for faculty participation in an operational Model have been suggested by the dissemination project resulting from the initial development of specification and feasibility studies. Many faculty members at each of the institutions involved have been widely used as consultants, locally and nationally. Operating Models can serve as demonstration centers and as continuing sources of consulting assistance, as these initial efforts demonstrate.

Graduate education students. The character of the Experimental Models Program, both in the development and implementation stages, assures that innovation and research activities are continually under way; that competent educational scholars and researchers will be continually required to assist professors and other development and technical staff in the Model Program. Opportunities to work at the theoretical stage of development will be continually available as data are collected, which must be analyzed, and put into a theoretical framework. From such a framework implications for further refinement and development of the Model can be drawn. Perhaps most important is the student's participation in an environment designed for the study and creation of change. The Model *is* change —guided, modified, explored. Today most of us read this word and accept it; few of us comprehend fully the extent to which the word change today can be used as a synonym for reality. The essence of society and of education is change. If we accept that, then the availability of a context of development and research, in which the first principle is change, is a primary benefit of the Experimental Models.

Benefits identified as available to faculty are also available to graduate students. Learning new instructional roles, and drawing on resources of a comprehensive system approach will aid students in decision making, hypothesis creation and testing, and projections for future programing.

Higher education. The Experimental Models Program, or something similar, could have been envisioned in any number of areas and at almost any instructional level. The 1967 request from USOE for preliminary specifications, however, was directed to teacher education. It may be that a professional education program, either in teacher education, engineering, medicine, or law, is more appropriate for initial work than is general education, but that is not certain. The success or failure of the Models Program will have implications for higher education in all areas; we can expect to find our colleagues across the disciplines watching critically, cautiously, and approvingly. Implementing the Models, in some form, is a crucial benefit in providing examples of success (or failure) in this area of educational projection. Throughout higher education, but especially on a campus where a Model is being implemented, a number of complementary applications may be expected to develop.

Problems for study in higher education are numerous. One of the first of these lies in the potential conflict between systems design and academic freedom. With the discussions currently under way and the trend toward planning–budgeting systems in higher education, we must expect much attention to be focused on this phase of the Models. Can faculty commit their efforts and energies to cooperative systematic participation in program implementation without surrendering some portion of their highly valued academic freedom? What problems will faculty be confronting? A major benefit of the Model to higher education, then, is the opportunity it provides us to make a case study of this relation between systems designs and academic freedom.

Individualized-personalized education is an obvious need; diverse efforts are under way to create such programs. In many instances these efforts are of limited scope; the change required is minimal. Probably the results will be minimal. The Experimental Models Program (in implementation) provides higher education the benefit of a comprehensive reorganization directed toward personalized education.

Accountability, Competency-Based Education, and behavioral objectives are all aspects of the program which will receive attention in higher education. Too much innovation at all levels is piecemeal; it is only too likely higher education innovation in the future will remain so. Needed are comprehensive, integrated thrusts such as those represented in the Models. Accountability concepts of Competency-Based Programs cannot be tested in a minimal, limited fashion. They must be tested in inclusive, realistic contexts. The benefits to higher education derive mainly from the comprehensiveness of the Models. Information derived from the Models will be useful to those who plan for education in the arts and sciences, in other professional schools, in technical schools, and in junior and community colleges.

The polarity represented by technology and human values is of special import to a wide higher education audience. Ways must be found to utilize technology to enhance the humanness of our educational endeavors at all levels. The difficulty of reconciling these emphases is due, in part, to limitations in our technological know-how; in part, to our inability to be creative in our search for harmonious solutions. We expect that initially those working with the Models will find it difficult, but not impossible, to resolve this polarity. Higher education will benefit through the demonstration of a working Model's various efforts to resolve this polarity.

Higher education is undergoing special scrutiny at this time of difficult budget problems. The systems design concept utilized in the Models provides a context for the student of economic efficiency in education. Such study will have broad implications throughout higher education. Any economic analysis of innovative practices begins with an analysis of costs and benefits of present programs. At present, these are too seldom available or too superficially done to be of substantial value in educational planning. Major steps have been taken within the past few years to move in appropriate directions on these problems; soon we may expect to understand more clearly the efficiency or lack of it in our current operating of institutions of higher education. The implementation of the Models provides an analysis of present practice, but it also provides a continuous flow of cost data which is relevant to other evolving educational programs. Both the demonstrable system for the study of economic efficiency and the findings which emanate from the system will provide benefits to higher education.

If universities and colleges are to change significantly, they will do so as a result of changing faculty roles. New institutions where faculty members only lecture as they have in the past, can hardly be called new. Buildings may be new; scheduling procedures may be new; student and faculty life-styles may be new; committee structures may be new; but none of this matters if the faculty member does not see himself in a new role. The Experimental Model provides the benefits of new staffing patterns and new roles for faculty. The nature of these roles and staffing patterns will evolve over time. Projections of their character can be made at present only tentatively. Needed now are illustrative environments; from these, accumulating evidence concerning the nature of needed innovations can be collected and disseminated.

The schools

The benefit audiences in the schools include instructional leaders, teachers, and pupils.

Instructional leaders. Those who assume responsibility for curriculum planning, development, and implementation in the schools benefit in a variety of ways through association with the Experimental Models. Through the close interaction of personnel in the universities and those in the schools, ideas evolve as each faculty draws on the experience and expertise of the other. The benefit to the schools is first: The university staff develops a better understanding of the schools philosophy and practice as it will be experienced by precertification students and in the assistance cooperating faculty can render. The parallel nature of teacher education and the school curricular programs creates a set of common problems; faculty can seek solutions at both levels. As faculty move easily back and forth between schools and the university through the medium of the Experimental Model, tentative solutions can be formed through cooperative action.

Perhaps the major benefit of the Experimental Models to the instructional leadership in the schools is the nature of the students who are becoming teachers. Their competencies are known; their goals are clearly established. The result is an improved relationship between these students, their teachers, principals, and others in leadership roles within the schools. Such understanding results in students who are better served by the schools as they learn; the students can be more appropriately directed for optimum effect on the students they will teach.

Teachers. The Experimental Models benefit teachers in the schools in a variety of ways. First, and most significant, are the advantages already identified for the precertification students. All of these advantages also accrue to the in-service teacher seeking improvement of her teaching skills or better understanding of her teaching role and her students. The Experimental Models include designs for in-service work. This in-service work extends the instructional mechanisms of the Models beyond the precertification level. The benefits already identified for precertification students will not be repeated here. However, those benefits (of individualization, personalization, and Competency-Based Programs) accrue to in-service teachers as well.

Beyond these direct benefits accruing to teachers working directly within the Models context, intertemporal benefits evolve as precertification students become teachers in schools everywhere. In that sense teachers in the schools experience a new set of benefits separate from those mentioned above. Teachers coming into the schools from the Experimental Models have a more comprehensive understanding of the schools, of learners in the schools, and of faculty roles and expectations. But the most important benefit is their perception of themselves as teachers. They have identified and developed a set of theories to guide their teaching practice, they understand the competencies they possess, and they understand that schools are changing as society changes. This appreciation of change provides what may be the most crucial benefit in the two or three decades ahead as graduates of today's universities help create schools for the twenty-first century. The entire Model is essentially a Confirmatory Mechanism; the student learns to use the continuous flow of data to make decisions relevant to an ever-changing school.

Pupils. Ultimately the benefits of the Experimental Model are designed to enhance the quality of education for the individual pupil in the school. The flexibility of the Model, the individualization provided for the learning teacher, and the teacher's resulting appreciation of the individuality of learners is a direct benefit to pupils. For too long schools have responded to pupils as though they were all of a kind. Provision for pupils with diverse backgrounds has been rare and continues to be rare in our schools. Pupils from minority groups—ethnic, cultural, racial, religious—have often found their identity ignored in schools geared to homogeneity. The Experimental Models provide teachers who have been dealt with as individuals and who have been helped to view learning as a very individual matter. They have come to appreciate the importance of varied learning environments to provide individuals with ideas or experiences which are personally useful. It is in this context that the Models contribute most significantly to the education of disadvantaged youth.

Teachers can be assigned according to their specific competencies; pupils will have teachers who recognize and appreciate their differences. Pupils will experience more effective teaching. Learners will benefit as schools move increasingly to individualize and personalize programs, and as they come in contact with teachers who understand and can implement such programs.

The community

Benefited audiences within the community are: parents, tax payers, public educational services, foundations, and commercial enterprises. All these derive benefits from the implementation of the Experimental Models Program.

All benefits to children (from the Experimental Models Program) are benefits to parents as well. More specifically, however, parents derive a number of other benefits. Perhaps most important is the opportunity parents will have of knowing how their children are doing. Parents will rely less on a teacher's opinion that tells them as much about the teacher as it does about the child. Instead, parents will be given assessments that specify the tasks to be learned and that evaluate progress in terms of the achievement of these specific competencies. Parents will understand better what their children are learning.

Since administrators will be able to select teachers with the specific competencies needed for a particular school, parents can be confident teachers have been selected on the basis of better evidence than in the past.

A fully operating Experimental Models Program with parallel development in the schools will provide parents with instructional models. These will make it possible for parents to better plan educational experiences for their own children. Certainly the school is not the only educating institution in the community. For some children the school is the major educational institution; for others it is but one of several, including the home, the church, and a variety of community organizations. Parents who better understand what the schools are contributing will be in a better position to plan for the use of other community resources in educating their children.

Finally, a major benefit of the Competency-Based Experimental Models Program for parents is that they will be able to use its resources for their own development. Parents wanting to know more about the mathematics program will be able to undertake independent introductory studies of it. The school can become a known educational quantity to everyone within its sphere of influence.

Tax payer benefits from the Experimental Models are difficult to analyze at this time for two reasons: Development and implementation costs are, as yet, unknown. Also, we cannot yet anticipate how widespread the effects of the program will be. The level of sophistication required of delivery systems for Competency-Based Programs is still unknown. Cost is related to that level of sophistication. Likewise, we need demonstration sites. These will provide evidence of the most efficient way to disseminate Competency-Based Programs to large numbers of learners. The main benefit to tax payers at present arises from the implications of systems designs for management and budgeting (of both development and implementation) of teacher-education programs. This systematic approach assures the tax payer of efficient use of available funding and provides him with data concerning what the costs are, what expected or actual benefits are, and how specific items are related to budgetary allocations.

Each community supports a large number of educational services. More often than not these services are totally uncoordinated and minimally used in relation to school programs. The Experimental Models will encourage coordination of these services. First, the Models provide a demonstration of effective and efficient management of a wide variety of learning resources within the formal educational community. Indeed, in many instances, these resources from the larger community may be built into the school's more formal network of resources through the activities of the Training Complex. Secondly, the specificity with which the school and the university define their responsibilities will make it possible for other educational institutions to review and re-define their own potential for supplementary contributions. The result is a community-wide consciousness of educational responsibilities. Schools can serve but a small proportion of them. The recognition and assumption of responsibility to coordinate this larger educational world for all citizens in the community is a major benefit that will result from several elements of the Models Program, implemented at the community level.

Foundations seek ways of supporting innovations to serve the common good. The foundations will benefit from the developing Models Program through the profusion of ideas generated by an evolving program. Foundations will find many of these ideas useful in their continuing search for useful educational alternatives.

Commercial enterprises—including hardware, software, and service organizations—will find many cooperative ways to work with and through the developing Experimental Models Programs. While they will find many benefits from such a cooperative arrangement, they also will make substantial contributions in terms of packaging, marketing, and servicing instructional materials. Their expertise in these areas will assure wide dissemination of the process and products developed by the Models Programs; as a result, the cost per learner/unit will be reduced over time. Thus, cooperation between the business and education communities can make the innovations resulting from the Models Program more economically feasible. It is expected that business dollar investments in education will be more economically sound than they have been in the past.

The profession

Audiences within the profession include state departments of public instruction, professional organizations, teachers unions, and certification agencies.

Several state departments are carefully investigating the potential of Competency-Based Certification. Such certification is nearly useless if it is not accompanied by Competency-Based Programs. Initial efforts to certify on such a basis may not be accompanied by Competency-Based Programs; if this happens, such efforts will fail. If we are to determine the validity of Competency-Based Certification, it must be accompanied by comparable programs. One of the benefits of the Models is the provision of such program bases.

Professional organizations in education represent a wide range of philosophies. The Association for Supervision and Curriculum Development, The Association for Educational Communications and Technology, The National Council of Teachers of English, and The National Council of Teachers of Mathematics may each take different positions on the issue of Competency-Based Education Programs. A major benefit of the fully implemented Models Program is that it will provide a testing ground for these positions. The Models can provide an opportunity to demonstrate the potential problems of Competency-Based Education. A widely diverse professional community will have the opportunity to observe, discuss, and debate the merits of an evolving entity at all levels.

Teachers' unions, themselves, hesitant but generally supportive of Competency-Based Education, will have an opportunity to study the nature of such programs through a series of fully operating programs. What new roles will be required of teachers; how teachers may be expected to prepare themselves for these roles; what impact cooperative group teaching procedures will have on the individual teacher; and the implications that recognized levels of teaching competency will have for the profession are all questions of substantial interest to teachers' bargaining agents. The use of the Models context in which to make such a study is essential to the effective integration of a wide variety of views on these issues.

Certification agencies at both college and local school levels utilize sets of standards developed over time, often informally. The certification of Competency-Based Programs will require a new approach to the establishment of criteria. A fully operating Model will provide bases for judgments on functional standards. Once certification by competencies becomes a major route into the profession, we expect the obvious benefits of such programs to encourage direct certification of the prospective teacher; current indirect methods will be unnecessary.

Benefits of Other Components of the Operational Plan for Program Development

Training Complexes, Protocols and Training Materials, and the Competency-Based Program of the Operational Plan for Program Development in Teacher Education are viewed as essential to the facilitation of the instructional environments provided by the Experimental Models. While the benefit section of this has concentrated primarily on the Experimental Models, we have assumed the support of other components.

It is through the Training Complexes that we expect to achieve much of the essential coordination between universities and schools, between formal and informal educational institutions of the community, between the local educational establishment and the professional organizations, between schools and the community. The Experimental Models require the extensive use of Protocols and Training Materials. Without them, the Experimental Models cannot exist. A plan would need to be developed to provide these materials if the Protocol and Training Materials program has not been established. The Confirmatory Mechanisms inherent in the Competency-Based Program are essential to the effectiveness of the Experimental Models. The essence of the Models is change. That change must be monitored and directed. It is through the Confirmatory Mechanism that the Models are kept in contact with reality. Part of the Confirmatory Mechanism is within the Models themselves; part is at the larger state and national levels where the Competency-Based Program assumes the responsibility.

Although the major focus of this paper is on the benefits of the Experimental Models, all benefits are dependent upon the interaction of these several programs. Direct benefits of Protocols and Training Materials accrue first to the Experimental Models; without both, neither functions. In the same way, the direct benefit of the Training Complex is the systematic coordination of all components of teacher education. Through this interaction—Training Complex/Protocols/Training Materials/Models—a fully operational, comprehensive teacher-education program comes into being.

The Competency-Based Program provides benefits in two directions. First, it provides continuing assessment of the effectiveness of various components of the Operational Plan. Second, it provides reports to the profession generally, concerning the nature of the evolving teacher-education programs exemplified in the Operational Plan for Program Development in Teacher Education.

Many of the various interactive benefits of the Operational Plan are also intertemporal. That is, benefits from the program generate other benefits later, as they are disseminated to other audiences. An illustration of an intertemporal benefit stream might be: Protocol Materials, as they provide direct benefits to the Experimental Models; in turn the Experimental Models provide benefits to precertification teachers; who, upon certification, provide benefits to their pupils.

SUMMARY

Because it is difficult to separate benefits derived specifically from each of the four or five major components of the Operational Plan we have focused here on the Experimental Models. The Experimental Models seem to provide the interface between the Operational Plan and learners in the schools. Other components feed benefits into a functioning model; through it benefits flow to precertification teachers and ultimately to the children they teach. It would be possible to focus on other aspects of the Operational Plan; either on the Training Complex or on the Competency-Based Program, for example. In such cases, the integration of these components with the functioning Experimental Model would have been assumed. The comprehensive nature of these thrusts and the commitment to total reform in teacher education they represent provide an extensive array of benefits; ultimately these benefits can be expected to redirect teaching and learning in many segments of educational endeavor.

A COST ANALYSIS FOR THE OPERATIONAL PLAN

Several alternative strategies may be employed to develop the Operational Plan. Each strategy offers differing benefits and has different costs. Policy choices must therefore be based on a study of the relationship of costs to benefits. This section develops cost estimates for the Operational Plan and then uses the estimates to formulate alternative development strategies. The presentation of strategies, with a discussion of their costs and expected impact, highlights the policy decisions which must be made regarding development of the Operational Plan.

While this cost analysis should be considered in relation to the statement of benefits provided by the Operational Plan, the analysis does not constitute a complete benefit-cost analysis. None of the benefits have been presented in quantified form. While the quantification of some direct benefits may be possible (for example, each CBP Center will have a direct impact upon 450 preservice and in-service teachers or their equivalents in part-time participants), the quantification of all interactive and intertemporal benefits is currently impossible. Too little is currently known about the exact impact of teachers on student behavior and student learning. In addition, the values in monetary terms which one might place on student learning, particularly at the elementary school level, would be arbitrary if not capricious. Nevertheless, the following presentation should assist in the intuitive evaluation of alternative development strategies.

Costs of a CBP Center

As a first step in determining costs of alternative development strategies, the costs of developing and implementing a CBP Center have been estimated. In preparing this initial estimate, program categories were selected which were consistent with the organization of the Operational Plan as five thrusts and with the interdependent functions which the thrusts would serve (Figure 4–2). The four categories employed here—Protocol and Training Materials, Training Complexes, Experimental Models, and Confirmatory Mechanism—also permit the examination of alternative development strategies later in this section.

Two distinct costing categories arise in preparing a five-year plan for the Operational Plan which will culminate in a functioning program: development and implementation. Development cost is defined as the cost of resources necessary to design, prepare, and test a "master copy" of all materials required for the Operational

Plan with one CBP Center. While some costs for development would obviously be devoted to pilot testing of materials with a group of students, development costs will depend principally upon the nature of the Model and not upon the size of the student body that will ultimately be participating in the program. Implementation costs are defined as the cost of resources required to install a fully developed CBP Center. It includes capital equipment and the reproduction of instructional materials. Implementation costs depend upon both the nature of the program and the size of the student population.

It will be observed in the following presentation of estimates that some of the program categories fall exclusively or predominantly into either development or implementation, while others have major components in each. Hence, the presentation of costs seems slightly artificial and redundant. The distinction between development and implementation has been made, however, to facilitate the presentation of alternative development strategies, where the number and size of participating institutions become important parameters.

The estimates of costs were derived from several sources, including *Teachers for the Real World,* various feasibility studies from institutions participating in the Models Program, and USOE reports. The following discussion describes the categories used to present estimates and indicates the manner in which the estimates were obtained. Table 4–1 summarizes these estimates.

Development costs

1. *Protocols and Materials Development:* preparation of mediated materials which are designed to develop cognitions or skills within teacher-education students. This category includes both capital equipment for production and technical personnel. The estimate of $4,500,000 shown here represents the estimate of a commercial firm for the design and production of mediated presentations which comprises 80 percent of the activities in a teacher-education program. This estimate does not reveal the fact that costs of Protocols and Training Materials would be ongoing; revisions and additions to the set of materials would imply an ongoing cost of a fraction of this total sum on an annual basis, once the Operational Plan was completely functioning. Depending upon the portion of the program selected for revision this year, this annual cost could range from 1/8 to 1/5 of the total development sum.
2. *Training Complex:* design of a system to coordinate the efforts of universities, schools, communities, and industry and to conduct certification activities. This category also includes the development of clinical experiences for teachers. The costs of the various functions identified here are drawn from detailed cost analyses by the universities of Massachusetts, Georgia, Toledo, and Wisconsin.

TABLE 4–1. CBP Center cost summary

Program Category	Five-Year Estimated Cost
Development	
1. Protocols and materials Development	$ 4,500,000
2. Training Complexes	
a. Development of Interinstitutional Systems	360,000
b. Development of Clinical Experiences Activities	256,000
3. Models	
a. Development of Instructional Programs	6,144,000
b. Design of In-service Programs	1,250,000
c. Management and Information Systems Design	1,900,000
d. Development of Student Assessment	1,000,000
4. Confirmatory Mechanism	
a. Competency-Based Program	300,000
b. Research on Instructional Effectiveness	1,100,000
Implementation	
1. Training Complexes	500,000
2. Models	
a. Media Presentation Equipment	1,033,000
b. Media Management System	750,000
c. Faculty Retraining	700,000
3. Confirmatory Mechanism	
a. Competency-Based Program	150,000
TOTAL	$19,943,000

a. *Development of Interinstitutional System:* The estimate of $360,000 reflects the assumption that the costs of developing an interinstitutional system over five years will be roughly comparable to that for developing an extensive management system for a complete teacher-education program at a single institution.

b. *Development of Clinical Experiences Activities:* The estimate of $256,000 represents development of the portion of the instructional program of the Experimental Models which includes activities in the schools. An arbitrary percentage was placed in the category on the basis of an examination of cost estimates.

3. *Models:* design of a professional education program to prepare teachers, culminating in a B.A. degree and at least a provisional teaching certificate. This category includes the design and development of a system to manage the instructional program and guide students through the program, as well as the costs asso-

ciated with designing instructional materials. Cost estimates here are taken from a report summarizing costs of all models.

a. *Development of Instructional Programs:* The estimate of $6,144,000 includes professional and supportive personnel, supplies, and space for five years to be used to identify, formulate, and develop materials to fulfill program objectives.

b. *Design of In-service Program:* The estimate of $1,250,000 is an average of the estimated costs of developing three extensive in-service programs. The figures ranged from $.5 million to $2.0 million. In each case, the in-service program was independent of the undergraduate teacher-education program.

c. *Management and Information System Design:* The estimate of $1,900,000 assumes the complete development of a system to manage instructional activities of participating students. It includes both software development and hardware time.

d. *Development of Student Assessment:* The estimate of $1,000,000 assumes design and testing of evaluative instruments to screen prospective students, assess students' progress, diagnose students' weaknesses, and, in some cases, permit students to bypass instructional activities.

4. *Confirmatory Mechanism:* formulation of research strategies to test all aspects of the Operational Plan's effectiveness in relation to teacher performance and impact upon students. The total estimate of $1,400,000 used here is the cost of developing an extensive research program to complement the development of a model undergraduate program. The research would study all aspects of program effectiveness and impact upon teacher behavior and pupil change.

   a. *Competency-Based Program:* The estimate of $300,000 repsents that portion of the total research effort which would be directed to studying means of ultimately attaining teacher accountability for pupil performances.

   b. *Research on Instructional Effectiveness:* The estimate of $1,000,000 is for costs of developing an ongoing system of research to complement the development, redevelopment, and pilot testing for the instructional program.

Implementation costs

1. *Training Complex:* The estimate of $500,000 used here for implementation costs for a Training Complex represents an arbitrary estimate of $100,000 for annual operating expenses. This is the only category for which operating costs as such are included in implementation estimates. These funds might be from federal, state, or local sources.

2. *Models:* the equipment to present and manage students' use of media in the instructional program.

   a. *Media Presentation Equipment:* The estimate of $1,033,000 shown here will serve the needs of 600 participating students for both A-V equipment and computer terminals in a highly mediated program. This estimate presumes extensive use of the Protocols and Training Materials. Approximately one-fourth of this figure is allocated to computer terminals.

b. *Media Management System (Dial Access)*: The estimate of $750,000 will provide an automated system which will enable students at terminals to request specific media presentation.

c. *Faculty Retraining:* The estimate of $70,000 represents the costs of a program for university faculty to acquaint them with the new roles imposed by a highly individualized, mediated program and to assist them in adjusting to a less autonomous role than they presently have. This cost would be less if the Experimental Models assumed a more traditional stance.

3. *Competency-Based Programs:* The implementation costs for Competency-Based Programs at a CBP Center are here considered to be the costs of maintaining the activities of an advisory board which will direct the research activities. The estimate of $150,000 represents estimated yearly costs of $30,000 throughout a five-year period. The annual costs are restricted to expenses for a twelve-member board.

Illustrative development strategies

Many alternative plans may be employed in developing a complete Operational Plan for Program Development in Teacher Education. Alternative development and implementation strategies may be designed by varying the number of schools participating in either development or implementation and the number and nature of the Training Complexes and Experimental Models which are being developed. These alternatives cannot be expected to be equivalent in either their effect upon teacher education or in cost. This discussion considers both effects and costs, in presenting three alternatives to the basic pattern of a single CBP Center.

For purposes of discussion, three different development strategies are outlined here. The three choices have been made to display the possible range of alternatives as well as the manner in which additional alternatives may be designed and priced. The alternatives are:

1. Develop ten CBP Centers using three Experimental Models.
2. Develop eight CBP Centers, each with a different Experimental Model.
3. Develop fifteen CBP Centers, using instructional materials from two Experimental Models.

Before the effects of these alternatives are discussed, together with their costs, some general guidelines should be presented.

Development effects. Alternative development strategies will substantially affect the type of benefits to be derived from any development activities. Three dimensions of the impact which will accompany a development strategy will be noted in the following discussion: the extent of the change which a strategy imposes on teacher education; the size of the population of teachers who are affected; and the characteristics of this population of teachers.

The range of effect which can be attached to each of these three dimensions is considerable. The extent of change imposed by activities may range from improvements in existing teacher-education programs to a radical restructuring of teacher education. The size of the population which is affected could vary from future teachers at one institution to comparable groups at several hundred institutions. Characteristics of the population immediately affected are likely to reflect the nature of the institution they attend, its size, and its resources.

Each of these dimensions must also be considered in relation to a time horizon; a maximization of the impact of one dimension may imply a time horizon different from that required for maximization of another dimension. Radical restructuring of teacher education on even a small number of campuses, for example, is not possible as rapidly as is the introduction of changes into existing programs.

Development costs. The cost estimates for a complete CBP Center have been used to estimate the total costs of the three alternatives presented here. In some categories, estimated costs were extrapolated directly from the base estimates. In several cases, however, allowances were made for additional costs which would be incurred by any development strategy which involves many institutions. These additional costs are greatest when the development or implementation of a single program are shared. Activities such as program coordination, program piloting, preparation of materials, and program conversion and faculty retraining will be repeated for participating institutions.

Estimated costs for each of the proposed alternatives are shown in Table 4–2. Numbers in parentheses indicate the multiples used to convert the figures from Table 4–1.

Benefits and costs of alternative strategies. Each one of the three alternative development and implementation strategies offers advantages which are not evident from a simple comparison of costs. This discussion examines the alternatives in terms of the three dimensions of effect: extent of change; size of affected population; and characteristics of the affected population. Additional comments suggest some advantages and disadvantages which may not be obvious from the discussion of effects.

TABLE 4–2. Operational Plan for Program Development in Teacher Education: development and implementation alternatives.

Program Category	1 Ten CBP's, Three Models		2 Eight Unique CBP's		3 Fifteen CBP's Using 2 Models	
Development						
1. Protocols and Materials Development	(1)	$ 4,500,000	(1.5)	$ 6,750,000	(1.5)	$ 6,750,000
2. Training Complex						
a. Interinstitutional Systems	(3)	1,080,000	(3)	1,080,000	(3.5)	1,800,000
b. Clinical Experiences Activities	(3)	768,000	(8)	2,048,000	(2)	516,000
3. Models						
a. Instructional Programs	(3)	18,432,000	(5)	30,720,000	(2)	12,289,000
b. In-service Programs	(3)	3,750,000	(5)	6,250,000	(2)	2,500,000
c. Management and Information System	(1.5)	2,850,000	(5)	9,500,000	(1.5)	2,850,000
d. Student Assessment	(3)	3,000,000	(8)	8,000,000	(2)	2,000,000
4. Confirmatory Mechanism						
a. Competency-Based Program	(10)	3,000,000	(8)	2,400,000	(15)	4,500,000
b. Instructional Effectiveness	(3)	3,300,000	(7)	2,100,000	(15)	3,000,000
Implementation						
1. Protocol and Materials[1]	(10)	2,000,000	(8)	1,600,000	(15)	3,000,000
2. Training Complexes	(10)	5,000,000	(8)	4,000,000	(15)	7,500,000
3. Models[2]						
a. Media Presentation Equipment	(7)	7,231,000	(5)	5,165,000	(10)	10,330,000
b. Media Management System	(7)	5,250,000	(5)	3,750,000	(10)	7,500,000
c. Faculty Retraining	(5)	3,500,000	(5)	3,500,000	(10)	7,000,000
4. Confirmatory Mechanism						
a. Competency-Based Program	(10)	1,500,000	(8)	1,200,000	(15)	2,250,000
		$65,161,000		$88,063,000		$73,785,000

[1] The arbitrary figure of $200,000 is meant to cover duplicating costs to supply a single program center with a complete set of materials.

[2] Anticipated scale economics or variations in needs for media presentation equipment are reflected in the multiples for the program category.

1. Ten CBP Centers using Three Experimental Models: $65,161,000.

The development of ten CBP Centers provides an opportunity to plan and carry out major changes in teacher education. Judicious selection of participating institutions, with attention to geographic and organizational diversity, will permit the introduction of changes in a variety of institutional settings, maximizing the demonstration effect of the program. The size and characteristics of the population which is immediately affected depends upon the nature of the participating institutions; obviously, considerable diversity is possible.

Comments: The channeling of resources from ten institutions into the development of three Models would provide a strong base for development activity. While there may be occasional communication problems, the expanded resource base should make the multiple-institution development a greater advantage than disadvantage.

The implementation of three Experimental Models at ten CBP Centers will facilitate the examination of each Model's effectiveness in a variety of settings. Multiple implementation of each Model will also reduce the possibility of program failure for strictly institutional reasons.

2. *Eight CBP Centers, each with a unique Experimental Model: $88,063,000.*

The development of eight unique Models should provide the maximum amount of change in teacher education in the long run, by insuring the availability on a demonstration basis, of a broad spectrum of programs. The size and characteristics of the student population which would be affected immediately would again be dependent upon the choice of participating institutions.

Comments: The implementation of each Experimental Model in only one CBP Center would reduce the tested generalizability of each Model. However, with such a range of programs from which to choose, adopting institutions might be encouraged to be more eclectic in their choice of programs, drawing from each the features which would contribute most to their own mode.

The development of eight unique Models will impose very heavy manpower requirements on developing institutions; handling this comparatively short-run phenomenon without incurring surplus staff later will pose a problem for each institution.

The population which would be immediately affected would be smaller with this alternative than with the preceding alternative. A comparison of long-range effects is not so easy; this alternative may have substantially greater impact by offering eight alternatives, not just three, to institutions interested in new approaches to teacher education.

3. Fifteen CBP Centers using two Experimental Models: $73,785,000

The development of two Experimental Models is not so likely to produce long-run major changes in teacher education as are the first two alternatives. The implementation of these Models at fifteen centers would, however, provide considerable opportunity to view each Model in a wide variety of settings. A large population of teachers would be affected immediately; their characteristics could be widely varied.

Comments: This alternative emphasizes one of the major policy decisions which must be made in choosing a development strategy: Whether long-run, radical change, or comparatively short-run, substantial improvement is preferred. The alternative provides the opportunity to work out many operational problems likely to arise with the CBP Centers, though it provides the Centers with less variety in the instructional program.

A five-year plan for the development and implementation of the Operational Plan

A five-year development strategy for the Operational Plan must consider not only the nature and magnitude of the impact which the total plan will have on teacher education, but also the interrelationships among aspects of the overall Operational Plan and their effect on development strategies over time.

The strategy outlined here presents costs for the development of five different Experimental Models and their implementation at fifteen CBP Centers. This alternative should both have considerable impact on the nature of teacher education and also affect large populations of students in the short run. The long-range demonstration effects resulting from the development of five complete and unique Models for teacher education will be highly significant. The implication of these Models at fifteen CBP Centers should afford considerable opportunity to examine the effectiveness of each Model in several environments and under a variety of institutional arrangements. This strategy may be compared with three other less costly alternatives which are presented and discussed in the preceding section.

The development strategy outlined here is designed to ensure the development of prerequisite portions of the Operational Plan and to preserve maximum flexibility within the development plan. Thus,

TABLE 4–3. Operational Plan for Program Development in Teacher Education: Proposed development and implementation strategy.

	Five Models, Fifteen CBP Centers					
Program Category	*Year* 1	2	3	4	5	*TOTAL*
I. Development	2%	20%	40%	35%	3%	
1. Protocols and Materials Development	$ 135,000	$ 1,350,000	$ 2,700,000	$ 2,362,000	$ 202,500	$ 6,750,000
2. Training Complex						
a. Interinstitutional Systems	21,600	216,000	432,000	378,000	32,400	1,080,000
b. Clinical Experiences Activities	20,480	204,800	409,600	358,400	30,720	1,024,000
3. Models						
a. Instructional Programs	482,320	4,823,200	9,646,400	8,440,600	723,480	24,116,000
b. In-service Programs	100,000	1,000,000	2,000,000	1,750,000	150,000	5,000,000
c. Management and Information System	152,120	1,521,200	3,042,400	2,732,100	158,180	7,606,000
d. Student Assessment	100,000	1,000,000	2,000,000	1,750,000	150,000	5,000,000
4. Confirmatory Mechanism						
a. Competency-Based Program	20,000	200,000	400,000	350,000	30,000	1,000,000
b. Instructional Effectiveness	60,000	600,000	1,200,000	1,050,000	90,000	3,000,000

Table 4–3 (*cont.*)

II. Implementation	*0%*	*2%*	*20%*	*40%*	*38%*	
1. Protocols and Materials	0	60,000	600,000	1,200,000	1,140,000	3,000,000
2. Training Complex	1,500,000	1,500,000	1,500,000	1,500,000	1,500,000	7,500,000
3. Models						
a. Media Presentation Equipment	0	206,600	2,066,000	4,132,000	3,925,400	10,330,000
b. Media Management System	0	150,000	1,500,000	3,000,000	2,850,000	7,500,000
c. Faculty Retraining	140,000	1,400,000	2,800,000	2,450,000	210,000	7,000,000
4. Confirmatory Mechanism						
a. Competency-Based Program	450,000	450,000	450,000	450,000	450,000	2,250,000
III. Administration	520,000	520,000	520,000	520,000	520,000	2,600,000
TOTALS	$3,701,520	$15,201,800	$31,266,900	$32,423,100	$12,162,680	$94,756,000

instructional materials are developed and tested before their integration into instructional systems and total implementation. Development activities are begun slowly to permit maximum "learning" related to operational considerations in the development period.

The program categories used in Table 4–3 to present the five-year plan are those developed in the previous section of this paper; a description of each category and the actitvities it includes is presented there.

Several additional alternative development strategies could also be formulated on the basis of cost estimates presented in the previous section. Table 4–4 offers estimated totals for implementing one highly mediated Experimental Model at varying numbers of CBP Centers.

TABLE 4–4. Operational Plan development alternatives: One model, varying number of CBP Centers

Number of CBP Centers	*Development Cost*	*Implementation Cost*	*Total Cost*
15	$21,660,000	$ 37,580,000	$ 59,240,000
30	21,660,000	75,160,000	96,820,000
60	21,660,000	150,320,000	171,980,000
120	21,660,000	300,640,000	322,300,000

CHAPTER 5

Notes on a School-University Consortium for Teacher Education

Benjamin Rosner

INTRODUCTION

The levers or mechanisms by which reform in teacher education can be attained come from five sources—the school, the community, government agencies, the university, and professional associations. The levers which are derived from the operation of the schools reflect the school curriculum and its organizational structures. The school curriculum contributes to much of the content of the teacher-education program; the school organization contributes to a definition of staffing patterns and roles of specific educational personnel.

Community here refers to the lay public. The levers which the community provides are statements of educational goals and financial support. Government agencies also provide levers for change. The levers associated with local, state, and federal agencies are financial support, and accreditation and certification of educational programs and personnel.

At the university level, a primary lever is associated with the governance of the institution. In addition, levers may be identified with admission practices; the reward structure for the teaching, scholarship, research, and public service functions of the faculty; and degree requirements. Finally, the activities of subject-matter associations influence the content emphases of school and college curricula, while professional teacher associations have marked impact on staff utilization, conditions of employment, and compensation.

Reform in teacher education must take into account the distribution of power among all sources. Reform based solely on the power inherent in any single source is inadequate. Identification of mechanisms which focus the power of all sources on common objectives is essential for the institutionalization of change in teacher education.

LEVERS FOR CHANGE

Levers may be identified by examining the pertinent policies and practices of the school, the university, the community, government agencies, and professional associations. Such examination suggests that changes in teacher education must be accompanied by changes in policy formulation, university admissions, university teacher-education curricula, personnel evaluation procedures, personnel certification procedures, school curricula, and school employment practices. More specifically, the levers may be defined as: parity (policy formulation), student recruitment practices (admissions), Performance-Based Teacher Education, exemplary school curricula, Confirmatory Mechanisms (evaluation), Performance-Based Certification, and staff utilization. The systematic manipulation of these levers will yield modifications in teacher training. Each of the levers for change is discussed below.

Parity

Parity effects change in teacher education by including representatives from the lay public, school administration, teacher associations, university liberal arts and education faculties, and students in teacher education on an advisory board influencing the governance of teacher training programs. The board would assist in the development of policy governing both school- and university-based components of the teacher-education program. This modification of policy formulating procedures tends to assure the responsiveness of teacher training to the publicly expressed objectives and priorities of the school and community.

Student recruitment practices

Recruitment serves as a lever by systematically manipulating the flow of human resources into teacher education. Such recruitment may be directed towards high school students entering colleges or universities, adults entering the schools at the paraprofessional level, and teachers aspiring to positions of educational leadership. Moreover, based on the assumption that many knowledges and skills are common to education and other professions, recruitment can be aimed at individuals with special experience and competencies to minimize the time and cost of training; e.g., some mathematics teachers may be recruited from engineering, and some school administrators may be recruited from government or business.

Performance-Based Teacher Education

Performance-Based Teacher Education is a lever for change because it requires the explication of the specific knowledges and skills that comprise the teacher-education program. Performance-Based Teacher Education requires systematic assessment of the student's performance at various stages of the program. A graduate of such a program would have demonstrated mastery of the knowledges and skills included within the training program to a specified level of competence. It is anticipated that Performance-Based Teacher Education would encourage modularization of the curriculum and personalization of the training process.

Exemplary school curricula

An exemplary school curriculum has two functions: to educate children and to prepare educational personnel. In its first function, the curriculum serves the needs of children. In its second function, the curriculum provides students of teaching with opportunities for practice within the framework of an internally consistent educational program. In this manner, the capacity of a school to serve the needs of children is prerequisite to its capacity to serve as a teacher training institution. The British Infant School and the Montessori School are two examples of exemplary curricula.

Schools vary in the quality of their educational programs and in their willingness to serve as teacher training facilities. If a school can be identified by a parity board as possessing an exemplary program and if the school is willing to serve as a teacher training institution, the objectives of the school-university teacher training program are mutually supportive. If a school is willing to become a training facility but does not provide an exemplary curriculum, the school curriculum would need to undergo transformation under the auspices of a parity board so that the school offers an effective environment for teacher education.

Confirmatory System

The Confirmatory System provides evidence of the effectiveness of each element of a training program, and for the program as a whole.

The Confirmatory System may operate at six criterion levels. At the highest level, the Confirmatory Mechanism assesses the degree to which teachers possessing specific knowledges and skills utilize them in actual classroom situations and whether these competencies produce changes in pupil performance. At this level, the Confirmatory System operates as an accountability system for school personnel.

At the lowest level the Confirmatory System offers evidence about whether trainees have acquired specific knowledges and understandings of concepts relevant to the interpretation and modification of pupil classroom behavior. At the middle level, the Confirmatory Mechanism speaks to the effectiveness with which trainees have acquired specific pedagogic skills and requires the development of specific school-based measures of teacher competence.

Certification

Both legal and "extralegal" certification are levers for reform. Legal certification establishes minimum standards of competence as a condition for seeking and retaining employment in the schools. Extralegal certification, functioning outside the direct control of state agencies, may establish standards of performance reflecting the highest levels of teacher competence.

The *form* of legal and extralegal certification manipulates the form of training. If certification is based on profiles of specific competencies, teacher-education programs will provide training addressed to these competencies. In addition, extralegal certification can facilitate experimentation with new modes of certification, establish a career line in teaching, and encourage the integration of the disciplines in the program of teacher education.

Personnel employment practices

Employment is a lever because it institutionalizes the roles and competencies of educational personnel. The creation of a new position, or the modification of existing positions, frequently requires personnel with new competencies. The demand for different skills establishes the need for new or modified training programs. For example, the introduction of teacher training positions in the schools would require some school personnel to assume new roles and acquire additional competencies. The need for competency as a teacher trainer would create the demand for new teacher-education programs.

The ideas mentioned above identify points at which leverage can be applied to effect reform in teacher education. The parity board and the exemplary school are powerful levers to reconnect teacher education with the schools and the community. Performance-Based Teacher Education and Certification make public the knowledge and skills expected of educational personnel. As a consequence teacher education needs to establish itself within the framework of a strong Confirmatory System. The development of this Confirmatory System is a major priority for teacher education.

A PARITY-BASED TEACHER-EDUCATION PROGRAM

The levers identified above may be manipulated in a variety of teacher training contexts. The Model proposed here begins with a school-university-community consortium. The consortium is represented by a parity board which advises on the formulation of policy governing the full range of teacher training. The training program calls upon the resources of a university or college as well as the resources of special schools identified as school training centers.

Undergraduate students enter the teacher education program through the university and gradually move to the school. Paraprofessionals enter the program through the schools and gradually move to the university. Both the university and the school provide routes for entry into the profession—the school-based training center route for paraprofessionals and the university route for general undergraduate students.

The college or university must provide each student with opportunities to become familiar with a variety of human service careers, including teaching. For those students electing education as a profession, the university is held accountable for their general education, their competency in one or more academic disciplines, and their mastery of concepts relevant to the diagnosis and treatment of human behavior in formal or informal learning situations. In addition, the university is responsible for assisting preservice students to acquire a degree of mastery in a number of critical pedagogic skills. Concepts and "entry-level" skills can be acquired in a laboratory setting using a variety of audiovisual materials, including Protocol and Training Materials, and microteaching procedures. A student would be held responsible for the acquisition of specified levels of pedagogic skill prior to his entry into the school training center for further skill development.

School training centers offer the real-world context for practicing and assimilating the skills acquired in the university laboratory. Opportunities for practice are offered by trained cooperating teachers (teacher trainers) under the supervision of a school-based director of training and his staff. A school serves as a training facility when it has installed an exemplary curriculum and its staff has been trained to use the school as a laboratory for the preparation of education personnel. Typically, a college would work with a cluster of four to six school training centers so that students would have practice opportunities within two or more exemplary schools. In this manner preservice (or in-service) teachers would become knowledgeable about several school curriculum and organizational patterns and avoid ideological indoctrination by exposure to a single point of view.

The university education faculty would divide their time between the schools and the campus. Some of the faculty would be housed primarily at the university (more than 50 percent of work load) and assume responsibility for the foundations of education (concept development), the installation and maintenance of the university-based Confirmatory System, and research relevant to teaching and learning. Others on the faculty would be principally housed in school training centers (more than 50 percent of work load) and would be concerned with development of the exemplary curriculum and skill development.

The goals of the school-based faculty are:

1. The establishment of the exemplary curriculum.
2. The preparation of cooperating teachers for the training of preservice teachers, paraprofessionals, and new teachers.
3. The development and installation of school training programs.
4. Acquisition of a new role as change agent and disseminator of innovative instructional practices and materials.

One of the major responsibilities of the education faculty is the design, installation, and maintenance of an exemplary curriculum. The faculty must work closely with community and school personnel to assist in the formulation of school objectives, the design of the school program, the selection of curriculum materials and resources, and the training of school personnel to implement the program. Responsibility for the maintenance of the exemplary curriculum preserves the school-university-community relationship and establishes the college faculty as change agents.

A second goal of field-oriented faculty is the preparation of the school staff for responsibility as teacher trainers. The faculty must sensitize school staff to their roles as teacher trainers in order that preservice teachers are assured sufficient practice for the acquisition of pedagogic skills. In addition, school staff must be trained to administer the School-Based Tasks (see Confirmatory System). One criterion that can be employed to determine whether or not a school staff has attained the competencies essential to their roles as teacher trainers is their ability to obtain extralegal certification as teacher trainers. Teacher trainers would be expected to take over the training responsibilities of the school training center within two or three years.

The training of cooperating teachers is but one aspect of the establishment of a center. The education faculty must assist in selecting and training key administrative personnel, establish a closed-circuit TV facility to observe practice sessions and the administration of School-Based Tasks, and develop a professional library and a curriculum materials center.

Upon the installation of the exemplary curriculum, the training of cooperating teachers, and the development and installation of the administrative and training components of the school training center, the education faculty would be assigned to a new school. It is anticipated that the transformation of education faculty from trainers to change agents will significantly reduce the lag between R and D and implementation. In addition, the process of systematically rotating college faculty to transform schools into training centers is viewed as a fundamental strategy for educational reform.

Figure 5–1 summarizes the school and university components of the teacher-education program. Although the design is primarily for the elementary school, it can be extended to the secondary school where individual departments assume the curricular and training responsibilities of a training center.

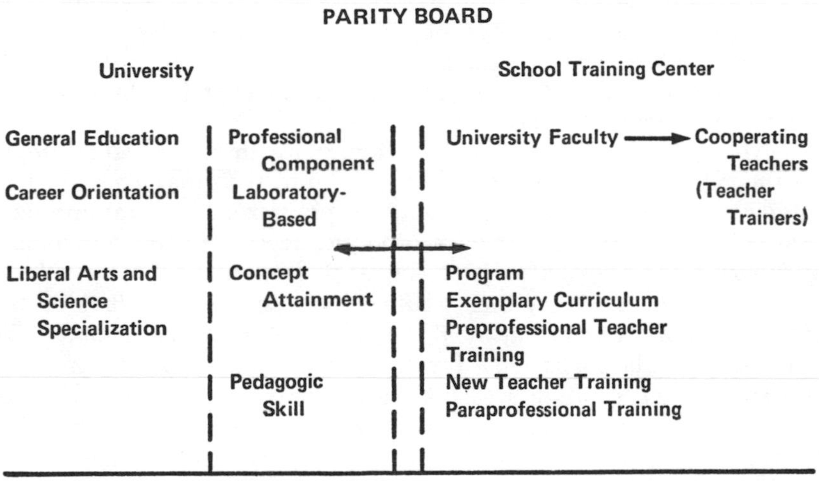

FIGURE 5–1. ***Parity-Based Teacher-Education Program.***

THE SCHOOL TRAINING CENTER

The selection of a school for conversion into a school training center is the responsibility of a parity board. The parity board needs to negotiate with local school boards, school administrators, professional teacher association, and the community at large in order that the training responsibilities of the institution and staff are thoroughly understood by all parties.

Initially, Centers might be selected from among schools with exemplary programs whose staffs express a strong commitment to teacher training and a willingness to prepare for the responsibility. Alternatively, Centers may be selected from nonexemplary schools on the condition that the schools are willing to undertake curriculum transformation and staff development. Parity boards may also offer incentives to exemplary schools which are unwilling to use their resources for teacher training. Such incentives might include the creation of district teacher-trainer positions with additional financial remuneration for the completion of training and acquisition of appropriate certification, adjunct faculty status, sabbatical leave with pay for preparation as teacher trainers, and payment of examination fees for teachers who are candidates for board certification as teacher trainers.[1]

A School Training Center has two major responsibilities: the maintenance of an exemplary program for service to children and the maintenance of a training program for preservice, paraprofessional, and beginning teachers. A third function of selected Centers is to serve the examination needs of Educational Specialty Boards. In addition, Centers can serve the Performance-Based Certification needs of state agencies. Finally, Centers can serve as sites for the field testing of new curriculum materials.

The staff of a Center includes personnel with major responsibility for the exemplary curriculum and a small unit with major responsibility for the training and examination program. The training and examining unit would include a director, several trainer-examiners, audio-visual technicians, and secretarial personnel.

The director of training would report to the principal of the School Training Center and hold the rank of assistant principal. The director would be responsible for assigning trainees to teacher trainers; supervising training sessions; supervising the administration of School-Based Tasks; maintaining liaison with the university, state certification agencies, and Educational Specialty Boards; maintaining the video facility, the professional library, and the curriculum resources center; and participating in the field testing of new training and examination materials and procedures. The director would be assisted by trainer-examiners who would share responsibility for specific aspects of the center's operations. Under the supervision of

[1] See the discussion of Educational Specialty Boards in M. Lieberman, *The Future of Public Education* (Chicago: University of Chicago Press, 1960).

the director, audiovisual technicians would maintain the center's closed circuit video facility.

Centers would be established in schools with 25 to 50 teacher trainers (cooperating teachers). Accordingly, each center could train between 50 and 100 preservice teachers annually. In addition, a center could accommodate 50 to 100 paraprofessionals. If a center does not offer training opportunities for paraprofessionals, the Center could accommodate 100 to 200 preservice teachers. The maximum number of preservice and paraprofessional personnel to be trained in a Center would depend on the Center's size and the staffing patterns appropriate to its exemplary curriculum.

Although School Training Centers are principally dedicated to the training of preservice and paraprofessional personnel, Centers may also serve as examining agencies for legal and extralegal Performance-Based Certification. Under the assumption that Performance-Based Certification would require evidence of a teacher's knowledge and skills, the Center's training unit and its closed-circuit video facility could arrange for and monitor the examination process.

THE CONFIRMATORY SYSTEM

Teacher-education programs, performance-based or otherwise, need to operate within the context of a Confirmatory System. A *Confirmatory System* is defined as the use of evaluation procedures to measure the effectiveness of each component of the program and the competencies of its graduates. Such an evaluation program is both formative and summative, since both the procedures and products of the training program must be continually assessed. In the present model, both the university and the school-based components are subject to the Confirmatory System. Figure 5–2 suggests the Confirmatory System operating in the service of a Parity-Based Teacher-Education Program. The criterion levels indicated are described in pages 3–6.

Examination of Figure 5–2 shows the Confirmatory System to be operating at both the university and school training center locations. At the university the Confirmatory System operates at Criterion Levels 4–6 to assess the program's effectiveness in the knowledge domain (Criterion Level 6) and in the development of specific skills under simulated and microteaching situations (Criterion Levels 5 and 4, respectively). Criterion Levels 4–6 comprise the accountability program for the university-based components of teacher education.

The training responsibilities of the Center require the installation of the Confirmatory System at Criterion Level 3. Criterion Level 3 confirms the attainment of competency in the classroom setting. It

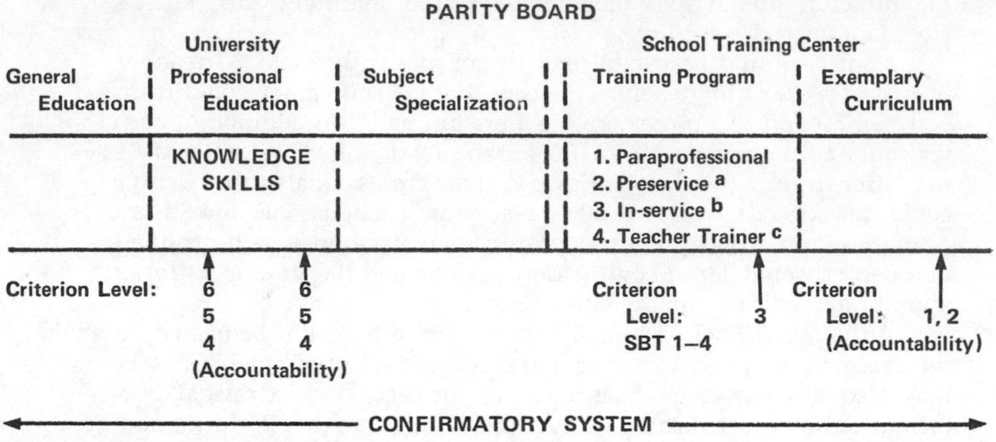

[a] Should contribute to decisions regarding provisional certification.

[b] Should contribute to decisions regarding continuing certification (permanent).

[c] Should contribute to decisions regarding extralegal certification.

FIGURE 5–2. *Confirmatory System.*

is recommended that these competencies be assessed through the administration of a series of standardized exercises, or School-Based Tasks.

It is suggested that four sets of School-Based Tasks (SBT) be developed. The first set of SBT would define the competencies of paraprofessionals, would contribute to a definition of paraprofessional job responsibilities, and would assist in defining the nature of the training program. The development of SBT (1) would have to take into account the varying responsibilities of paraprofessionals in different exemplary programs.

SBT (2) would be developed for preservice teachers. These tasks would probably include a number of tasks from SBT (1) but would require demonstration of a higher order of skill. In addition, SBT (2) would include tasks unique to the role of professional teachers in various exemplary schools. Just as SBT (1) would serve to clarify the competencies required of paraprofessionals, SBT (2) would assist in defining the skills of entry-level teachers. Obviously, SBT (2) would also help to shape the nature of the preservice training program.

A third set of tasks would need to be developed for teachers preparing for continuing or permanent certification, that is, teachers with one to three years of teaching experience. Again, it is likely that SBT (3) would include many tasks from SBT (2) but with expectations of greater skill mastery. It is also likely that SBT (3) would contain some tasks defining the unique responsibilities of more experienced teachers.

Finally, a fourth set of tasks would be developed for teacher trainers. SBT (4) would not only define the skills expected of teacher trainers, but would also contribute to a sharper definition of the training program.

Although the four sets of School-Based Tasks might be developed by individual school-university teams, it is recommended that the development of SBT (1–3) be coordinated by a single agency in order to assure compliance with a common set of technical specifications and to minimize duplication of effort and cost. In addition, a national program of SBT (1–3) development would provide a set of standardized exercises to facilitate research on teacher education. Lastly, sets of School-Based Tasks (1–3) would encourage experimentation with Performance-Based Certification at the paraprofessional, provisional, and permanent levels.

It is also recommended that the development of SBT (4) be the responsibility of the extralegal Educational Specialty Boards. SBT (4) would function at the level of teacher trainers. If Educational Specialty Boards develop examinations to reflect the highest levels of competence in the field, recipients of extralegal certification should be qualified as teacher trainers. The competencies required of teacher trainers should, therefore, be built into the Specialty Boards for each field.

The Confirmatory System operating at Criterion Levels 3–6 is concerned exclusively with the assessment of knowledges and skills. At Criterion Levels 1 and 2, the Confirmatory System is concerned with the effectiveness of the exemplary curriculum. Criterion Levels 1 and 2 introduce an accountability program for the school. In turn, Criterion Levels 1 and 2 provide a yardstick by which to measure the effectiveness of skills associated with Criterion Level 3. Similarly, School-Based Tasks at Criterion Level 3 offer a criterion against which to measure the effectiveness of the university components of the training program. In general, the Confirmatory System assists both the university and the School Training Center to review and revise each component of the parity-based school-university teacher-education program.

CHAPTER 6

BEPD, NCERD, and Teacher Education that Makes a Demonstrable Difference

H. Del Schalock

INTRODUCTION AND OVERVIEW

The Bureau of Educational Personnel Development, U.S. Office of Education, has established within the past two years a number of program development thrusts that have come to be thought of as basic or foundational to other BEPD program efforts. These include the Protocol Materials Development Program, the Training Materials Development Program, the Training Complex Program, and the Performance-Based Certification Program.[1] In addition, BEPD has assumed responsibility for the Elementary Teacher Education Models Program—a developmental effort of the National Center for Educational Research and Development, U.S. Office of Education—that was taken by NCERD through its design and feasibility testing stages.

In September, 1970, Dr. Don Davies, Associate Commissioner of Education and then Director of BEPD, established a task force internal to BEPD—Task Force '72—to study the implication of the five foundational thrusts for the structure and operation of the Bureau. The primary responsibility of the Task Force, headed by Dr. Allen Schmieder, is to submit alternative recommendations relative to the development of the five program thrusts outlined above, plans for implementing the alternative recommendations, projected costs associated with each plan, and the implications of each plan for other BEPD programs.

To help in the execution of its work, Task Force '72 has estab-

[1] For a definition of Protocol Materials, Training Materials, Training Complexes, and other related terms see the Glossary, page 155.

lished an external working committee that is to generate a primary set of inputs for Task Force consideration. These inputs are to take the form of position papers prepared by a number of persons familiar with one or more of the thrusts being considered by the Task Force. The present paper is one of that set.

The direct charge to those preparing position papers was fourfold:

1. Present one or more proposals as to the "mix" of the five thrusts being considered by Task Force '72 that will optimize their impact, either individually or collectively, upon American education particularly.
2. Spell out the implications of the mix(es) proposed for the operation of schools, for children within schools, for Educational Personnel Development Programs, for statewide certification procedures, for the Bureau of Educational Personnel Development, and for OE generally.
3. Set out a plan of procedure, including tasks and timelines, for implementing the proposals made.
4. Project cost estimates for carrying out the implementation plan.

While straightforward enough on the surface a number of assumptions underlie the charge, and a number of issues emerge from it. Two basic assumptions are (and these seem to underlie all of the efforts of BEPD and Task Force '72) (1) that American education is in need of reform and (2) that Educational Personnel Development Programs provide a primary vehicle by which to effect such reform. Some of the issues that arise are (1) Do the five thrusts under consideration provide the necessary and sufficient conditions for the design of Educational Personnel Development Programs that have the leverage to reform American education? (2) If they do constitute such conditions, how are they to be organized into operational preparatory programs? (3) If they do not constitute the necessary and sufficient conditions to effect reform in American education through more effective preparatory programs, what conditions would? (4) If Educational Personnel Development Programs could be developed that effect the kinds of change in elementary and secondary education desired, what would be needed to effect such changes across the nation? A public stance in relation to such matters would seem to be an additional charge that those preparing position papers must meet.

The plan of the paper is relatively straightforward. As a point of departure, and as a backdrop to the proposals made in the paper, a position is presented with respect to the assumption and issues outlined above. Within the context of this position a "preferred" proposal relative to the mix of the five thrusts with which the paper is to deal is presented. Implications of the proposal are then traced, in cost-benefit terms, for staff and students, in a preparatory program so designed, for school personnel, for state departments of education, for children and the adult members of a community, and for several bureaus within the U.S. Office of Education.

The rationale for and organization of the paper rests upon a careful definition of the five thrusts with which the proposal deals. These definitions are presented in an attached Glossary, and the reader is encouraged to study them carefully.

BACKGROUND NOTES

1. The Bureau of Education Personnel Development (BEPD) has responsibility by law for providing assistance in and leadership to the preparation of educational personnel in the nation. It is constrained by law from the execution of research—and perhaps evaluation and development as well—yet it is committed intellectually to the necessity of these activities for the effective discharge of its legal responsibilities.
2. As it is currently organized BEPD has a number of "targeted population" programs, e.g., Rural-Urban and TTT; a number of "nontargeted" programs, e.g., Teacher Corps and COP; some experimental or demonstration programs, e.g., the Site Concentration and Performance-Based Certification efforts; and some foundational or basic programs, e.g., Protocol Materials, Training Materials, and Training Complexes. It also has inherited the Elementary Models Program.

   To an outsider looking in it is not clear how these various efforts relate to one another. The purpose of Task Force '72 is to make recommendations in this regard, particularly as to how the basic or foundation thrusts relate to one another and to other programs within the bureau.
3. The National Center for Educational Research and Development (NCERD) has responsibility for providing assistance in and leadership to all aspects and levels of education in the nation through the application of research and development activities. Although it currently sponsors training programs in the areas of educational research, development, evaluation, and diffusion, it is not generally responsible for the training function.
4. As one of its developmental activities NCERD sponsored the design of new Models for elementary teacher education. Upon completion of their design and feasibility testing they were transferred to BEPD for development and implementation. NCERD interest in the Models remains, however, partly because of interest in seeing that its initial investment bears fruit and partly because the Models have built into them a strong R & D component. As such, Model-based teacher-education programs represent extremely promising contexts for the pursuit of education R & D activities that have recognized significance.
5. A remarkable research finding has just been reported: Experienced teachers in the areas of social science, auto mechanics, and

electronics were unable to bring about greater learning gains in high school pupils in those subject areas—as measured by "performance items" of a paper and pencil variety—than were college students studying social science or tradesmen working as mechanics or electronic equipment repairmen.[2]

PART I: A POINT OF VIEW

In this section of the paper a point of view is developed with respect to the assumptions and issues that underlie BEPD operations generally and the task of Task Force '72 specifically. Since it seems inescapable that the position one takes with regard to these assumptions and issues will influence the position one takes as to the most desirable mix or mixes of the five thrusts being dealt with, it would seem important that the reader of the paper be provided information as to where the writer stands on these matters. It also seems essential that this be done if the proposals with respect to the structure, function, content, and interaction of the five thrusts which follow are to be fully understood.

Is elementary and secondary education in the United States in need of reform?

In spite of the curriculum development and classroom reorganization efforts of the late 1950s and early 1960s, the desegregation of the schools, the rather dramatic increase in literacy in the nation, the increased emphasis upon the individualization of personalization of instruction, and the increasing emphasis upon accountability, there is general agreement across the land that genuine reform in elementary and secondary education is sorely needed.[3] The severe problems which persist in the area of reading, the inadequacy of occupational preparation and planning, and the perceived "irrelevance" of much that is offered as education by its consumers speak to the need for fundamental reform at the elementary and secondary level. So, too, does the political unrest within the schools, the revolt of the tax payers at the ballot box, and the increasing concern on the part of legislators, the Congress, and the federal administration with the governance of education. Silberman's concept of the "mindlessness" of American education captures as well as any other the characteristics of the total system that cry for its reform.

[2] James W. Popham, "Performance Tests of Teaching Proficiency: Rationale, Development and Validation." *Amer. Educ. Res. J.*, 1971, vol. 8, no. 1, pp. 105–117.
[3] See, for example, Charles Silberman, *Crisis in the Classroom: The Remaking of American Education* (New York, Random House, 1970).

In addition to such general concerns there are a number of specific concerns that are increasingly in demand of attention: (1) the lack of clarity as to the goals and the indicators acceptable as evidence of the realization of those goals for education generally or for the various populations of learners for which a particular school is responsible (which contributes, of course, in a major way to Silberman's concept of mindlessness); (2) the apparent narrowness of the goals that are operating within the schools either implicitly or explicitly—in relation to the needs of children and youth in today's world; (3) the failure of the schools to provide systematic evidence on the relationship of program costs to program benefits; (4) the failure thus far to implement fully the ideal of individualized or personalized education; and (5) the relative lack of community participation in the entire enterprise. All these aspects of elementary and secondary education seem appropriate targets for change, and in this sense the basic assumption of BEPD as to the need for educational reform would seem to be justifiable.

Can educational personnel development programs be effective tools for educational reform?

This is a more difficult question to answer than the first, and it would seem that an honest response would be "it depends." If Educational Personnel Programs are designed to perpetuate what IS instead of create what OUGHT TO BE, or poor models are provided as to what ought to be, then it is hard to see how educational reform can be effected through them. If, on the other hand, there is some degree of clarity as to what education in the future ought to be, and there is clarity as to the role and task responsibilities of personnel within that context—and there is a commitment to and a methodology for insuring that personnel can in fact assume such roles and perform such tasks—it then seems reasonable to believe that preparatory programs could in fact effect reform in the larger educational arena. Such a stance assumes, of course, that the goals of education for various populations of learners are clear, that the indicators acceptable as evidence of the realization of those goals have been made explicit, and that both have been agreed to by all participating in the educational enterprise.

What characteristics must educational personnel development programs assume if they are to become effective instruments of educational reform?

In addition to being clear about the purpose of education and the nature of the schools needed to bring those purposes about, Educational Personnel Development Programs must assume a number of additional characteristics if they are to effect change in the broader educational picture. Some of these are discussed in the paragraphs which follow. While not exhaustive they do provide guidelines for the development of preparatory programs that are likely to make a difference.

1. A shift from an experience-based to a performance-based mode of operation

Two broad strategies for the design and operation of teacher-education programs are currently in competition: that which can be called an *experience-based* strategy and that which is being called a *performance-based* strategy. Most teacher-education programs in operation today can be considered to be experience based, for by and large they involve a specified number of courses or course hours in specified areas of study. They are "performance based" in so far as the requirement of a particular grade point average in courses taken can be considered a performance measure, but they do not specify in precise terms what it is that is to be taken from such experiences. They do not specify what prospective teachers need to know or be able to do or be able to accomplish in order to become certified.[4]

Performance-Based Programs differ from those that are experience based in that the outcomes expected to derive from them are specified. Operationally this means that the knowledge, skills, attitudes, sensitivities, competencies, etc., that prospective teachers are expected to have upon completion of a teacher-education program, and the indicators acceptable as evidence of the realization of those outcomes, are specified and made public. Performance-Based Programs do not deny the significance of experience, but they openly recognize and treat experience as a means rather than an end. They treat experience as a variable to be manipulated in the realization of given ends, rather than as an end in itself. By so doing, Performance-Based Programs are open to continuous change on the basis of feedback as to the success they are having in realizing the ends that they are committed to accomplish. By clearly specifying the ends for which they are to be held responsible Performance-Based Programs meet the

[4] In spite of some performance language, a large share of the recommendations appearing within the 1970 Standards and Practices statement are still largely experiential in nature. Specifically course work in the area of general studies, content of teaching specialty, humanistic and behavioral studies, teaching and learning theory with laboratory and clinical experience, and a "practicum" experience are recommended. For details see *Recommended Standards for Teacher Education* (Washington, D.C.: The American Association for Colleges of Teacher Education, March, 1970).

requirements of "an accountability model" in the fullest sense of the term. By and large Experienced-Based Programs do not.

Even further from a performance-based or an accountability model is the historic concern with institutional resources as a basis for accreditation, for example, concern that a certain proportion of a faculty hold a Ph.D. degree, concern over the scholarly performance of faculty, concern over the "quality" of students admitted to a program, library facilities, etc. (see pp. 7–12 of the *1970 Standards for Teacher Education*). While there is some logic to such an approach—that is, in order to provide the experiences needed to bring about the outcomes desired a sound resource base must exist—the problem with it is that the provision of such a base in no way assures the realization of the outcomes desired. As a consequence, while Performance-Based Programs must be deeply concerned with the resources that they can bring to the task they face, assessing the resource base of a Performance-Based Program becomes critical only when the outcomes expected from that Program are not being met.

In terms of their relationship to an accountability model resource-based, experience-based and performance-based strategies in teacher education can be conceptualized as in Figure 6–1.

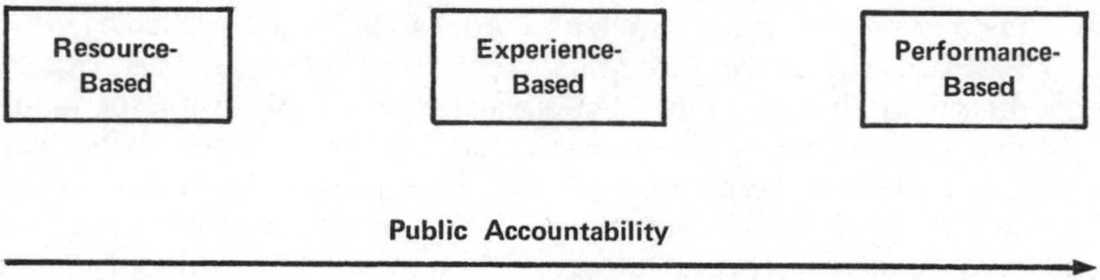

FIGURE 6–1.

2. A shift from a primary focus upon knowledge and skill mastery to a primary focus upon output

Assuming the desirability of moving to a Performance-Based Model of Operation within teacher education, the designers of such programs must decide upon the focus they wish to give them. In broad terms Performance-Based Programs can assume any one, or any combination, of three foci: the mastery of knowledge, the mastery of skill, or the demonstrated ability to apply the knowledges and skills mastered to effectively carry out the tasks that need to be performed within a particular school setting. As used here the completion of tasks involves the production of tangible outputs, that is, the completion of instructional tasks results in specified learning outcomes in children and the completion of instructional support tasks results in outputs such as a "unit" of instruction, an examination, a curriculum guide, a course evaluation plan.

Historically, teacher-education programs have focused heavily upon *knowledge* as the primary basis for certification. As a consequence courses within the discipline that constitutes one's teaching specialty, in the liberal arts, in teaching methods, and in human learning and child development have become standard requirements throughout teacher education. Often they represent the only requirements for certification, save a one-term or one-semester student teaching experience. The basic assumption underlying such an approach is that knowledge of subject matter, teaching methods, childrens' learning, etc., as measured—coupled with a brief testing of the ability to apply what is known in a student teaching situation and a subjective judgment as to the acceptability of a particular student to the teaching profession—is a functional basis for predicting the success of a prospective teacher. The reverse assumption is also applied: There is no need to systematically gather evidence as to the ability of a prospective teacher to behave in specified ways, or of his ability to carry out the functions for which he will be responsible within a school once he is certified. Schematically, such an assumption can be illustrated as in Figure 6–2.

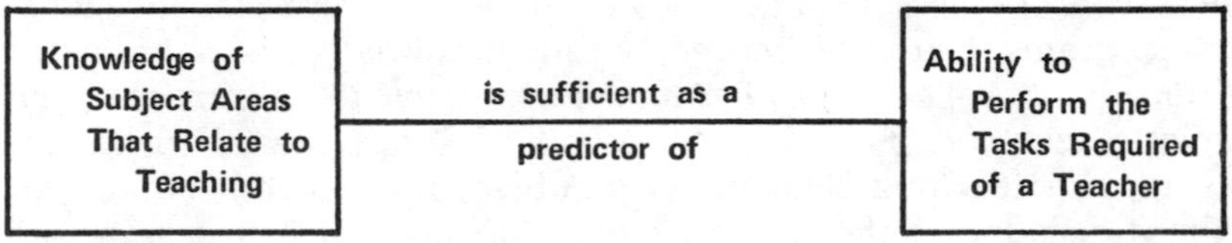

FIGURE 6–2.

While such an assumption is becoming less and less acceptable to many in the profession, it is still acceptable to some. Accordingly, some teacher-education programs can be considered to be performance based but focus only at the knowledge level—providing of course that the desired knowledge outcomes are specified and the indicators to be used as evidence of the realization of those outcomes are made public.

The criterion level set for performance has nothing to do with a program being or not being performance based.

As indicated above, an increasing number of persons in the profession are unwilling to accept the assumption that because one knows something he can necessarily apply it. Or, put in other terms, an increasing number of persons in the profession are becoming uncomfortable with the magnitude of inference between knowing and doing, and are asking for evidence that prospective teachers can do that which is expected of them as well as know that which has been specified for them. The move to focus upon what a prospective teacher can do as well as what he knows rests on four interrelated assumptions:

1. Knowing, and the ability to apply what is known, are two different matters, and the certification of teachers should focus as much upon what a prospective teacher is able to do as it does upon what he knows.
2. The criteria for assessing that which a prospective teacher can do should be as stringent, as systematically derived, and as explicitly stated as the criteria for assessing that which he knows.
3. The assessment of both that which is known and that which can be done must be carried out and described systematically.
4. When a prospective teacher has demonstrated that he knows and can do that which is expected of him, and only then, will he be granted certification.

Accepting the reasonableness of such assumptions, there is still the problem of deciding what is meant operationally by a prospective teacher "being able to do." As interpreted by most teacher-education programs that have moved beyond knowledge as a basis for certification *being able to do has meant being able to perform specified teaching behaviors*. Such a focus parallels closely the emergence of the study of teaching behavior as a subject for research,[5] and with it the translation of the categories of behavior used in research into training systems to be mastered by preservice or in-service teachers, or to be used by supervising teachers. The arguments for adopting teaching behaviors as a basis for certification are roughly as follows:

1. The reasonableness or logic of focusing upon what a teacher does instead of what he knows, believes, or feels, since what he does is a reflection of what he knows or believes or feels.
2. Since it is a teacher's behavior that is the primary determinant of teacher influence, it is important that prospective teachers be able to behave in ways that are desirable.
3. The research that has been done on teacher behavior has laid out categories of behavior that are observable, measurable, and relatively easily mastered; and, because such a focus has a good deal of common sense about it and because it permits systematic

[5] Cf. Anita Simon and E. G. Boyer, eds., *Mirrors for Behavior, An Anthology of Observation Instruments,* vols. I–XIV (Philadelphia, Pa., Research for Better Schools, Inc. 1970).

measurement, it provides one means for meeting the requirement of "accountability" in teacher education.

The assumptions outlined in the paragraph above can be illustrated as in Figure 6–3.

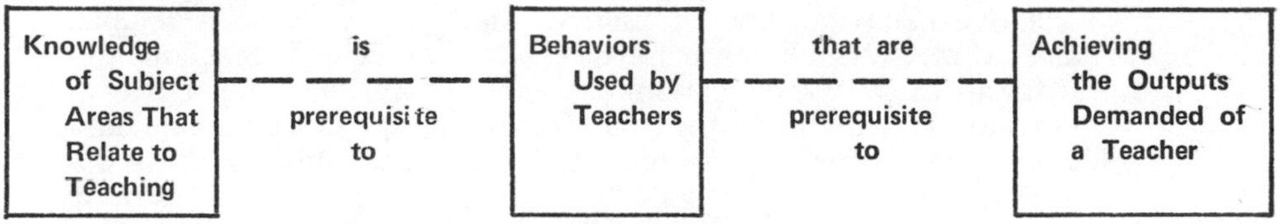

FIGURE 6–3.

A program derived from such assumptions will have two foci: knowledge and teaching behavior. If it is to qualify as a Performance-Based Program, it will have to make explicit the knowledge and teaching behaviors that prospective teachers will have to demonstrate, and the indicators acceptable as evidence of their realization.

While a teacher-education program that incorporates both a knowledge and a teaching behavior focus satisfies most persons in the profession at this point in time, there are some who hold that such a program still involves too much inference making. Those who take such a point of view argue that simply because a prospective teacher is able to behave in certain ways is no assurance that he will be able to effect the outcomes for which he will be responsible in an ongoing educational setting. They further argue that teacher-education programs should, therefore, adopt still another focus, namely, the requirement that prospective teachers demonstrate that they can bring about such outcomes as a basis for certification. The rationale underlying this argument is simply that if a teacher is to be accountable for bringing about specified classes of learner outcomes or noninstructional outcomes subsequent to certification, it would seem reasonable to require that they demonstrate that they can bring about such outcomes prior to certification. While such a point of view does not take all inference making from the relationship between performance prior to certification and performance subsequent to it, it does reduce it significantly.

There are a number of advantages to such a position:

1. It represents a logically defensible criterion of teaching effectiveness, program effectiveness, and teacher and program accountability.

2. While doing so, it accommodates individual differences in teaching performance or style in that it allows for wide variation in the *means of achieving the outcomes* for which teachers will be held responsible once they take a job.
3. It allows for the fact that at this point in time we are not at all clear about the specific teaching behaviors that bring about specified outcomes in pupils, or the specific behaviors that bring about selected noninstructional outcomes, but it does require that effective behaviors and/or instructional programs be developed and utilized (which is precisely the circumstance of teachers).
4. It forces the entire educational system, as well as teacher education, to be clear about the goals or objectives of education, and to become clear about the means for the realization of those objectives.
5. It takes much of the guesswork out of hiring new teachers, for each teacher would have a portfolio which summarizes in detail what he can or cannot do at the time he is certified.

If pressed to defend the position on the basis of education not being clear about its goals or objectives, or not being clear about how the means by which the objectives that it is clear about are to be realized the answer is simply "then that's a task that education must get on with, and a teacher-education program so designed will contribute to that task." The relationship between program characteristics, performance criteria, and identifying labels is summarized in Figure 6–4.

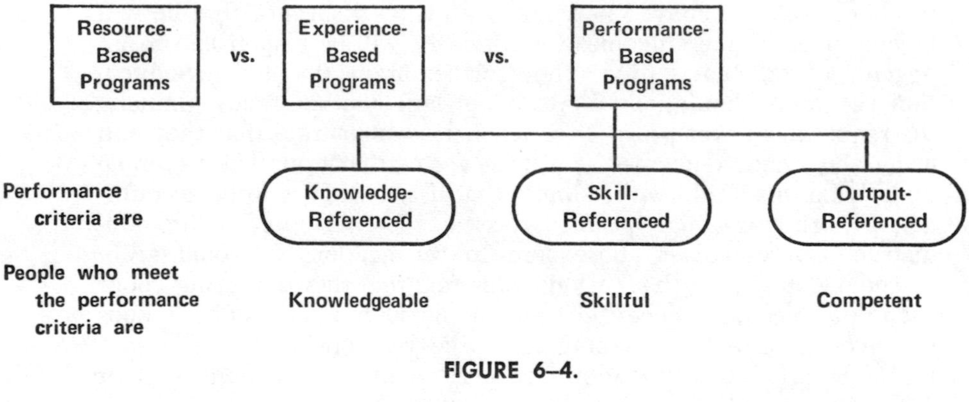

FIGURE 6–4.

A number of problems are inherent in implementing an output-referenced personnel development program. The most obvious one has already been alluded to, namely, the necessity of being clear about the educational outcomes that we want from our schools, the difficulty in measuring such outcomes, and the fact that the discipline is not at all clear as to the factors that contribute to the development of particular learning outcomes in particular kinds of children. Without clarity about such matters it obviously will be difficult to implement such a program. On the other hand, it is precisely these matters that education must be clear about. Adopting a stance in teacher education that forces the discipline and the profession to confront its weaknesses in this regard would seem to be a reasonably good strategy for eliciting movement within the profession as a whole. It goes without saying that the teacher-education programs so designed would be at best a bit "rickety" until the conceptual, methodological, and empirical base needed to support them has been established, but is there any reason to believe that as rickety as they might be they would be any less productive than the programs that are currently maintained?

Three additional problems need to be considered briefly: (1) the inability to attribute in any absolute sense success or failure in pupil learning to a teacher's performance in a school setting: (2) the apparent denial by an output-referenced approach of the utility of a prediction model in training; and (3) the whole issue of the economic feasibility of such an approach.

The problem of linking classroom learning to teacher-performance for purposes of certification is obviously troublesome, but no more so than it is for the schools as they attempt to assess the effectiveness of staff performance for purposes of rank or salary or tenure considerations. As a consequence, there would seem to be little justification for ducking the issue at the teacher-education level. But what conditions must exist if teacher influence is to be linked to learning outcomes? At least three would appear to be necessary:

1. Be clear about the nature of learning outcomes that can be expected to be influenced in a demonstrable way by what occurs in the school and those which cannot be expected to be so influenced—especially in a reasonably short-time basis.
2. Construe the matter of influence to be a function of teacher-materials-context and system interaction rather than a matter of teacher influence alone.
3. Adopt a sensible position with respect to what is meant by success. Operationally success as a teacher will probably have to be defined in terms of the frequency with which a given proportion of students achieve particular kinds of outcomes, with kinds of students working towards kinds of outcomes under kinds of conditions being systematically varied. It will also require sensible measures of student learning, for example, individual patterns of growth in reading skill across time rather than average grade level scores for a first or second or third grade. Such assessments will obviously require a great deal of sophistication in both their conceptualization and in the sampling of contexts within which they are to be taken. In the writer's judgment, however, the

sophistication needed is available if and when teacher educators wish to draw up on it.[6]

The apparent problem of inefficiency in an output-referenced program is especially bothersome to the scientific community. Their argument, which is essentially the argument that has been dominant in teacher education since the writer can remember, is the logical one that says in effect that since the ability of a teacher to bring about given outcomes in the schools depends upon some set of knowledges and skills preparatory programs should focus upon the mastery of such knowledges and skills. While the logic is sound, and there is little disagreement with the desirability of developing training programs that focus on the mastery of knowledges and skills as predictors of success rather than as its uncertain enablers, the fact of the matter is that at this point in time there is no firm evidence as to the knowledge or skill base needed to effect desired educational outcomes. The hard reality is that if one wishes to have confidence that prospective teachers can in fact effect learning outcomes in pupils prior to certification there is little alternative to moving to an output-referenced program. This does not mean, however, that as a discipline education should cease to work towards a model of training that has greater efficiency. But the training model based upon knowledge and skill mastery assumes predictable relationships between that which has been mastered and successful performance as a teacher, and at the moment these relationships are unknown. Moreover, perhaps the best way of establishing such relationships is to move to the kind of product-referenced training model that has been proposed. By moving to such a model it will be possible over time to establish the kind of empirically demonstrated relationships between knowledges, skills, and task performance that ultimately may permit a more efficient model to operate, but until that time—at least if certifying or hiring agencies wish to have evidence that prospective teachers can in fact perform the tasks for which they will be responsible as professionals—there is little option to moving to other than an output-referenced training program.

More will be said in subsequent paragraphs about how such empirical relationships might be established within the context of ongoing training programs.

The economics of operating an output-referenced program are also bothersome to many. The cost of collecting output related information (assuming that it can in fact be collected), and the cost of moving students to the point of being able to effectively produce

[6] Some of the shifts in thinking about measurement that will be required to implement an output-referenced teacher-education program are put forth by the writer in the chapter on measurement in *The National Research Training Institute Manual* (Monmouth, Oregon: Teaching Research, 1969).

expected outputs, would seem to force such programs to be more costly than traditional teacher education. Once such a program has been developed this is not necessarily the case. Feasibility studies have shown that the cost to colleges of operating such a program can be no greater than traditional, Experience-Based Programs, as schools are willing to assume many of the costs associated with them.[7] Development costs are high, however, so the economic issue is a real one. In the end, the decision to support the development of such programs will rest upon the value that is given the increased clarity and order that they would introduce to the field of education generally.

3. A shift from an essentially data-free to an essentially data-dependent mode of operation

Most teacher-education programs operate today on a minimum of information. Little is known about student interests or abilities or background or projected plans; little is known about the effectiveness of a given instruction-learning experience for students who vary on any of these qualities; and little is known about the appropriateness or usefulness of the learning objectives established for the preparatory program, from either a short-term or long-term point of view. Even students in preparatory programs rarely know whether what they are doing has genuine utility for their performance as professionals. Upon close analysis it can honestly be said that a great many Educational Personnel Development Programs operate without being at all clear as to what it is they are attempting to do, why they are attempting to do it, and whether or not they have been effective in doing whatever it is they are trying to do. Students within such Programs tend to suffer similar fates.

Such conditions cannot endure under a performance-based, output-referenced preparatory program. Under such a program the outcomes that students are to be able to effect if they are to succeed in the program must be specified, the indicators acceptable as evidence of their realization spelled out, the conditions that bring about such outcomes identified, the knowledge and skills and sensitivities assumed to be needed by personnel to create such conditions hypothesized—and then evidence systematically gathered as to whether or not all of the above hold. Most critically the collection of evidence starts with an assessment of whether the students of teaching are able to

[7] See, for example, the final report on the feasibility study of the ComField Model. Schalock, Kersh, and Horyna, eds., *A Plan for Managing the Development, Implementation and Operation of a Model Elementary Teacher Education Program.* Final report of a Phase II study in the U.S.O.E.-sponsored Elementary Models Program (Washington, D.C.: Superintendent of Documents, U.S. Government Printing Office).

effect the outcomes for which they are being held responsible. Data are also needed, however, on the effectiveness of each of the various elements within the program in bringing about the learning outcomes for which it has been designed. By systematically collecting data at all levels of program operation empirically based decisions can be made about either the plans of individuals within the program or the program as a whole as it moves through time.

By and large the kind of data being called for here are data that serve on-line decision making and are thereby best thought of as data that derive from either formative or summative-comparative evaluation activities rather than research activities. (See the definitions of evaluation and research in the Glossary.)

4. A shift from an essentially training function to a research, development, and training function

The need to identify increasingly more powerful conceptions of teaching and learning, the need to establish a more efficient preparatory system than one that depends upon indicators of output for certification purposes, the need to establish strong "principles of instruction" on which to build teacher-education programs—that is, empirically demonstrated relationships between instructional strategies or tactics or moves and the emergence of desired learning outcomes for given kinds of learners in given kinds of settings—and the need to understand the emergence and interaction of different kinds of learning outcomes in different kinds of pupils over time are all matters of greatest urgency in education and teacher education. They are matters, however, that will find their solution primarily through research and development activities (see the Glossary for definitions of these terms) rather than evaluation activities. It follows that the effective, efficient operation of Educational Personnel Development Programs over the long term is dependent upon such activities, and it is proposed here that a performance-based, output-referenced, and Data-Dependent Training Program provides the best possible context within which to mount research and development programs that will be able to provide answers to such questions. The essential conceptual frameworks, the organizational structures, and a significant portion of the data base needed to carry out such R & D functions will be available as a necessary adjunct to training programs so designed. It would represent a terrible waste if such contexts were not utilized to their fullest.

5. A shift from an essentially impersonal, instructor-oriented learning environment to one that is personalized and student oriented

The plea for the personalization of the instruction-learning process in teacher education comes from many sides. On the part of students there is the plea to "increase the relevance" of teacher-education programs, where relevance is defined personally and from the point of view of the broader social context within which education functions. They plea for a greater opportunity to exchange on a personal basis with instructors and other students; for an opportunity to take from a program that which makes sense to them in terms of their individual interests, plans, and preferred mode or style; and for the right to have the assessment procedures that are applied to them and their work be appropriate in terms of the goals, objectives, and contexts within which that work is taking place.

The experience of the writer has been that teacher educators also wish to personalize the instruction-learning process—both for the sake of making the learning experience as meaningful as possible to each individual involved in it and for the sake of increasing the probability of personalizing the instruction-learning process at the elementary and secondary level. Educators are increasingly of the opinion that in order for instructional staff to personalize instruction at the elementary-secondary level they probably will have to have experienced a personalized program in the course of their own educational history.

There is also a concern on the part of students and educators that a "performance-based, output-referenced, and data-dependent" mode of operation in teacher education will force programs and students within them into a stereotype or common mold. To persons first introduced to the language of such programs this appears to be a genuine danger, and as a consequence an insistence upon the personalization of learning within them assumes major importance.

Actually, the designers of such programs have little option but to personalize both the instruction-learning and the assessment process, for the demonstration of the ability to effect desired educational outcomes is always situation specific. To illustrate the concept, consider two demonstrable outcomes: getting a six-year-old child in a group of ten who is bright but visually handicapped to be able to distinguish between all letters of the alphabet and getting a thirteen-year-old boy of average ability in a class of thirty, with little exposure to cultures other than that of his own relatively isolated mountain community, to place value in cultures other than his own. Competence in bringing about such outcomes simply cannot be thought of in an abstract or generic sense; competence in a prospective teacher must always be thought of in terms of the ability of that teacher to bring about a specific outcome for a specific child or set of children who have specific characteristics and who are operating in a specific instruction-learning context. Operationally this means that competence in effecting educational outcomes is always defined in terms of an idiosyncratic mix of output-oriented operations, the nature of the output to be effected and the context within which it is to occur.

What does the translation of such concerns into program management look like? What are the dimensions of personalization? Schalock and Garrison[8] have suggested that seven conditions must be met in order for a preparatory program to become genuinely personalized:

1. Person-to-person experience must be a part of the planned program.
2. A variety of instruction-learning options must be available to meet individual needs within the planned program.
3. Students must participate in the design of their own programs.
4. Students must have the opportunity to participate in the design and development of the overall teacher-education program.
5. There must be a mechanism, for example, sponsorship, negotiation, or performance contracting, that will carry the personalization process.
6. Students and staff must hold perceptions that permit the personalization mechanism to operate.
7. There must be an approach to assessment that is consistent with the philosophy of personalization.

6. A shift from an essentially college- or university-centered program to a field-centered program

If a Performance-Based Program adopts output criteria as its point of reference there is little option but to have a significant portion of the program take place within a field setting. For a prospective teacher to demonstrate that he can bring about a particular learning outcome in a particular child or set of children he must have access to children, preferably in a school setting. Moreover, the access must be of a continuing nature over a relatively long period of time in order to demonstrate that meaningful learning outcomes on the part of pupils can be effected. To establish such close and continuing contact with the schools requires essentially that colleges and universities enter into partnership with the schools in the operation of the teacher-education program. While it is possible for Performance-Based Programs that are knowledge referenced to operate within the context of a university,

[8] H. D. Schalock and J. Garrison, "The Personalization of Teacher Education Programs," in *New Directions in Teacher Education: Problems and Prospects Ahead,* M. Vere Devault, ed. (In press.)

and it may even be possible through the adept use of simulation strategies such as microteaching to operate skill-referenced programs within a university, it is literally impossible to operate an output-referenced program within a university context alone.

7. A shift from a relatively narrow and essentially closed decision-making base to one that is broad and essentially open

Historically, decision making in teacher education has rested largely within the colleges and universities. State departments of education, as agents for teacher certification, have obviously had some influence upon the field, and so have professional education and teacher-education associations, but by and large influence outside of the colleges has been relatively weak. Increasingly this picture is changing. Professional groups within education, teachers' unions, community groups, and students in preparatory programs are demanding an increased voice in decisions relative to the conduct of such programs.

The adoption of an output-referenced, performance-based strategy for teacher education would serve to further broaden this decision-making base. As has been pointed out repeatedly, such programs rest squarely upon the explication of the kinds of learner outcomes expected from the schools, and this requires some degree of consensus between the colleges, the schools, the community, the state boards of education, and the students and pupils involved. So too does agreement as to the indicators acceptable as evidence of the realization of such outcomes, and the role of prospective teachers in bringing them about. It is also likely that such programs would lead to increased involvement of professional education associations in the business of teacher education, in part because of the same issues that draw other groups into the decision-making structure of such programs, but also because of the implications of such an approach for professional licensure and job maintenance over time. As a consequence, one of the major tasks that output referenced, performance-based, teacher-education programs will have to face is the design of a decision-making mechanism that provides for representation from these various groups, and which orchestrates their input with the design and operation of the program.

Do the five thrusts constitute the necessary and sufficient conditions for teacher-education programs to meet the requirements outlined above?

In the writer's judgment the answer is an unqualified YES, provided that the potential of each of the five thrusts is fully utilized! The Performance-Based Certification thrust provides the wherewithall to move on to an output-referenced mode of operation, and thereby move teacher education to a level of accountability that will force not only teacher education to be certain that it is preparing personnel who can in fact bring about the goals set for education but to force education as a whole to become clearer about its goals. The thrust represented by the Elementary Models provides the wherewithall to move to a Data-Dependent Mode of Operation and to integrate research and development with training. They also provide for the design and operation of preparatory programs that are committed to output as a point of reference for certification, for the integrated use of Protocol and Training Materials throughout the instructional process, and for the personalization of the instructional process. The Protocol and Training Materials Development thrusts can provide the conceptual and theoretical leadership needed in establishing the content of teacher-education programs, as well as leadership in the design, fabrication, and development of the materials base needed in support of such Programs. Finally, the Training Complex thrust provides the structure within which to establish the necessary working relationships with the field and within which to establish the broadly based decision-making mechanisms needed to reach concensus as to the products to be developed within the field.[9]

In the writer's opinion the crux of the matter is the criterion level set for certification. If it is set at only the knowledge level the five thrusts in combination will produce little more than teacher education now produces. If it is set at the knowledge *and* skills level the potential contribution of the five thrusts will be more fully exercised, but as pointed out in the discussion of the desirability of an output-referenced criterion the education profession would still be lacking the essential element that would give it leverage to "turn itself around," and a base for confirming that having turned itself around it is making a difference in the lives of children and youth. The criticalness of the criterion issue has been elaborated more fully by Turner in a paper prepared for Task Force '72 entitled, "Programmatic Themes and Mechanisms in Teacher Education."

What is needed to effect the kind of change envisioned for teacher education on a national scale?

Assuming optimal utilization of the five thrusts within any given personnel development program, and by so doing implementing preparatory programs that will truly make a difference in the education

[9] Several of the Elementary Models also provide a framework for linking to the community and a more broadly based decision-making structure. Syracuse University's "Proto-cooperative" notion, Florida State University's "Portal Schools" notion, and the ComField Model's concept of "coalitions" are cases in point.

of children and youth, there is the second order problem of diffusing that which has been developed throughout the nation as a whole. This is a concern that is obviously of high priority to the Office of Education but to the writer's knowledge it is a concern for which no formal solutions have been either sought or found. The Office of Education has systematically attacked one aspect of the problem, namely, the dissemination of information through its ERIC system, but dissemination is only one dimension of the diffusion process. (For a definition of diffusion see the Glossary.) For the majority of teacher-education programs in the nation to adopt the kind of program that has been described, the on-line demonstration of such programs will in all likelihood be required, banks of Protocol and Training Materials that can be drawn upon fully and easily will be needed, resources to provide the necessary support systems for such programs will have to be found, and elaborate information and materials exchange networks will have to be established. It is probably fair to say that at present education has no good examples of nor models for such a massive diffusion effort. Accordingly, in the "preferred plan" that is outlined in the pages which follow, considerable attention is given to the nature of the diffusion mechanism that is likely to be needed if a major diffusion effort is to be a success.

And where does one start in relation to all the above?

With first questions first! In the writer's judgment it is inappropriate to take as a point of departure in the design of Education Personnel Development Programs the question, "What kind of training programs do we want?" In the language of the everyday this is simply getting the cart ahead of the horse. Training programs must be responsive to the question, "What kind of personnel do our schools need, and what competencies should such personnel possess?" But this too is out of order as a place to begin. The first questions to be asked, and they are the questions from which all else must flow, are, "What do we want our children to learn? How do we want them to feel or believe? What should they be able to do? What adults do we want to become? What should they know or be able to do or be able to accomplish? And toward which of these ends should the schools contribute?"

Once answers are in, in relation to first-level questions, second-level questions can then be asked. "What kind of schools will it take to achieve the desired ends? And how do we want such schools to function? Are schools to make explicit and public their goals and objectives? What indicators are to be used as evidence of the realization of such? In what sense are the schools to be held accountable for realizing their goals and objectives? Are they to present evidence as to cost/benefit relationships for alternative goals or for alternative programs in relation to a particular goal?" As answers to second-level questions begin to emerge, it then becomes possible to ask third-level questions, namely, "What kind of personnel are needed to operate schools of the kind required to achieve the ends desired?" When answers are finally obtained to this level of question it then becomes possible, but only then, to sensibly design an Education Personnel Development Program that has some hope of providing the personnel that are needed to operate the schools that are needed to effect the outcomes that are desired by a community (or a state or a nation) for its children.

Rather obviously, ongoing Education Personnel Development Programs do not have the time or the human and financial resources to carry out such fundamental analyses prior to or while they proceed with their training function. Nor do school systems. Nor can such an analysis be done once for example by a state, or a region or the federal government, and have it translate functionally into the variety of Personnel Development Programs that crisscross the nation. While the latter may be a place to start, simply as a means of providing a real-life example of how such an analysis works and the power it generates once it has been done, in the end each training program in concert with representatives from the community it is intended to serve must make its own analysis and design its own program on the basis of it. Anything less denies the reality of the differences that exist within and between training programs, within and between communities and the strength of the tradition in America that insures local control of education.

So again, where does one start? Again the answer, "With first questions first!" And in the opinion of the writer, the federal government, each state, and each Personnel Development Program in conjunction with representatives from the community it serves should begin with such questions. If the kind of analysis suggested were undertaken simultaneously by all of the above, it is likely that enough progress could be made and enough wisdom gained to permit preparatory programs to become relevant, functional units within the larger education enterprise. Without such progress, however, it is questionable whether this will ever be the case.

PART II: A PREFERRED PROPOSAL

The proposal which follows represents an attempt to integrate the five thrusts with which the paper is to deal within a statewide teacher-education program that reflects the characteristics outlined in the previous section of the paper. Specifically, the proposal has five purposes:

1. Develop broad specifications for a prototype Education Personnel Development Program that combines within it the essential features of the five foundational thrusts within BEPD in such a way as to optimize their impact in relation to the point of view expressed previously.
2. Link to these specifications a plan by which to incorporate the research, development, and evaluation functions that will be needed to ensure effective operation of the proposed program.
3. Develop specifications for a statewide network of such programs.
4. Suggest ways in which the costs involved in the development and operation of a statewide network be shared among federal, state, and local agencies.
5. Suggest ways in which statewide networks could be linked nationally and to industry in order to insure maximum spread effects.

The proposal is set forth in a series of guidelines that speak to the five purposes.

Guideline #1: Define certification standards in terms of PERFORMANCE CRITERIA and set those standards at the OUTPUT rather than the KNOWLEDGE AND/OR SKILL level.

Of the five thrusts to be dealt with in the paper the concept of Performance-Based Certification has within it the greatest leverage for change. This is especially so when certification criteria are set at the output rather than the knowledge or skill levels. By insisting that preparatory programs spell out in advance what it is that prospective teachers or administrators or instructional support personnel be able to accomplish in an ongoing educational context prior to certification, and insisting that each candidate show evidence that he can in fact effect such accomplishments, there is little opportunity for anyone to "weasel" on their obligations.

1. Persons responsible for preparatory programs must make explicit that which graduates of their programs will be able to accomplish in the schools; they must make explicit the indicators they will accept as evidence of such accomplishments; and they must devise a program that ensures the majority of students in it are able to develop to the point where they are able to realize such accomplishments. They must also make explicit the kind of systematic linkage called for in the previous section of the paper between the expected outputs of their program and the personal needs of schools, and these in turn to the outcomes expected of schools.
2. Students who wish to become certified must show that they can "put it all together." They cannot just talk about it; they cannot win brownie points by regurgitating the contents of books or lectures or discussions; they cannot make it with a few highly

developed "performance skills." Performance-Based Certification at the output level requires that they know what it is that they wish to accomplish with the children they wish to work with, and that they can in fact accomplish those things with at least the majority of children with whom they do work. Anything less and certification will simply not be forthcoming.

3. State department personnel must be responsible for ensuring that such is the case or else the entire process will be a mockery. These are harsh guides to action for everyone involved, but such is the leverage of Performance-Based Certification with criteria set at the output level.

In the writer's judgment none of the other thrusts being dealt with has anywhere near the power to effect change of such magnitude and on so many fronts simultaneously as does Performance-Based Certification. As a consequence the position can be taken, as it is in fact in the present paper, that the remaining four thrusts are simply means to effect the conditions established by Guideline #1.

While powerful as a lever to effect change, and therefore attractive to those who wish to bring change about, it needs to be reiterated that Performance-Based Certification at the output level carries with it some extremely complex problems that are in need of solution before it is free to fly. Many of these have already been alluded to, for example, the necessity of explicating the goals of education, and designing educational systems that have a high probability of realizing those goals, as prerequisites to the design of Personnel Development Programs; the need to involve the schools and community in such an effort; the need to personalize the entire preparatory process so as to furnish a negotiated choice for students as to school contexts within which to work, and, the outcomes to work towards within those criteria and criteria by which to be judged successful or unsuccessful in bringing about such outcomes.

There are also other problems. One of the most critical of these is the certification of persons who demonstrate markedly different sets of competencies. Given the need to personalize output-referenced programs, and the fact that such programs will vary by the nature of the schools to which they link, it is probable that persons from preparatory program A, which is linked to school districts that are pressing toward open classrooms, individualized learning programs for pupils, and decisions about pupils resting upon performance or other recorded data, will present portfolios of demonstrated competencies markedly different from those of persons from a preparatory program that is linked to schools reflecting a different mode of organization. This is the case even when the students applying for certification have worked with reasonably similar groups of pupils toward reasonably similar kinds of outcomes with reasonably similar materials. When kinds of pupils vary, for example by grade level and ability, and kinds of outcomes and materials and school contexts vary, and when these all interact with the differences that exist in prospective teachers and the personnel responsible for operating preparatory programs, the variation in the portfolio of demonstrated competencies that will be presented to the state department for certification purposes staggers the imagination.

How is the state department to cope with such variance? Will the vehicle of the approved program handle it? Probably not in the way it presently operates, for it is a vehicle designed primarily to handle variance only between course-oriented, experience-based preparatory programs, not between individual candidates who vary in demonstrated competencies. Will the "committee" strategy developed in the State of Washington handle it? Perhaps, but only so long as the data base required about performance is minimal. If hard performance data are required as a basis for certification, the committee strategy will have to be supplemented to accommodate the generation of such data and its use in decision making. Considerable attention must be directed to the solution of this problem if output-referenced, Performance-Based Certification procedures are to be implemented.[10]

Another serious problem that is encountered immediately when attempting to implement an output-referenced program is the fact that such a program requires a significantly different structure, content, and mode of operation than does an Experience-Based Program at the knowledge and/or skill level. So long as Experience-Based Programs are defined primarily in terms of courses, or Performance-Based Programs focus only at the knowledge level, the business of teacher education can go on relatively unchanged in the college and university setting. It can even continue there when performance criteria are defined at the level of skills provided, creative uses of "simulation" or "microteaching" techniques are used, and the criteria of skill demonstration are kept rather simple, i.e., without regard to the performance of skills within the context of real-life educational settings with real-life children who may or may not be responsive to a particular skill. *Teacher-education programs cannot remain cloistered if they adopt an Experience-Based Mode of Operation that places students in contexts outside of the college or university, or if they adopt a Performance-Based Mode of Operation with certification*

[10] Performance-Based Certification Programs with criteria set at the knowledge and/or skill levels do not face such severe difficulties, for it is possible to insist (and even convince some people) that all students in preparatory programs should know whatever it is they need to know about children, methods, subject-matter fields, etc., and that all students should be able to perform essentially the same *set of skills—since such knowledges and skills are assumed to be essential prerequisites to effective teaching.* Because some tough issues can be avoided by choosing intermediate performance criteria for certification purposes, at least for a little while, it is not a good reason, in the writer's judgment, to do so.

criteria set at the output level. In the first case, students must have access to other contexts, whatever they may be. In the second, they must have access to schools and students within schools. Such a requirement forces preparatory programs to link functionally to contexts other than the college or university, and that fact forces a set of structures and operating procedures on such a program that represents essentially "a new ball game."

But this is not the only kind of change that adoption of an output-referenced certification strategy forces on program operation. As indicated previously, it forces the personalization of the program, attention to data, attention to self-correction, attention to schools and schooling, attention to children, attention to the community, and attention to what life is all about. All these matters have major implications for program operation, and they are simply inescapable. For those who wish details of the Oregon College of Education adaptation of the Teacher Education,[11] see Schalock, Kersh, and Horyna, eds., *A Plan for the Development, Implementation and Operation of a Model Elementary Teacher Education Program.* Final Report of the Phase II study in the U.S.O.E.-sponsored Elementary Models Program. Superintendent of Documents, U.S. Government Printing Office, Washington D.C.

Guideline #2: As a context within which to implement an output-referenced, Performance-Based Certification plan, establish on a cost-sharing basis illustrative state-wide networks of Training Cooperatives, with each Cooperative having the organizational characteristics of a TRAINING COMPLEX and the structural, functional, and operational characteristics of one or more of the ELEMENTARY MODELS.

As suggested in the previous section of the paper, adoption of an output-referenced, performance-based approach to certification forces preparatory programs to assume two dominant characteristics: (1) a functional linkage to the field, and (2) a data-dependent or "confirmatory" mode of operation. A functional linkage to the field is demanded by the requirement that such programs rest upon an explication of the kinds of learning outcomes a community wants for its children, the kinds of schools needed to effect those outcomes, and a context within which prospective teachers can demonstrate that they can or cannot bring such outcomes about. A reliance upon a Data-Dependent or Confirmatory Mode of Operation is forced by the commitment to performance as a basis for certification. Within such

[11] The ComField Model is one of the nine Elementary Teacher-Education Models developed under the sponsorship of NCERD. It is the only Model of the nine to advocate output-referenced criteria as a basis for certification.

a framework each candidate for certification must provide evidence of acceptable performance in relation to the established criteria for certification. Also, given the responsibility of the Programs to prepare personnel to meet these criteria within a reasonable length of time with a reasonable outlay of energy, it is essential that evidence be obtained on the contribution of each component within a program to the realization of the goal or goals that it is designed to serve, the success of different types of students with the component, etc. It is also essential that evidence be provided on the appropriateness of the goals pursued by the Program, and on its long-term consequences, for example, its impact on the personal growth of teachers three or five or ten years after graduating or on their impact on children and the schools at those points in time. Operationally, a functional linkage of a Personnel Development Program to the field involves a full-fledged partnership between a community and its schools, and a college or university responsible for the preparation of education personnel.[12] The implementation of a Data-Dependent or Confirmatory Mode of Operation within such a Program involves reliance upon the principles of systems design and operation.

Fortunately, through the work that has been done on Training Complexes and the Models guidelines for such partnerships and for the application of systems principles to the design, development, and operation of teacher-education programs already have been established.

On the basis of the conceptual work done thus far the idea of a teacher-educational model, as this has been explicated in the Elementary Models, and the idea of a Training Complex, as this has been explicated in *Teachers for the Real World* and subsequent design efforts, seem to be mutually supportive. In general terms, the Training Complex provides a context within which a systematically designed and operated teacher-education program resides, and the Elementary Models provide first approximations to the structure, function, and operation of such programs. As indicated earlier, while some of the Elementary Models proposed structures somewhat akin to a Training Complex none took those ideas as far in their development as has Bunny Smith and others in their thinking about Training Complexes. Contrariwise, those who have been concerned with Training Complexes have not pushed their thinking as far in regard to the actual structure, function, and operation of the training programs to be housed within as have the Elementary Models directors. By combining the work of both groups it would seem that the efforts of each would be strengthened. The combination of the two ideas can be illustrated schematically as in Figure 6–5.

[12] It is this partnership that has been labeled in Guideline #1 as a Training Cooperative.

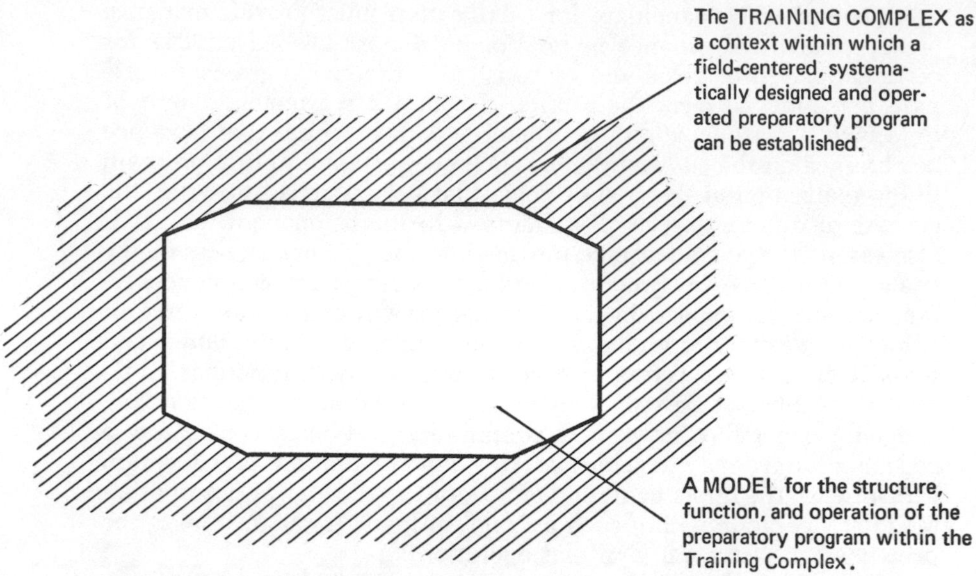

FIGURE 6–5. ***The basic components that make up a Training Cooperative for the preparation of educational personnel.***

In the design of Training Cooperatives three sensitivities should be kept in mind:

1. A Cooperative is seen as an integral part of all teacher-education programs within a state, that is, it is not simply an illustrative or demonstration program for a state or region.
2. It is a school-community context within which only selected aspects of any given personnel development program will be housed.
3. It will always be developed around exemplary or illustrative elementary-secondary programs.

Given these conditions it follows that (1) in order for a state to adopt a competency-based plan of certification it must first establish a network of Cooperatives where desired competencies can in fact be defined and demonstrated; (2) that each Cooperative involve minimally a community, a school within that community, and a college or university responsible for the preparation of education personnel; and (3) only communities that possess one or more exemplary schools, with exemplary being defined as a school that is clear about its objectives and that has been designed with the realization of those objectives in mind, will be invited to become a part of a Training Cooperative. As presently conceived the following activities will occur within each cooperative:

1. Identify the outputs to be realized by prospective educational personnel within the Cooperative.
2. Identify the indicators acceptable as evidence of the realization of those outputs.
3. Carry out the instruction that leads to the actual development and demonstration of the competencies, required to bring about such outputs, including the skills associated with them.
4. Carry out the formal assessment required in all of the above.

The mastery of the knowledge that is prerequisite to skill and competence demonstration, and to some extent the mastery of skills—to the extent that this is possible through simulated training conditions—will be carried out within the college setting. A statewide network of such Cooperatives is illustrated schematically in Figure 6–6.

Four further points need to be discussed: (1) the rationale for utilizing a community and its schools as the locus of a Training Co-

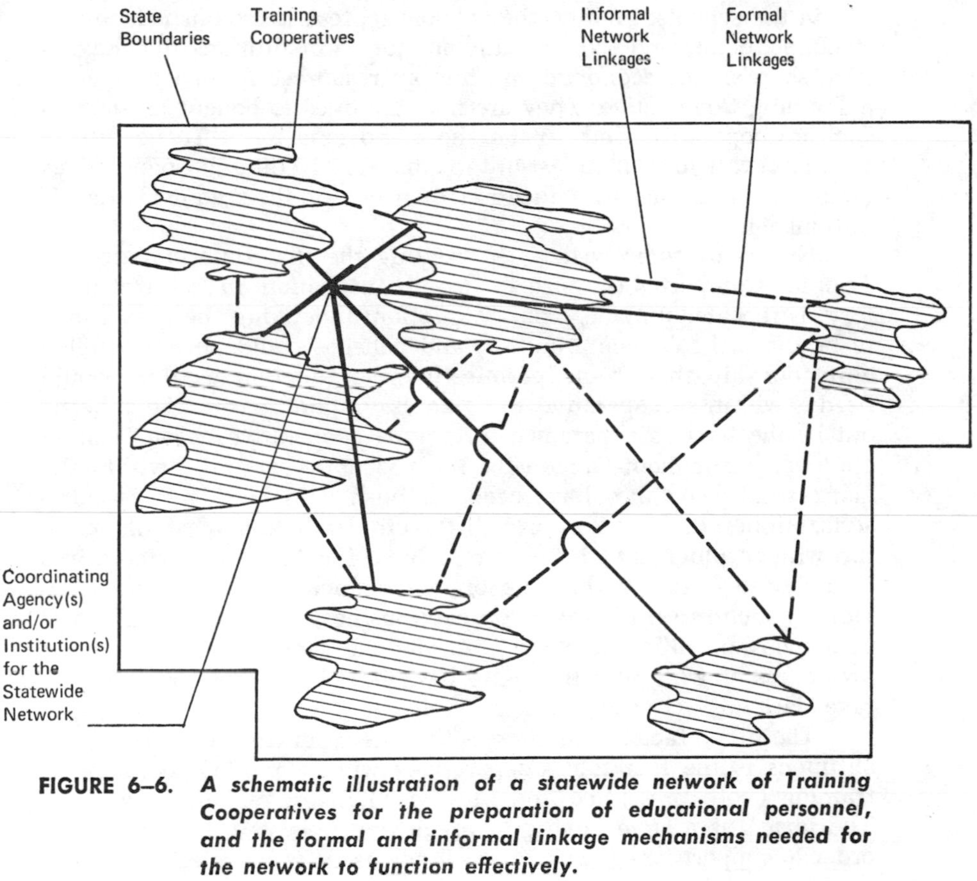

FIGURE 6–6. ***A schematic illustration of a statewide network of Training Cooperatives for the preparation of educational personnel, and the formal and informal linkage mechanisms needed for the network to function effectively.***

operative rather than creating a new institution on a "neutral ground"; (2) the rationale for using a state as the primary organization for Cooperatives rather than a region; (3) the rationale for cost-sharing in the development and operation of Cooperatives; and (4) the rationale for establishing a nationwide network of illustrative statewide networks.

1. *The rationale for utilizing a community and its schools as the locus of a Training Cooperative rather than creating a new institution to house it*

The rationale is relatively straightforward: Communities are where the action is. Also they are the governmental units that provide the bulk of funds for the support of elementary and secondary education in the nation; they are the units that have the schools; they are the units that have the greater reason to care about the well-being of schools; and they are the units that ultimately control what happens within the schools. Finally, the schools represent established, understood, politically and economically supported institutions that have a good share of the economic and human resources needed to operate a Training Cooperative. They are also the ones to benefit most from such a Cooperative, both in the short and long term. To not utilize such resources to their fullest in the creation of Training Cooperatives (including intermediate education districts, or their equivalents) is unthinkable.

Not so by some writers. In reading the materials prepared on Training Complexes the plea for a new institution on "neutral territory" is repeatedly made. The assumption underlying the plea seems to be that schools, communities, and colleges could never establish a relationship that would permit them to function as they would need to within a Cooperative. Such an assumption has not been borne out by the writer's experience. Prototype cooperatives have been in operation throughout Oregon for the past ten years, and within the last several years they have been established in Florida, Massachusetts, Minnesota, New York, North Dakota, Utah, and Washington. In the writer's judgment, the only real hope for Training Cooperatives is their integration within the ongoing educational enterprise. Obviously, such integration is a complex business and can run aground in a thousand different places, but if done sensitively and with an awareness of what it is that is to be gained by all concerned it can take place.

The other factor that presses for the utilization of existing institutions is the fact that Cooperatives will be needed to facilitate training (both preservice and in-service) in all regions of a state. The image of a state having to create multiple new institutions in order to support its education personnel needs is disquieting at best.

The likelihood of the success of such a venture, given the financial circumstances of the times and the history of the Regional Laboratories and R & D Centers, is probably next to zero.

2. *The rationale for establishing a state as the primary unit of organization, rather than a region*

Granting the proposition that a Training Cooperative or something akin to it is needed to support each training program in teacher education, and recognizing that at this point in time the certification of teachers is a responsibility of the states, and recognizing that legislation, funding sources, communication networks, and other support systems to teach education are defined primarily by state boundaries (although there are obvious moves afoot to increase the planning and operation of human service programs on a regional basis) it seems reasonable to think of the state as the primary unit of organization for such Cooperatives. As a means of facilitating nationwide resource sharing and communication flow across state lines within a region makes some sense, but beyond that the notion of organization along regional lines would seem to have little to offer.

3. *The rationale for cost-sharing between participating institutions in the Cooperatives and the state and federal governments*

Colleges currently have budgets that support Education Personnel Development Programs. School districts have budgets for in-service education. Increasingly schools want beginning teachers who have had a wide range of experience with children. Colleges are following suit by seeking such experience for their students, and for earlier and longer periods of time. As schools move to open classrooms, individualized instruction, team teaching, differentiated staffing, and the like they have more and more need for persons in the schools with different backgrounds and capabilities. College faculty are increasingly of the opinion that persons in the schools have a great deal to give in relation to the preparation of teachers.

In most instances the community and the state department of education view these events with pleasure.

So should the designers of Training Cooperatives for they provide not only the interpersonal and interinstitutional groundwork for Cooperatives, but they also provide the avenue for their financial base as well. A number of schemes have been worked out whereby a school district and a participating college have pooled their human and financial resources so as to effectively create a prototype Cooperative, and these seem to be working to the satisfaction of all concerned.[13] If such arrangements could become widespread, and there is no reason for believing that they could not, a relatively firm financial base already exists for the development and operation of Cooperatives.

Given the projected functions of these "new institutions," however, it is unlikely that such a financial base would be adequate for their full development and operation. As always, one place to turn for additional financial help is the state and federal governments. Assuming that the installation of fully functioning Training Cooperatives of the kind proposed would significantly influence education throughout a state and the nation, and assuming that district and college contributions would cover operating instructional costs, a state might be willing to pick up the cost of program evaluation and instate diffusion and the federal government might be willing to pick up the cost of the research and development needs associated with launching a statewide network of Cooperatives as well as the cost of nationwide diffusion efforts.[14] Whether federal monies for the support of such activities should be assigned to states on a "project" or "block-grant" basis, or some other basis, is an open question, but the idea of shared costs at the federal and state level, in conjunction with shared costs at the college and local level, seems sound.

4. *The rationale for establishing a network of illustrative statewide networks*

Much will need to be learned in the operation of Cooperatives both individually and on a statewide basis before they become fully functional components within the education enterprise. It seems reasonable to assume, therefore, that some organizational structure which links the developing statewide networks would be most useful. Through such a structure they could share on a regular basis the issues that they face and the solutions that they find.

Similarly, by pooling that which emerges from the various state networks and making it available to teacher education at large the utility of such networks would be greatly enhanced. Given the national scope of such an effort it seems reasonable to assume that the Office of Education would be the agency to effect such coordination.[15]

[13] For information about such arrangement contact Dr. Jim Ellingson, Oregon Board of Education, Salem, Oregon or Dr. Bill Drummond, Washington State Department of Education, Olympia, Washington.

[14] The research, development, evaluation, and diffusion needs associated with Cooperatives as well as more detailed suggestions for cost-sharing relative to them are outlined under Guideline #4.

[15] It is also possible that each statewide network initially funded could serve as a "pilot" or "lead" state in relation to a region, and thus insure a more intimate network for communicating the results of the overall de-

Guideline #3: Utilize within the proposed preparatory program all PROTOCOL, TRAINING, AND INTEGRATING MATERIALS that are *available to and consonant with that program.*

Strictly speaking, a teacher-education model is devoid of substance or content. It lays out specifications for the structure, function, and operation of a teacher-education program, but the specific content to be included within it when fully developed is left to the designers of that program (and thus the general utility of a model). Given this condition a program of the kind proposed becomes a ready consumer of the Protocol, Training, and Integrating Materials that are available to it. The incorporation of these materials within the operation of a center is illustrated schematically in Figure 6–7.[16]

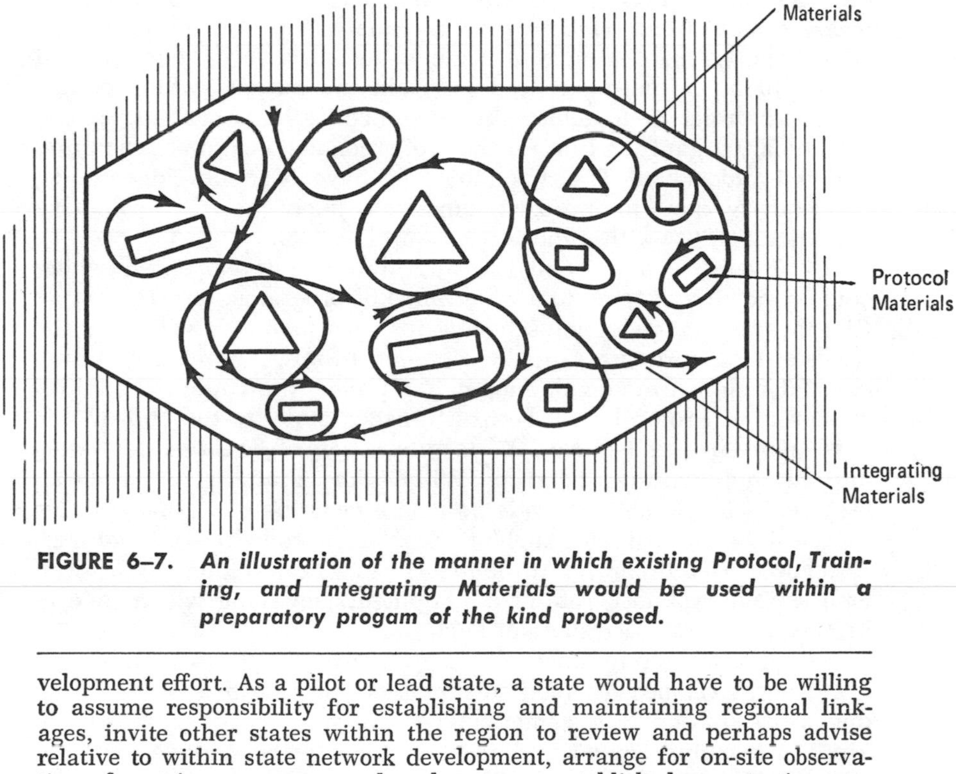

FIGURE 6–7. ***An illustration of the manner in which existing Protocol, Training, and Integrating Materials would be used within a preparatory progam of the kind proposed.***

velopment effort. As a pilot or lead state, a state would have to be willing to assume responsibility for establishing and maintaining regional linkages, invite other states within the region to review and perhaps advise relative to within state network development, arrange for on-site observation of ongoing programs, and perhaps even establish demonstration programs within other states. Additional details are provided in this regard under Guideline #7.

[16] Strictly speaking, a large share of the available Training and Protocol Materials will probably he used in the college setting, though many may also be used in or as adjuncts to the field setting provided by the cooperative. In this sense the schematic is a pictorial convenience.

While the principle just stated and illustrated in Figure 6–7 is appropriate as a principle, a host of operational questions revolve around it.

1. How likely is it that Protocol and Training Materials produced in other centers or in other preparatory programs would be adopted by or would be able to be fit within a second program? To the extent that a program focuses upon knowledge and skill outcomes (which would run counter to the proposal made in the present paper), it is possible that "ready-made" materials would receive wide use. This assumes, of course, that the conceptual base for both Protocol and Training Materials has been well established, that such materials have been well produced, and that there is evidence that they in fact bring about the outcomes that they are intended to achieve. If the second program is output based, however, it is likely that Protocol and Training Materials developed elsewhere—at least if they have been developed independently of an analysis of the outputs that educational personnel have to bring about—will have more limited utility. In an output-referenced program the outputs which educational personnel are to achieve in a given educational context become the primary organizing unit for the professional education curriculum, and if Protocol and Training Materials have been developed independently of those intended outcomes it is likely that they will have a restricted utility within the curriculum.[17]

2. Even if Protocol and Training Materials developed elsewhere could be readily adapted to a wide range of programs, how likely is it that the present production schedule for such materials will meet the needs of such programs? At the moment a limited number of Protocol Materials are under development (probably no more than fifty or so sets of Protocols will be in a finished state by the end of this academic year) and plans for the production of Training Materials are only now getting underway. While some Training Materials already exist in the field, there is no where near the mass of materials that will be needed ultimately to support a fully operational Performance-Based Program. At the present rate of development, or even at a tenfold expanded rate of development, how long will it take to accumulate the needed mass of such materials?

3. At the present time no integrative materials (see Glossary) are being developed. In fact, so far as one is able to determine, no one in the nation is systematically addressing the question of the kinds of learning outcomes that educational personnel are expected

[17] The implications of a Performance-Based, output-referenced program in teacher education for concept identification and organization is spelled out in detail in a paper by the writer entitled "Tasks to Be Performed by Teachers as a Basis for Identifying and Ordering Concepts in Teacher Education." The paper was prepared for use as a discussion vehicle within the Protocol LTI. February, 1971.

to develop to facilitate the realization of learning outcomes.[18] Given the definition of Integrating Materials, it is quite obvious that they cannot be developed until questions of this kind have been answered. If certification criteria and preparation programs are to become output-referenced, there is simply no way to avoid dealing with such issues for they constitute the beginning and end of both curriculum development and competency assessment.

Assuming the correctness of this assessment it seems essential that a task force comparable to that which exists for Protocol and Training Materials be established to begin the process of identifying the outcomes expected of schooling, the kinds of school arrangements needed to effect such outcomes, the criteria to be used in judging whether prospective teachers are able to bring them about, the measures to be used in assessing performance relative to those criteria, and in the nature of the learning experiences that must be engaged in by prospective teachers to develop the competence to perform them. Within this context learning experiences will need to include those designed to sensitize the prospective teacher to all the above.

4. Given such concerns, should the proposed illustrative statewide networks of Training Cooperatives become primary producers of Protocol, Training, and Integrating Materials? If so, how should production responsibilities be divided amongst them? And what critical mass of human and nonhuman resources would be needed to support the development of such materials within a reasonable time frame? If heavy production were commissioned for the cooperatives, what would their responsibilities be for producing multiple copies of the materials for distribution? For actually distributing or marketing the materials that they do produce? For coordinating their development? If the cooperatives were not to become involved in production would they in fact be field-test centers for producers? More is said under Guidelines #6 and #7 about the production and distribution of such materials.

Guideline #4: Incorporate within one or more of the Training Cooperatives within each state the functions of RESEARCH, DEVELOPMENT, EVALUATION, and DIFFUSION.[19]

[18] Since writing this an RFP has been discovered that has been let by BEPD (RFP #71-27) for "The Design and Conduct of a Program to Qualitatively Assess the Educational Needs of Children Through a Broadly Based Literature Review and to Determine Quantitatively the Implications for Educational Manpower." This is surely a much needed step in the right direction.

[19] This section of the paper, and the three sections which follow, deal with topics that extend beyond the five thrusts with which the paper is intended to deal. They have been included in the paper, however, because of their criticalness as adjuncts to the five thrusts in the overall

The major research, development, evaluation, and diffusion activities that need to be carried out within a Training Cooperative, or within a statewide network of cooperatives, have been alluded to at various places and in various ways throughout the paper. The rationale for including such activities has also been advanced in pieces and parts. The purpose of this section of the paper is to summarize these proposed activities and the rationale for them in one place, and to speak of their distribution within a statewide network of cooperatives.

1. Development. In the previous section of the paper, questions were raised about the generalizability or the transportability of materials, be they Protocol, Training, or Integrating, across programs. It will be recalled that, in the writer's judgment, the bulk of materials designed to support Educational Personnel Development Programs will be submitted to some degree of modification by each program that relies upon them. If this is true it will mean that each program will have to assume responsibility for some adaptive developmental activities in order to arrive at an integrated use of materials that become available through multiple producers. Since this is not a major developmental activity, however, it will not be dealt with further at this time.

A more critical issue for the purpose of this discussion is whether major program development efforts, such as the one that has been proposed in the present paper, should be considered as a primary locus for materials development. The history of experience in the protocol projects and in the development of instructional modules in support of Teacher Corps efforts suggests that the process of materials development is much more complex than people initially realized. This has also been the experience of the Regional Laboratories. Accepting the complexity of the task, would it make sense to add such a responsibility to all the other responsibilities that will accompany a program development effort of the magnitude that has been proposed? In one respect, yes, for the development of such a program represents a natural context within which to launch the development of the materials needed to support it. Also, if the program development effort is viewed as exemplary, then materials developed within it should be optimally useful. In another respect, however, the requirements of materials development could be so severe as to threaten other aspects of program development and operation. This is an issue that needs to be tested on a trial and error basis.

Assuming that a Training Cooperative or a network of such Cooperatives should become involved in the production of materials, the next question is whether all three kinds of materials, that is,

---

design and operation of Personnel Development Programs that have some hope of making a difference.

Protocol, Training, and Integrating Materials, should be produced at a single site? One of the inevitable problems that would arise with multiple centers producing multiple products is that of overlap or duplication. If exemplary programs were to assume major responsibilities for materials development, some coordinating mechanism would have to be established at the national level to oversee such efforts.

Another development problem exists in relation to an output-referenced, Performance-Based Teacher Education Program which has not been spoken of heretofore. That is the problem of the design and development of the support systems needed to operate such a program. Generally speaking, these pertain to the design, development, and operation of the instructional program: the generation of information to support instruction and the assessment of its results: the management of information: the selection, preparation, and maintenance of staff: and the provision of facilities and supplies, costing, program management, and policy setting.

One of the results of the feasibility study conducted in Oregon on the implications of adopting the ComField Model was the finding that the development and operation of the systems needed in support of instruction were roughly equivalent in cost to the development and operation of the instructional program per se.[20] Since each program must develop its own support systems in order to operate, it is likely that these will be developmental costs that cannot be significantly reduced through "system sharing" across programs. This is not to say that design and development costs could not be reduced by having exemplary systems available, but it is to say that support systems are not likely to be able to be transported and used by operating programs in the same way that instructional materials can be.

In summary it is likely that every Performance-Based Teacher-Education Program will encounter some adaptation developmental costs in relation to instructional materials and that they will encounter considerable costs of this kind in relation to support systems. If the decision is made to have exemplary programs become the locus of materials development efforts, or as the locus for the development of exemplary support systems, developmental costs will climb accordingly. Because of the highly specialized human resource requirements involved in such activities, and because of the relatively limited supply of such resources, it is not likely that many programs will be able to be mounted that will be able to assume major responsibilities for development.

2. *Evaluation.* For purposes of the present paper *evaluation* has

[20] See the report of the feasibility study that is cited elsewhere for a detailed description of the mechanisms needed in support of such a program and the costs projected by the mechanism.

been defined as that set of activities that generate information in service of on-line decision making (see the Glossary). Ignoring the function of evaluation within developmental activities, it would assume at least the following functions within a program of the kind proposed:

a. Determine for purposes of certification the success or lack of success of each student in realizing each outcome for which he is responsible.
b. Determine the contribution of each element within the program to its intended outcome.
c. Determine the effectiveness with which each element makes its intended contribution, that is, determine the range and proportion of students that achieve the learning outcomes that they are expected to achieve after engaging with a particular program element.
d. Determine the range and proportion of students that are able to reach the criteria required for certification as a function of engaging with the program as a whole.
e. Determine the amount of time and energy required to reach the criteria of certification.
f. Determine the long-term effects of students who have moved through the program upon the schools in which they work and the children with whom they interact.
g. Determine the long-term effects of the program upon the personal development and well-being of the students who have gone through it.
h. Continuously review the appropriateness of the goals of the program, especially those having to do with the learning outcomes desired for children.

One of the great strengths of a Performance-Based Program is that it has within it the data base that permits such evaluations to be made without undue effort. Without such information the Program as a whole and individuals within it suffer from an inability to adapt wisely.

Evaluation efforts, like other instructional support efforts, will involve program specific development costs. While it is possible that exemplary systems can be developed, and to some extent adapted to the demands of individual programs, it is likely that they will not have the same degree of transportability that instructional materials will have. It is also likely that they will require a greater outlay of resources to operate for the information that derives from them must be processed, stored, and made available for retrieval upon call. While the costs associated with these activities can legitimately be considered as instructional support costs they do require considerable resources to develop, install, and operate, and that fact should not be overlooked in planning for program development.

Since evaluation activities provide data that are designed to have utility only for on-line decision making, and are therefore not intended to be generalizable beyond the context within which they are collected, a question is often raised as to the defensibility of spending as much money as it takes to obtain such information. Questions are also raised as to whether or not such information might not be of use to other programs even though it is not gathered against the constraints of a design that is intended to force its generalizability. With respect to the first question, the answer is simply that if one is to adopt a Performance-Based Mode of Operation, and it is to be other than a mockery of the concept, there is no alternative to the systematic collection of evaluation data of the kind outlined. While it is true that such information does not have the properties that permit it to be generalizable that is not the intent of such information. Its purpose is to support decision making in relation to ongoing program operation and that should not be confused with the knowledge generation purpose of research.

The second question is obviously related to the first and carries an answer that can alleviate some of the anxiety reflected by it. In the writer's judgment, evaluation information, if carefully prepared and presented as documentary rather than the results of research, has considerable information value to persons beyond the program in which it is collected. The results of another's experience can be studied, whether that experience is similar or dissimilar to that incurred in one's own program; procedures that have been used in generating, presenting, or utilizing the information presented may be of value to someone else; and the fact that documentation has occurred insures that some record will be preserved that can be viewed by others who at a later time may be thinking of pursuing a similar course. Information of this kind does not have the same utility that generalizable knowledge possesses, but it has some utility. For this reason it would seem advisable, at least at a state level, for Training Cooperatives to maintain such documentation and share it with one another. Since case histories have been found to be highly useful documents in other disciplines, considerable utility may be found in sharing such information nationally.

3. *Research.* Given the output focus of the proposed program, the multistate linkage of the program to those outputs—that is, through schools designed to bring about such outputs, the personnel needed to maintain such schools, etc., and the necessity of evaluation data relative to the adequacy of all the linkages that have been made—an extremely rich "natural" context for research on human learning and instruction becomes available. To not take advantage of such a circumstance would be a phenomenal waste.

From the writer's point of view, the great advantage gained by such a context is that it provides a relatively natural setting within which to conduct the kind of multi-variate research that ultimately must be done if principles of instruction are ever to be identified. As used here, *an instructional principle* refers to an empirically demonstrated relationship between one or more classes of instructional strategies and one or more classes of learner outcomes when the characteristics of learners and the conditions under which learning is taking place are known (within such a scheme the substantive content that links to a strategy is considered as part of that strategy). By forcing explication of classes of learning outcomes and by systematically gathering data as to their realization, an output-referenced preparatory program provides the critical content needed for such research.

The nature of the research that could be undertaken within the program that is being proposed need not be limited, of course, to the kind just outlined. Research into the nature of learning environments, the nature of learner characteristics, the dimensions of instruction, small-group processes, or any other dimensions of social behavior and settings would be appropriate as foci of investigation. To prevent researchers from jumping into such a context too quickly, however, with what could turn out to be a discordant array of research activities, it needs to be recognized that any ongoing educational program can tolerate only so much activity above and beyond the business of its operation. Thus, while a wide variety of research is possible within a context of the kind proposed, and the tolerance of the program for research activities is likely to be much greater than that found in traditional programs, there is obviously an upper limit to the range and amount of research that can go on there. For this reason researchers who enter such contexts should choose well their research priorities.

In the writer's judgment, the kind of research that has been proposed should receive the highest of ratings in this regard. Somehow, more powerful paradigms for research on teaching and learning must be developed than we presently have at our disposal, and they must be applied in a context and with a level of support that offers some hope of results that have immediate payoff. As things now stand the development and operation of education programs and teacher-education programs have to take place essentially without benefit of empirical data, and that is a circumstance that cannot be permitted to exist. If the proposals made in the present paper were acted upon it could begin its alteration.

4. *Diffusion.* If a Training Cooperative is designed as an illustrative program within a state, or if a statewide network of such Cooperatives is designed as illustrative for a region or nation, the realities of the diffusion process must be faced. As used in the present paper, *diffusion* refers to that set of activities that lead to the adoption by another of that which is attempting to be spread. (See the Glossary.)

As such diffusion involves a great deal more than simply the dissemination of information. While it is not clear what in fact the diffusion process requires in order for it to be effective,[21] it is probable that in addition to the dissemination of information it must also involve demonstration, testing on a trial basis, support during implementation, and service following adoption. If this is true, diffusion becomes a very complex and costly business, and in the mechanisms to carry it must be extremely carefully constructed. Because of the complexity of the matter Guidelines #6 and #7 are devoted to the topic specifically.

Given the nature of the RDD&E activities proposed for inclusion in a Training Cooperative, what is the optimal distribution of such activities within a statewide network of Cooperatives? Undoubtedly this will vary by state, depending upon the extent to which information management capabilities crosscut an entire state, the distribution of research, development, and evaluation capabilities within a state, etc., but something on the order of that which follows seems reasonable: One or perhaps two Cooperatives in a state become identified as "lead" institutions, and in that role assume major responsibility for receiving resources for research, development (including the development of an exemplary evaluation system), and diffusion. These institutions would be expected to carry the brunt of the research and development efforts needed within a state, and also the major responsibility for instate diffusion of those efforts. Other programs would receive some support for research and development, on the assumption that situation-specific demands will always force some adaptation on materials or systems developed elsewhere, and on the assumption that research needs to be an ongoing process in all contexts. Each program would receive also some support for the diffusion function, and all programs would receive essentially equivalent funding for the execution of the evaluation function. Such a formula reflects several related assumptions: (1) that resources of the kind needed for initial developmental work can best be utilized by "bunching" them within a single or limited number of contexts; (2) that some contexts are better equipped to accommodate such resources than others; and (3) that different contexts within a state will be ready to engage in RDD&E activities at differing points in time. While some may feel that such a plan is elitist and doomed to failure because of the politics of interinstitutional cooperation, it can only be pointed out that at least one state has supported such a plan and is of the opinion that it is functional.[22]

[21] See, for example, R. Havelock, *A Comparative Study of the Literature on the Dissemination and Utilization of Scientific Knowledge,* ERIC Document No. ED 029171 (Ann Arbor: Michigan University, Institute for Social Research, 1970).

[22] See Chapter 3 in Part I, and Part VII in Volume I of the Final Report on the ComField feasibility study.

Guideline #5: Federal funds for the operation of each statewide network of Cooperatives, and for the coordination of the various statewide networks at a national level, should come jointly from various bureaus within the Office of Education.

The concept of shared funding between local school districts, cooperating colleges, and the state and federal governments has already been outlined. The purpose of the present discussion is to suggest a way in which federal funds could be shared across bureaus within the Office of Education so as to integrate several related thrusts within OE and at the same time optimize resource availability for a training program.

It will be recalled that the cost-sharing strategy called for school district and college resources to be directed primarily to the costs of instruction within the program, the extra resources of the state to be directed to the costs of evaluation and to some extent the costs of development and diffusion, and federal resources to the major costs associated with research and development and to the costs of diffusion at the national level. With this as a point of departure it is proposed that BEPD and the Experimental Schools Program share in both development and diffusion costs, and that NCERD assume responsibility for research costs. Such a division would seem to fall logically within the domains of responsibility for these three operating units, especially in the light of the new organizational structure within the office. The opportunity to participate in an activity that would hold so much joint interest should provide a convenient vehicle for cross-bureau programing.

In terms of OE's history, cross-bureau activities have never been particularly common, and those that have been tried have never been particularly successful, so the hopefulness about such cooperative efforts has to be viewed with restraint. Nevertheless, there are seeds for such activity afoot and there is the expressed desire to let such seeds flower, so there is some reason to be hopeful about its possibility. An output-oriented model of teacher education, with its linkage to schools and the intended outcome of schools, should be ideal as a place to begin. It would be unfortunate if a vehicle so right for exploitation at the bureaucratic level was bypassed.

Guideline #6: As a means of bringing the knowledge and capability of the private sector to bear in support of the diffusion process each statewide network of Cooperatives should link to industry for assistance in the design and development of its instruction and support systems.

As discussed previously, the diffusion process is one which is not well understood and, with the exception of its ERIC program, one in which the Office of Education has not had a great deal of experience or success. In part this is undoubtedly due to a limited understanding of what is required to carry out diffusion successfully. In the writer's judgment, however, even if the requirement of an effective diffusion effort were known, the likelihood of carrying out such efforts with federal funds is minimal. It is simply too costly a process. For this reason it seems in the best interests of education to turn to the private sector for help.

Given the notion of packaged and, therefore, reasonably transportable instructional materials being available for use in preparatory programs in the future, a number of questions as to the diffusion of such materials arise: (1) After being developed, how are they to be mass produced and distributed? (2) How is a demand for their use to be created? (3) Once a demand has been created, who is going to see that the demand is met? In the judgment of the writer, the only feasible way to mass produce and distribute (market) such materials and provide the services needed in support of their adoption and use is to involve the private sector. These are precisely the kind of services that private enterprise is accustomed to providing, and they have the financial wherewithall to carry them out.

While the nature of the working relationship that would have to be struck between industry, the Office of Education, and the initial producers of materials is unclear it could assume something like the following:

1. Education materials production firms would consult with the initial producers of materials during their development (each producer should probably work with a different representative from industry).
2. Once developed and appropriately field tested, the distributing firm will "package" the materials, reproduce them in the quantities needed, market them, and provide the service functions needed in support of their adoption and utilization.
3. As materials become available for distribution the distributor will provide ERIC and the regional laboratory network with detailed description of the materials that are available, the requirements for their utilization, cost, how they might be obtained, etc. This information can be disseminated through ERIC and the laboratories as well as through the channels ordinarily used by industry.
4. Each of the training cooperatives within a state or region that is a part of the nationwide development-diffusion network will develop an efficient and effective means of demonstrating the materials being distributed for those who wish to make an on-site inspection of them in operation.

Whether such a procedure would prove to be functional is open to debate, but given the magnitude and significance of the task it seems critical that OE begin to explore seriously something approximating it.

Guideline #7: In addition to a national pool of transportable products to be used in Performance-Based Teacher-Education Programs, made available largely through industry, regional dissemination-diffusion networks should also be established.

As indicated previously, one of the key elements in the diffusion process seems to be an opportunity to see that which is being considered for adoption in operation. Translating this to teacher education, it requires that demonstration programs be reasonably available in terms of distance from satellite programs so that persons who wish to get to them can. Granting this necessity, it would seem that demonstration programs must be provided on at least a regional basis. By linking such programs to ERIC, and perhaps to regional laboratories, the more personal aspects of the dissemination function might work as follows:

1. Each demonstration institution would assume responsibility for developing prototype materials that describe the program being implemented.
2. Staff from the ERIC Clearinghouse on Teacher Education would take these prototype materials, refine them, and reproduce them in quantities sufficient for distribution by ERIC, the laboratories, and the demonstrating programs.
3. Each of the regional laboratories would be responsible for personally informing each of the teacher preparation institutions in their region about each of the illustrative programs underway, how additional information might be obtained about those programs, how they might gain access to specific materials and/or procedures developed within them, etc.
4. Each of the demonstration institutions, and their sister institutions within a state, would establish a procedure whereby persons coming for on-site inspection of the program could be accommodated efficiently and effectively.

Again, while it is not at all clear that that which has been proposed will work, the issue to which the proposal is addressed is critical, and the Office of Education must develop a plan to deal with it seriously.

As a first approximation to such a plan, a proposal made by the writer as a followup to the feasibility study on the ComField Model is attached as Supplement I. It needs to be pointed out that the proposal is dated and that it contains the language of the models, but in its time it was intended as a relatively complete proposal.

PART III: SOME IMPLICATIONS OF IMPLEMENTING A PROGRAM OF THE KIND PROPOSED

The major implications of the proposals that have been made for program operation have been spelled out in the preceding pages or in the supplements attached to the body of the paper. Implications have not been spelled out specifically, however, for those involved in or affected by the program. The purpose of this section of the paper is to do so, and attempt to do so in cost/benefit terms. In order to keep the analysis short and as easy to read as possible, costs and benefits are put forth in summary form for each group of individuals affected. Only those implications *which must necessarily follow* from the implementation of such a program have been listed; possible or hoped for implications do not appear.

Implications for institutions responsible for program operation

It will be recalled that the operation of an output-referenced, performance-based personnel development program requires a partnership between a community, one or more schools within that community, one or more colleges or universities, and the state department of education. It will also be recalled that the partnership functions within the context of a Training Cooperative. The implications for members of this partnership are the first set to be summarized.

The schools

BENEFITS

1. An increase in clarity as to the goals of education and how those goals are to be translated into the goals or objectives of individual schools.
2. An increasingly better fit between a school and its programs and the goals or objectives it is to realize.
3. An increased awareness of the expectations which members of the community have for their schools.
4. The contribution of all of the above to a vital, continuing in-service education program.
5. A prototype system for the assessment of a school as a whole or any of the elements within it against desired pupil outcomes.
6. A prototype model for the operation of schools that are output-referenced, performance-based, personalized, field-dependent, data-dependent, etc.
7. A continuously available supply of new personnel with

known capabilities so far as performing the functions required within a particular school is concerned.

8. A relatively inexpensive source of personnel to fill positions at the lower end of a differentiated staffing structure.
9. A built-in, rational change mechanism.
10. Direct and active involvement in the preservice as well as the in-service development of education personnel, at the levels of policy, management, and operations.[23]

COSTS

1. The added responsibility of and additional resources required for participation in such a program, though resource requirements will be offset by the availability of students to fill supporting staff roles and the contribution of the program to in-service training.
2. Having to share with the community and a college or university decisons relative to the goals of education and the nature of schools and schooling as it pertains to the realization of those goals.
3. An increased number of adults in the schools.
4. The hard work of having to continuously engage in decision making relative to the goals of education and the nature of the schools and schooling that will lead to the realization of those goals.
5. The intellectual and emotional wear and tear that is attendant to work in a context that is committed to continuous, data-dependent change.
6. The demand placed upon continuously updated in-service education that accompanies work in an institution committed to continuous change.
7. The threat of a data-dependent, output-referenced mode of operation–both philosophically and in terms of personal performance.
8. The potential threat of incoming staff having demonstrated levels of competence.

The residents of a community

BENEFITS

1. All the benefits that accrue through the schools (see above).
2. A prototype system for generating information as to the success or lack of success that the schools are having in bringing about the outcomes expected of them.
3. A prototype system for obtaining cost/benefits indices relative to the operation of programs within a school as well as a school system as a whole.

[23] The implications cited are in no particular order, and they are not intended to be exhaustive.

4. An opportunity to influence the utilization of a broad range of resources within a community and state in the service of the education of children.

COSTS

1. All the costs, to the extent they are real rather than perceived, that accrue to the schools (see above).
2. The expenditure of the time and energy required as full participants in the preparatory program.
3. The shared responsibility for seeing that the schools, the personnel that operate the schools, and the programs that prepare those personnel are of a quality to ensure the realization of the outcomes desired of schooling.
4. The shared responsibility for ensuring the resource base needed by (3).

The college and/or university

BENEFITS

1. All of the benefits that accrue to a community and the schools within it as a strengthened base on which to design, develop and implement a preparatory program.
2. The resources of the schools and the community in assisting with the design, development, and implementation of a program.
3. The provision of the real-life context within which an output-referenced, performance-based program must function.
4. The functional integration of the preparatory program within the profession that it serves.

COSTS

1. Having to share the responsibility for decision making about teacher education with other institutions and agencies within the Cooperative.
2. No longer having the luxury of conducting a preparatory program within the walls of a college or university.
3. Having to engage in the continuing and difficult intellectual task of identifying the pupil outcomes desired from schooling, the nature of schools with the greatest probability of bringing about such outcomes, etc., as a basis for the design, development, and implementation of the preparatory program.
4. Having to establish new structures and modes of operation, both within and without the college and university, and having to adopt significantly different role behaviors within them.
5. Having to perceive students in the preparatory program as

individuals able to make decisions relative to their own ends, and the means to get to them, and then act in terms of it.
6. The threat of data relative to the effectiveness of a program, and the effectiveness of one's own performance in relation to it.
7. The emotional wear and tear that is an accompaniment to a program that is designed to be continuously adaptive.

The state Department of Education

BENEFITS

1. All of the benefits that accrue to the schools, participating colleges and universities, and the residents of participating communities.
2. An information base which permits an analysis of the outcomes desired from education on a statewide basis.
3. An information base which permits an analysis of the kinds of schools deemed appropriate for the realization of those outcomes.
4. An information base which permits the projection of personnel needs on a statewide basis for the manning of such schools.
5. An information base which permits the assessment of the competencies of existing education personnel on a statewide basis.
6. An information base which permits an analysis of the contribution of existing personnel development programs in a state to projected personnel needs.
7. An information base which permits an analysis of the adequacy with which ongoing preparatory programs are preparing needed personnel.
8. An information base which permits the linkage of all the above to the effectiveness with which the schools in the state are able to bring about the learning outcomes expected of them.
9. An information base which, given all the above, would permit a state department to rationally and systematically coordinate educational activities so as to effect optimally the learning of children within a state.

COSTS

1. Assuming that the benefits outlined above wish to be exploited, a complex information generation and management system must be developed and maintained, with its attending resource requirements.
2. Still assuming that all possible benefits wish to be exploited, a state department would have to assume an even more active and pervasive coordination/leadership function that it now assumes, with its attending resource requirements.

3. The working out of a solution to the problems associated with certification when certification is based upon situation specific demonstrations of competence in effecting desired educational outputs rather than the completion of program specific course sequences.

Implications for students in the program

Thus far a great deal has not been said about the specific implications of such a program for students in it, although it is likely that the reader of Parts I and II of the paper sensed that the nature of learning experiences within such a program would be considerably different than they are within existing programs. Three major differences would appear: (1) students would be spending a great deal of time with real outcomes; (2) knowledge and skills would be seen only as enabling conditions in relation to certification, rather than criterion conditions; and (3) the whole process of instruction within such a program would be highly personalized. Beyond these points, however, little has been said as to the actual operation of the program from the point of view of students and personnel within it.

In order to provide additional information along these lines, two pages of narrative from a synopsis of the Oregon College of Education's adaptation of the ComField Model have been reproduced. These pages are intended to introduce the reader to both the structure and function of output-referenced programs, though obviously the Model presented is only one of a variety of arrangements that could be followed. With this minimal background, and with the background gained through reading parts I and II of the paper, it is anticipated that the reader will be able to make reasonable sense of the implications statements that follow the insert.

> The program involves three relatively distinct phases of work: the *general studies phase*, the *clinical studies phase*, and the *intern phase*. Operationally, the general studies phase is defined as that aspect of the program that does not involve responsibility for the learning of children; the clinical studies phase as that aspect of the program that involves responsibility for the learning of children under simplified (laboratory or simulated) conditions; and the intern phase as that aspect of the program that involves supervised responsibility for the learning of children in fully operational, real-life educational settings. As such, the general studies phase of the program corresponds most closely to that which has been traditionally labeled the "professional development" or "laboratory" dimension.
>
> The intern phase has no parallel in traditionally designed teacher-education programs, and it in no way resembles the "intern" programs currently in vogue. As used in the program pro-

posed by the OCE Coalition a prospective teacher enters the intern phase only after he has demonstrated a specified set of competencies under laboratory conditions, and his task within the intern phase is to demonstrate the same or a higher order set of competencies under real-life conditions. As an intern a prospective teacher is to assume supervised responsibility for the full range of functions for which he will be responsible as a teacher, and he will be held accountable for the systematic demonstration of those functions.

Two levels of certification are included in the preservice program: INITIAL and CONTINUING.[24] These correspond, respectively, to the competition of the clinical studies and the intern phases of the program. As used in the proposed program INITIAL certification designates a level of competency which permits the assumption of supervised responsibility for the learning of children (a teaching intern), and CONTINUING certification designates a level of competency which permits the assumption of full responsibility for the learning of children. Certification criteria and processes are described in greater detail in Part III of the report.

As currently planned, no firm time lines are attached to program phases but, in general, for students declaring an interest in teacher education upon entry as freshmen, the general studies phase will last for a year or two, the clinical studies phase a year or two and the intern phase a year or two. Some students may extend or shorten these estimates, and students transferring from other colleges or students declaring an interest in teacher education after a year or more at OCE will undoubtedly move through the program on another time schedule. On the average, however, most students will likely spend three or four years completing requirements for initial certification and one or two years completing requirements for continuing certification.

A schematic representation of program structure, the probable number of years required to move through the program, and the certification levels within it are presented in Figure 6–8. The broken lines in the figure represent relatively flexible entry-exit requirements; solid lines represent relatively inflexible entry-exit requirements.

BENEFITS

1. As a consequence of the programs linking to desired learning outcomes in real-life learning contexts:

[24] A third level of certification, that of CONSULTANT, is also used in the program, but it is reserved for persons in the field who have demonstrated the competencies needed to perform as Clinical Supervisors. As such, this is a level of certification that occurs outside of the preservice program and is not dealt with in the present context. It is planned, however, that certification at the CONSULTANT level will be as stringent and systematic a process as it is at the preservice level.

a. Students would be able to gain first-hand experience with children.
b. There would be an oportunity to determine whether they can or cannot effect the kinds of learning outcomes desired for children, and to continue their learning until they are able to do so.

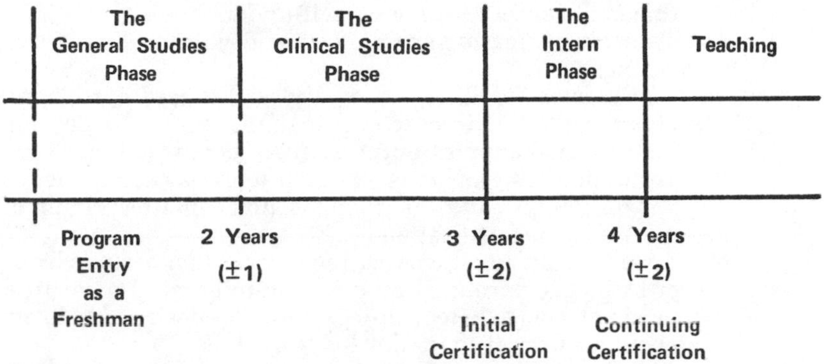

FIGURE 6–8. ***A schematic representation of the structure of the preservice Elementary Teacher-Education Program proposed at OCE.***

c. There would be an opportunity to determine preferred contexts, that is, level and type of children with whom to work, the educational settings in which to work, the subject or discipline areas in which to work, etc.
d. There would be an opportunity to struggle seriously with the unending question of the outcomes desired from schooling.
e. There would be increased meaningfulness of "relevancy" of the preparatory experience as a result of all the above.

2. As a function of the personalization of the instruction-learning process there is:
   a. An assured one-to-one or small-group contact with staff and other students.
   b. An opportunity to contribute meaningfully to the design and development of the program as a whole.
   c. An opportunity to negotiate that which is to be taken from the program as a whole.
   d. An opportunity to negotiate the settings within which competence is to be demonstrated and to negotiate the criteria by which judgment about competence is to be made.
   e. An opportunity to assess continuously the relevance of the objectives that have been negotiated and the rele-

vance of the learning experiences being pursued in relation to those objectives.

f. An opportunity to progress through the program at a rate and in a sequence that optimizes the relationship between objectives, past experience, and present circumstances.

g. An opportunity to develop a minimal level of self-understanding as a basis against which to make judgments of the kind required in all the above.

h. An opportunity to develop an overall "style" of teaching that is in concert with one's self-understanding.

3. As a function of treating knowledges and skills as enablers of competence:

   a. The mastery of knowledges and skills needed to bring about a particular outcome in children, or to develop instructional support outputs, such as curriculum units, evaluation designs, or assessment tools, is each student's responsibility[25] and, as such, is not a matter of direct relevance for certification.

   b. A student already in possession of a particular knowledge or skill, as determined by criterion-referenced measures, need not engage in learning experiences designed to bring about mastery of that knowledge or skill.

   c. A student has the opportunity to demonstrate a particular competency prior to or independently of the demonstration of mastery of the knowledges and skills that are assumed to relate to the demonstration of a particular competency.

   d. A student has an opportunity to cycle repeatedly through attempted competency demonstration or the mastery of knowledges and skills assumed to facilitate that demonstration.

4. As a function of all the above, with their emphasis upon personally appropriate and self-directed learning experience, *it is assumed:*

   a. That prospective teachers will develop into independent, self-directed, continuing learners; and, that systematic, personalized and self-directed instruction of the kind encountered in the preparatory program will transfer to the education of children in the school.

COSTS

1. The increased responsibility placed on students in such a program for their own learning.
2. The harshness of certification criteria.
3. The indeterminate time required to complete criteria for cer-

[25] It is, of course, the responsibility of those in the program to provide the learning experiences that will ensure that the knowledges and skills needed to bring about a given output are in fact available within the program.

tification (sometimes this may extend considerably beyond the four years now typically associated with certification, but it may also require fewer years than this).

4. The emotional wear and tear that may accrue as a result of being free from the constraints (and security) of the highly structured course approach that now dominates preparatory programs.

Implications for others in society that would be directly affected by the program

While the implications that emerge from a program of the kind that has been proposed are most far reaching for those responsible for its implementation, or for students enrolled within it, it also carries with it implications that spread throughout a relatively large sector of the social system. In the paragraphs which follow some of the more obvious of these are spelled out for a selected set of persons who would feel its impact.

Pupils in the schools

BENEFITS

All of that which would accrue from the benefits accrued by others who make a difference in the lives of children, and results of implementing in the schools the kind of systematically designed, data-dependent and personalized approach to instruction that characterizes the preparatory program. It will be recalled that such an approach to instruction is likely to result in relatively independent, self-directed learners—two benefits of the highest priority.

COSTS

Assuming the adoption by schools of the approach to instruction that has just been outlined, it is likely that pupils would respond to it in much the same way that college students are expected to respond (see above). Also, as in the case of students in the preparatory program, pupils at the elementary-secondary level will in all likelihood encounter some emotional wear and tear during the time that a shift in program operation is underway.

Parents and citizens of a community, a state, or the nation

BENEFITS

All the benefits which accrue to the children in the schools of a community or state that moves to such a program, or which accrue to the personnel who operate such programs (see earlier statements). Another kind of benefit stems from being able to hold schools and preparatory programs accountable, in a costs/benefits sense, for effecting the kinds of learning outcomes which are held collectively to be of importance.

COSTS

All the costs encountered by pupils affected by such a program (see earlier statements) and the possible increase in dollar costs to support such programs.

Schools and school personnel generally

BENEFITS

In time all the benefits that accrue to the schools that are members of a Training Cooperative should extend to schools throughout the educational system of a community or a state or the nation.

COSTS

Using the same logic all the costs that schools are likely to assume as partners within a Training Cooperative should also be encountered by other schools in a community or a state or the nation as they enter into similar working relationships. It may be, of course, that over time the costs assumed will diminish as new means are found to help the transition, but it is unlikely that costs will ever be able to be attenuated completely.

Colleges and college personnel generally

The rationale in relation to both benefits and costs outlined for schools would seem to hold in relation to colleges. For a summary of the benefits and costs likely to be encountered by colleges and college personnel, see pages 145–146.

Professional Education Associations and/or Unions

BENEFITS

All that would accrue from the increased status of the education profession if it were able to perform in the way anticipated as a consequence of initiating the kind of program that has been proposed. Whether this would forge an increasingly important or less important role for professional education associations and/or unions within the overall conduct of education, however, is an open question.

COSTS

The loss of traditional bargaining points, such as number of working hours, reduced class size, and vacation rights to such matters as the learning outcomes most appropriately the responsibility of the schools, the resources required to effect those outcomes, and personnel benefits such as salary and staffing positions as a consequence of the realization of given outcomes. In a sense the loss is one of moving from the relatively comfortable, nonthreatening environment of a nonaccountable model of education to the harshness of an accountability model.

Implications for the U.S. Office of Education

As indicated at the outset of the paper, two bureaus within the Office of Education and the Experimental Schools Program, are particularly appropriate sources for support in implementing a program of the kind proposed. In the paragraphs which follow the implications of such a program are summarized specifically for these units, as well as for the office as a whole.

The Experimental Schools Program

BENEFITS

The requirements that an output-referenced preparatory program take as a point of departure the nature of learning outcomes desired from schooling, and the nature of schools required to effect those outcomes, would parallel in effort the kind of thrust that is represented by the Experimental Schools Program. That Program is centrally concerned about the consequences of schooling and the nature of schools that can effect those consequences, and they must have evidence that schools so designed are in fact bringing about the consequences desired. Functionally this means that all which derives from the Experimental Schools Program should be of immediate and critical use to the kind of preparatory program that has been proposed, *and vice versa.* It is also clear that neither program would be able to wait upon the results of the other. Operationally, then, it would seem essential that both efforts maintain intimate contact, if not sharing the funds.

COSTS

It is unclear where any costs would be encountered by the Experimental Schools Program unless some of the resources that would ordinarily be used to support such a school within the context of an output-referenced personnel development program.

The Bureau of Educational Personnel Development

BENEFITS

1. An integrated application of the five basic thrusts currently emerging within the bureau.
2. Through the application of those thrusts the development of a generic preparatory program which would serve as a primary source of input to the target programs within the bureau.
3. The linkage of all preparatory programs supported by BEPD to schools and the process of schooling.
4. The legitimizing of a research, development, evaluation, and diffusion within BEPD operations (through cooperation with NCERD and the Experimental Schools Program).
5. All the benefits that accrue a state department, multiplied by fifty (see pages 146–147).

COSTS

1. Assuming that the benefits outlined above wish to be exploited, a complex information generation and management system must be developed and operated, with its attending resource requirements.
2. Continuing to assume that the benefits outlined above wish to be exploited, the bureau would have to provide a more active and persuasive coordination/leadership function than it now provides, with its attending resource requirements.

The National Center for Educational Research and Development

BENEFITS

The essential benefits that would derive for NCERD from such a venture is the context that would provide for the pursuit of the R&D activities that are functionally dependent upon such a context. Some of the specific benefits that would emerge from the conduct of R&D within an output-referenced personnel development program have been spelled out on pages 133–139.

COSTS

No undue costs to NCERD are apparent. There would have to be resource allocations, of course, in the support of R&D activities within the context of preparatory programs, but these are funds that would be channeled in support of activities elsewhere so no "direct costs" are seen accruing in that sense.

The U.S. Office of Education generally

BENEFITS

1. An instance of cross-bureau coordination that is more than perfunctory.
2. An instance that illustrates the functional integration of on-line schooling, the preparation of personnel to man those schools, and the pursuit of RDD&E activities that relate thereto.
3. An instance of all the above activities being linked directly to specified learning outcomes in children, and in a real sense being accountable for the realization of those outcomes.
4. An instance of partnership in funding at the state, local, and federal levels that seems to be economically feasible, and sensible from the point of view of the differentiated use of resources.
5. An instance of an economically feasible and sensible linkage of industry to federal, state, and local education efforts.
6. A basis for a natural experiment on the effectiveness of a nationwide diffusion strategy.

COSTS

No apparent costs other than those normally encountered in support of similar activities (for an estimate of cost by supporting agency see Part V of the paper) and for some possible emotional wear and tear that could accompany the "reordering of priorities" or "rethinking of strategy" of "the establishment of cross-bureau linkages" within the Office of Education as a result of moving to a cooperative effort.

GLOSSARY

Development: the generation of technology (procedures, hardware, materials, organizational frameworks) that have a known degree of success in bringing about a particular outcome or in performing a particular operation.

Diffusion: the generation of linkages (dissemination and installation networks) that lead to the adoption and utilization of knowledge, technology, and/or information.

Evaluation: the generation of information that facilitates decision making in a specific context within a given time frame.

Integrating Materials: "packaged" and thereby sharable or distributable sets of instructions and suggestions that have a known degree of reliability in getting prospective teachers with particular characteristics to be able to demonstrate that they can produce *a particular output or set of outputs that they will be responsible for producing as professional educators.* Examples of educational outputs include bringing about desired learning outcomes in pupils, developing a particular curriculum segment, and designing a particular evaluation scheme.[26]

Performance-Based Teacher Education: a teacher-education program where the learning outcomes that are to emerge and the indicators acceptable as evidence of the realization of those outcomes are specified and made public. Learning outcomes may be at:

1. The knowledge level (the result of interacting with Protocol Materials).
2. The skill level (the result of interacting with Training Materials).
3. The output level (the result of interacting with Integrating Materials).

Protocol Materials: "packaged" and thereby sharable or distributable learning experiences that lead to the mastery of *a particular concept or set of related concepts* by a given class of learners with a known degree of reliability, and with assurance that the concept that is mastered has meaning in terms of "real-life" referents. A basic assumption underlying Protocol Materials development is that the "real-life" referents necessary for concept mastery can be provided through simulation technology, i.e., through films, tapes, video-tapes, and the like.

Research: the generation of knowledge (facts, principles, generalizations, theories, laws) that can stand the test of empirical verification.

Teacher-Education Model: an integrated set of specifications that establish boundaries or parameters for the structure, function, content, and operation of a teacher-education program. A model

[26] Educational outputs are always situation-specific, that is, the realization of pupil outcomes always pertains to a specific outcome or set of outcomes for a specific child or set of children under a specific set of learning conditions; the development of curriculum always pertains to the statement of goals, objectives, and learning experiences for a specific body of knowledge for specific sets of children under specific sets of learning conditions, etc. As a consequence the demonstration of the ability to effectively carry out professional responsibilities must be done in real-life settings where there are real pupils learning, real curricula to be developed, and real evaluations to be designed.

As in the case of skill mastery, practice and corrective feedback are critical to the development of the ability to produce particular sets of educational outcomes and a large proportion of the "packaged" materials designed to bring about such abilities assume the form of instructions and suggestions.

is not an operational program; it simply provides a framework within which operational programs can be created. Fact, theory, and accumulated wisdom dictate the *substance* or *content* of model-based programs, and as a consequence—because different people have access to or accept different sets of facts, theories, and accumulated stores of wisdom—each model-based program will vary in its substance. All model-based programs, however, will share the parameters established by the model on which they rest.

Training Complex: a social institution designed to serve teacher education by providing "neutral ground" on which all institutions and agencies that have an investment in teacher education—especially the colleges, the schools, and state certification agencies—can direct their resources toward the improvement of that enterprise. An essential feature of the institution is the concept of "parity" or "equality of representation" for those participating within it.

Training Materials: "packaged" and thereby sharable or distributable learning experiences that have a known degree of reliability in getting a particular class or learner to execute *a particular skill or set of related skills* at a particular performance level in a particular instruction-learning context. The demonstration context may be simulated, for example, a microteaching situation or it may be a real-life situation. In either case practice and corrective feedback—two essential elements in skill training—must be able to be provided.[27]

[27] It should be noted that those aspects of "packaged" training materials that deal with practice and corrective feedback will assume the form of instructions and suggestions rather than substantive materials with which to interact.

SUPPLEMENT I

NOTES ON MAXIMIZING THE INFLUENCE OF DEMONSTRATION PROGRAMS ON TEACHER EDUCATION REGIONALLY AND NATIONALLY

H. Del Schalock
Teaching Research

From the outset the strategy of the OE Models Program has been straightforward and sound: through competitive proposals generate a set of alternative models for elementary teacher-education programs; through a second set of competitive proposals undertake careful feasibility studies of the implementation of the initial set of Models, or any combination of them; and, finally, if the feasibility studies are at all encouraging, implement two to four model-based programs as exemplary programs for elementary teacher education in the nation. The rationale underlying the strategy for the first two phases was basically one that relied upon the productivity of competition, governed by the strengths of carefully planned projects. The rationale underlying the third phase is that which underlies all demonstration or experimental programs, namely, the power of ideas in operation. John Dewey built the case for such programs before the turn of the century:

> . . . I heard once that the adoption of a certain method in use in our school was objected to by a teacher on this ground: "You know that it is an experimental school. They do not work under the same conditions that we are subject to." Now, the purpose of performing an experiment is that other people need not experiment; at least need not experiment as much, and that they may have something definite and positive to go by. An experiment demands particularly favorable conditions in order that results may be reached both freely and securely. It has to work unhampered, with all the needed resources at command. Laboratories lie back of all the great business enterprises

> of today, back of every great factory, every railway and steamship system. Yet the laboratory is not a business enterprise; it does not aim to secure for itself the conditions of business life, nor does the commercial undertaking repeat the laboratory. There is a difference between working out and testing a new truth, or a new method and applying it on a wide scale, making it available for the mass of men, making it commercial. But the first thing is to discover the truth, to afford all necessary facilities, for this is the most practical thing in the world in the long run. We do not expect to have other schools literally imitate what we do. A working model is not something to be copied; it is to afford a demonstration of the feasibility of the principle, and of the methods which make it feasible. So (to come back to our own point) we want here to work out the problem of the unity, the organization of the school system in itself, and to do this by relating it so intimately to life as to demonstrate the possibility and necessity of such organization for all education.

Assuming that the Phase I and II strategy has been successful, that is, that strong models have been developed and that it is feasible to implement them, the long-range success of the Models Program depends upon the impact which the demonstration program will have upon the educational community. In the judgment of those who have been responsible for working with the ComField Model thus far, maximum impact will not come from simply establishing an exemplary program at an institution and then making it known to the educational community that such an institution exists. Rather, the widespread diffusion of an educational change as far reaching as that proposed in most of the models will require more than a purely demonstration and dissemination effort. The purpose of this section of the report is to set forth a proposal as to how the impact of the third phase of the Models Program can be maximized.

THE PROPOSAL IN BRIEF

Fund at least two and preferably three or four exemplary programs; establish a functional information and materials exchange network between exemplary programs; nest each of the exemplary programs within a statewide plan for implementation; and nest all of the exemplary and statewide programs within an integrated network of the regional laboratories and private enterprises. Operationally the plan calls for (1) two to four exemplary programs to be established across the nation (the criteria for selection of such pro grams are yet to be established); (2) implementation of each exemplary program on a statewide basis; (3) link each exemplary and statewide demonstration program to all regional laboratories for the dissemination of information about them to all institutions within a region which have elementary teacher-education programs; and (4) link each exemplary and statewide demonstration program to the educational publishing industry for the mass production and marketing of the materials and/or procedures developed by those programs and for the services required by institutions in attempting to implement them in their own programs. In addition, each exemplary program would need to link effectively to the research and development efforts occurring within the nation that contribute to either elementary education or elementary teacher education. The interdependencies between the exemplary program, the statewide implementation of those programs, the regional laboratories, the educational publishing industry, research and development activities in education across the nation, and teacher-education programs throughout the nation are illustrated schematically in Figure 6–9.

RATIONALE UNDERLYING THE PROPOSAL

The central assumption underlying the proposal just sketched is that to effect change in elementary teacher education on a national scale, such change will have to be carefully planned for, and all the resources available in the nation in support of such change will have to be brought to bear in a finely coordinated fashion. This includes not only the coordination of exemplary programs, but the coordination of teacher-education programs within the states in which the exemplary programs rest, the coordination of the regional laboratory network in a massive dissemination effort, and the coordination of education-related industry with all of the above. Attending assumptions are:

1. That the basic development work in support of the exemplary programs needs to be carried out within the context of the institution responsible for the implementation of the program.
2. That the materials and procedures developed within the exemplary program need to be validated against a wide variety of institutions before they are made available generally to teacher-education institutions throughout the nation.
3. That private enterprise is best able to take the prototype materials that have been developed within the exemplary and statewide programs, refine them, mass produce them, market them across the nation, and provide the supporting services (including in-service education) required for their utilization in other teacher-education programs.
4. That the ERIC Clearinghouse on Teacher Education is best

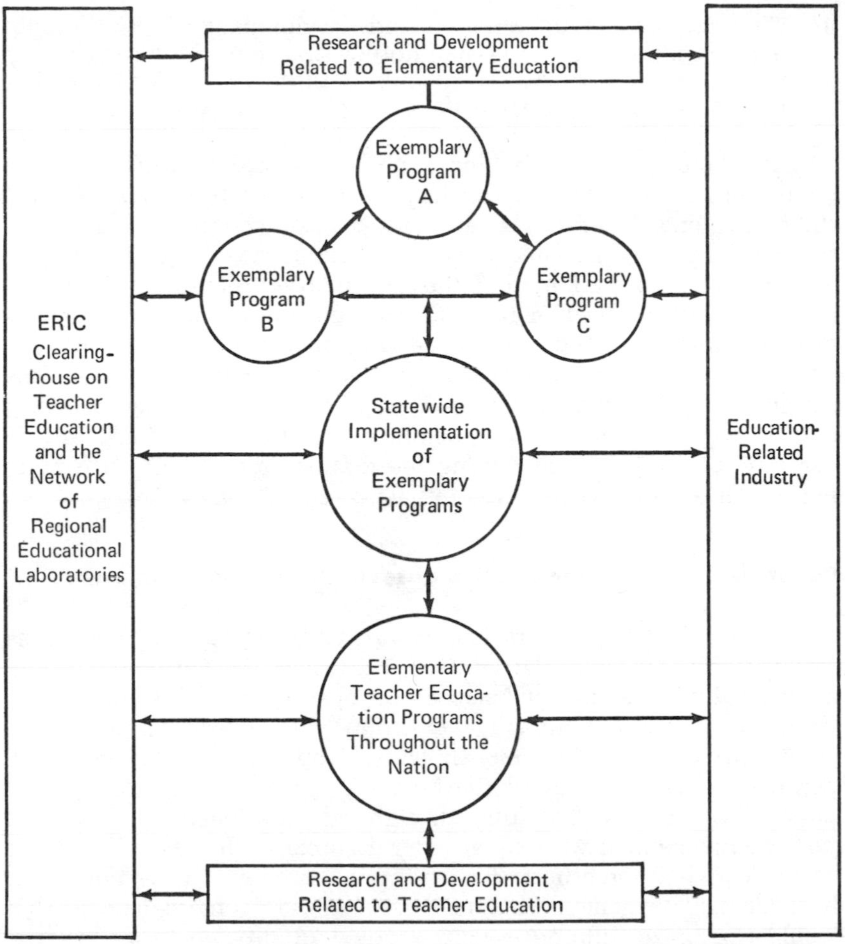

FIGURE 6–9. ***A schematic illustration of the interaction of institutions and agencies in a plan designed to maximize the impact of Phase III of the OE Models Program in Elementary teacher education in the nation.***

equipped to take the prototyped materials describing the exemplary programs and the materials that have derived from them, refine them, and prepare them for use in nation-wide dissemination.

5. That the regional educational laboratories are best equipped to utilize the materials developed by ERIC in a nationwide effort to disseminate information about the exemplary programs and the products that have derived therefrom (the efforts of the laboratories will be supplemented by advertising efforts on the part of the materials publishers).

6. That the products of research and development efforts throughout the nation have to be monitored consistently for their utility in the exemplary programs, and in those institutions utilizing materials that derive from the exemplary programs.

It is recognized in making such a proposal that none of the institutions mentioned carry on in pure form the functions assigned them: Regional laboratories carry out developmental as well as dissemination functions; education-related industries disseminate huge amounts of information; and the exemplary programs will, in all likelihood, be involved in research as well as developmental activities. Nor does the proposal assume that such an interplay of functions will cease. It does assume, however, that the institutions assigned a primary function in the plan are those that are best able to carry out major responsibility for those functions, and if carefully coordinated could bring those functions to bear in a manner which would maximize the impact of the overall effort.

Rationale underlying the creation of several exemplary programs

As a general rule, planners find it dangerous to "put all their eggs in one basket." This is particularly true when the various "baskets" available have not as yet been tested operationally for their effectiveness. At the present stage of knowledge, and in light of the complexity of the various models being proposed, it would seem imperative to test as many of the Model Programs as is economically possible. Since it is likely that all eight of the Models available will not be implemented with equal federal support, choices will have to be made. While the criteria for making such choices have not as yet been defined, a general rule to follow would seem to be one that would maximize differences, given equal quality on other criteria. Another factor to consider, again assuming equality on other criteria, is the geographic location of the exemplary programs selected. Geography is a significant variable politically, logistically, and as a source of identification. What weight it should have in the matter of institutional selection for implementation purposes is unclear, but it is a variable that must be considered.

Rationale underlying the creation of an information and materials exchange network between exemplary programs

The magnitude of the materials development task facing those implementing exemplary teacher-education programs, the commonality of the logistical and operational procedural problems to be overcome, and the commonality of the subject matter around which instructional materials are to be developed suggests that considerable economy could be effected if those responsible for implementing a given program had free access to that which was being developed in other programs. This is not to imply that all materials developed in one program will be directly or indirectly applicable to another. It does imply, however, that much of what is done in one program will have some degree of utility in another, and whatever savings in time and resource expenditure can be effected thereby, should be effected.

Given this rationale it could be argued that institution A should be responsible for developing one aspect of an overall program, institution B another aspect of the overall program, etc. On the surface there is a logic to such an arrangement and the likelihood of considerable economy. Operationally, however, it is doubtful that it would be an effective way to proceed. While there will be obvious commonalities between programs each will be relatively idiosyncratic with respect to how such commonalities are put together. Also each program will have characteristics unique unto itself. The major strength in the entire Models development effort has been the opportunity to synthesize and integrate the knowledge and ideas and procedures that are common to the field into a unique and interdependent whole that represents a given Model. To not honor that integrity at the time of implementation would be to deny the fundamental strength that has derived from the Program up to this time. Farming out pieces and parts of a program to various institutions to develop, or attempt to develop only those pieces and parts that are common to all Models, would lead in effect to a kind of dismemberment of each of the Models that would destroy the strengths inherent in them.

Rationale underlying the implementation of exemplary programs on a statewide basis

To have maximum impact upon elementary teacher education nationally, demonstration programs must have high visibility. They must also have high credibility. The proposal being made suggests that one of the best ways possible to gain both is to implement the program on a statewide basis. Such a strategy would provide evidence as to the feasibility of implementing the program under a variety of contexts, it would provide a range of alternative institutions with which an adopting institution could identify and/or work, it would provide a natural setting for the field testing of materials before they were marketed, and it would be of sufficient political significance that it would not be ignored nationally, etc. The full range of arguments in support of statewide implementation have been provided in Chapter 3 and Part VII.

Rationale underlying linkage to the network of regional laboratories

While implementation on a statewide basis would provide for program visibility and credibility, there remains the problems of getting detailed information about the program to institutions interested in its adoption. Are the demonstration institutions to carry out the dissemination function? Will the ERIC Clearinghouse on Teacher Education? While both will undoubtedly play major roles in the dissemination effort, it is doubtful that they would be able to reach all institutions in the nation that prepare elementary teachers in a way which lets those institutions come to fully understand the nature and scope of the exemplary efforts.

Another logical resource available to the dissemination effort is the regional laboratory network. The involvement of the laboratories in such an effort would be in keeping with the original intent of the system, and would make use of the extensive information networks that most laboratories have established with teacher-education institutions. It would also permit the dissemination process to be more personalized in that personnel within a laboratory are generally knowledgeable of the idiosyncrasies of the institution within their regions having elementary teacher-education programs, and they could help interpret the demonstration programs accordingly.

Operationally, by linking the demonstration institutions and ERIC to the laboratory network, the dissemination function could work as follows:

1. Each demonstration institution would assume responsibility for developing prototype materials that describe the program being implemented.
2. Staff from the ERIC Clearinghouse on Teacher Education would take these prototype materials, refine them, and reproduce them in quantities sufficient for distribution by ERIC, the laboratories, the demonstration programs, etc.
3. Each of the regional laboratories would be responsible for informing each of the institutions within their region that prepare elementary teachers about each of the exemplary programs underway, how those institutions might get additional information about such programs, how they might gain access to specific materials and/or procedure developed within those programs, etc.
4. Each of the demonstration institutions, and their sister institutions within a state, would establish a procedure whereby persons coming for onsite inspection of the program could be accommodated efficiently and effectively.

Rationale underlying linkage to the educational publishing industry

While the dissemination of information about the demonstration programs is a necessary condition to widespread impact, it is not a sufficient condition. In addition to information, adopting institutions must have access to the materials and procedures needed to make such programs operate. A critical question to be faced is how such access is to come about.

As in the case of dissemination, the demonstration institutions will simply not be equipped to produce and distribute materials on a scale that would support wide-scale adoption. While resources are expected to be made available in support of materials and procedural development within demonstration institutions, that which derives from them will be in "homemade" form and in a limited number of copies. Even if materials were available for wide-scale distribution, demonstration institutions would be in no position to provide the consultants, training, and follow-up services that will be needed by adopting institutions to effectively integrate the new materials and procedures into their ongoing programs. If the fruits of the implementation efforts are to have maximum payoff nationally there must be provision for the production and distribution of the materials that emerge from the demonstration programs on a scale which will make it possible for every institution in the nation desiring their use to be able to do so. In the collective judgment of those who have worked with the ComField Model the only feasible way to produce and distribute the materials and services needed in support of widespread program adoption is to involve the private sector.

Operationally the relationship between industry and the other institutions involved in the implementation effort might be as follows:

1. Educational materials production firms would consult with demonstration institutions during the development of the materials and procedures needed in support of program operation (each exemplary institution would probably work with a different representative from industry).
2. Once developed and appropriately field tested, the producing firm that has been monitoring their development will "package" them, reproduce them in the quantities needed, market them, and provide the service functions needed in support of their utilization.
3. As materials become available for distribution, the producer will provide ERIC and the regional laboratory network with detailed descriptions of the materials that are available, the requirements for their utilization, cost, how they might be obtained, etc. This information can be disseminated through ERIC and the laboratories as well as through the channels ordinarily used by industry.
4. Each of the exemplary institutions and the institutions within a state committed to the implementation of a model-based program will develop an efficient and effective means of demonstrating

the materials being marketed for those who wish to make on-site inspections.

Rationale underlying the linkage to research and development activities across the nation

By and large the Elementary Teacher-Education Models that have derived from the phase I and II efforts have a minimal empirical base. Also the materials to be used within the program are by and large in a "projected state" rather than an existing, empirically tested state. This is not the fault of the model builders, for in all cases they have used that which has been available to them. It does suggest, however, that all of the proposed programs are only approximations of what they could be, and in order to continuously grow in effectiveness they will need to continuously expand the knowledge base, the materials, and the methodology on which they rest. This can be done by closely monitoring that which emerges from educational R & D efforts around the nation and by carrying out a vigorous research and evaluation program within context of the demonstration effort.[1]

MANAGEMENT PROCEDURES NEEDED TO IMPLEMENT THE PROPOSAL

Specifying that linkages of the kind described should occur between institutions and agencies of the variety proposed is one consideration; developing the wherewithall that permits such linkages to function

[1] Actually, the implementation of the demonstration program will provide a unique opportunity to extend our understanding of the educative process *because in all cases the models are data dependent.* Without exception the models are committed to systems design principles, and this requires that empirical data be continuously gathered on the effectiveness of program operations. As such, vast amounts of data will be available to those who operate the program, and it would be an indefensible waste of resource if that information is not used to its limits in extending our base of understanding in the teacher-learning process. While it is true that much of the information that will be collected within the context of the program will be done so outside of the constraints of traditional research paradigms, and therefore may be lacking in its generalizability, the absence of such rigor in design does not render such data useless. Assuming that the measures used are valid, and that the questions being asked are of a kind that do not require the rigor of experimental design, great amounts of information can be obtained that has high usability to both persons attempting to operate the program and to extend the empirical base of the discipline.

through time is another. Obviously, an extremely complex management system would be required to make such relationships work. Some preliminary ideas as to what such a management system might look like are outlined in the paragraphs which follow.

A structure that could be used to link demonstration programs

An informal structure characterized by frequent "coordinating contacts" between project directors and the director of the Models Program in the U.S. Office of Education; periodic cross-site visitations by key personnel within each of the implementing institutions.

A structure that could be used to link demonstration programs to statewide implementation efforts

The structure proposed to support the statewide implementation effort in Oregon (see Chapter 3 and Section VII) provides an example.

A structure that could be used to link demonstration programs and statewide implementation efforts to the ERIC Clearinghouse for Teacher Education and the network of regional educational laboratories

A formal structure wherein the individuals responsible for dissemination functions within the demonstration programs would meet periodically with representatives from each of the regional laboratories, the ERIC Clearinghouse for Teacher Education, and the director of the Models Program from the Office of Education, to plan and coordinate the national dissemination effort. This body could be labeled the "Dissemination Council."

A structure that could be used to link demonstration programs and statewide implementation efforts to the educational publishing industry

A formal structure wherein the persons responsible for overall program development and dissemination within each of the demonstration institutions, representatives from the private sector working with demonstration institutions, director of the OE Models Program meet regularly to plan and coordinate materials distribution and program support efforts. This structure might be called the "Products Development and Utilization Council."

A structure that could be used to link demonstration programs to national research and development efforts

A formal structure wherein the person responsible for overall program development within each of the demonstration institutions, a representative from each of the federally supported research and development centers across the nation, and the director of the OE Models Program meet periodically to review emerging knowledge and/or products that might have utility to the Models Program and to make known the needs of the Models Program to those charged with responsibility for R & D efforts. This group might be called the "Research and Development Council."

A structure that could be used to coordinate all facets of the dissemination and diffusion effort

A formally constituted structure wherein the project directors at each of the demonstration institutions, a representative from the network of regional laboratories, a representative from the network of federally supported research and development centers, a representative from the industrial firms supporting the dissemination-diffusion effort, a representative from the ERIC Clearinghouse for Teacher Education, a representative from each of the states committed to implementing the demonstration program, and the director of the OE Models Program meet at regular intervals to establish policy governing the overall implementation-diffusion effort. The group might be called the "Coordinating Council."

EVALUATING THE EFFECTIVENESS OF THE OVERALL DISSEMINATION-DIFFUSION EFFORT OF THE OE MODELS PROGRAM

Because of the magnitude of the dissemination-diffusion effort, its criticalness, and its potential contribution as a model for other nationwide educational change efforts, the entire procedure needs to undergo careful and continuous evaluation. In this regard it would seem appropriate to let independent bids for the evaluation effort, thereby assuring the best evaluation design possible within the present limits of our knowledge and a relatively independent or unbiased assessment of that which actually emerges from the program. Minimally, however, the request for evaluation proposals should require an evaluation design that is "formative" in nature—that is, continuous in its provision of corrective feedback from the initiation to the completion of the project—and "summative" in nature—that is, a final assessment of the impact of the overall program upon teacher education in the nation. In addition the request for proposals should require that the evaluation design attend specifically to the operation of each of the institutions and/or agencies contributing to the overall effort, as well as the effort as a whole.

ALLOCATING RESOURCES FOR THE MANAGEMENT AND EVALUATION OF THE DISSEMINATION-DIFFUSION EFFORT

It is assumed that resources must be set aside within the OE Models Program to accommodate the energy required to carry out such management functions.

CHAPTER 7

Facilitating Local Options and Coordination of Programs

Charles E. Stewart

It is clearly evident that the training of an educator is never completed. The process begins long before the career decision is made and continues—systematically or not—as long as the educator remains in the profession. Such a concept of teacher education as a continuing process has an obvious advantage in that it permits a local school system to assist in designing training programs to fit local needs, limitations, and resources. It also permits a cooperating higher institution to make use of inservice training activities as a basis for the assessment and redesign of preservice programs.

Indeed the notion of gearing training programs to local needs is so crucial today that many educational leaders have come to the rather extreme view that local school systems—especially large cities—should assume a teacher-education function. For example, Chandler and others have said, "In effect, cities must produce their own teachers and school administrators. Metropolitan colleges and universities must join with urban school systems to design programs of preparation for educational personnel that are geared to the educational problems and opportunities present in cities."[1]

This is not to suggest that a "good" teacher in a large-city school classroom will look or behave sharply different from her counterpart in a rural school, although many would argue that this must be the case. What is crucial here is the requirement of differing arrangements for training, involving new cooperative roles and relationships which will vary among school-university partnerships across the country.

The reassessment of role and function for the various members

[1] B. J. Chandler, L. J. Stiles, and J. I. Kitsusue, eds., *Education in Urban Societies* (New York: Dodd, Mead and Co., 1962), pp. 259–260.

of the partnership is, in itself, a formidable task among institutions whose record of successful cooperation has been a sometime thing, highly individualized and personalized, according to the tastes of those choosing to participate at any given time. Moving towards the sounder basis of *institutionalized collaboration* in continuing teacher education certainly will require great skill in, and commitment to, the task of building the partnership at the local, regional, or state level. But it will need also all the nurture and assistance to be gained from a maximum flexibility in any design for allocating national resources to this purpose.

It is perhaps axiomatic to state that a variety of regional influences, including urban-suburban-rural factors, must be allowed to have an important bearing upon program design and implementation at the local level. Moreover, as pointed out elsewhere in this report, one must take into account existing patterns of school-community-university relationships as illustrated by a large-city university deeply involved with its immediately surrounding urban complex of school systems, as opposed to the more widespread service area of, for example, a large Midwestern university area—or a sparsely settled state which looks to its state department of education for strong organizing and planning leadership.

Beyond these factors, however, is the hard reality that there are as many important differences among large cities as there are between the large city and the small. To begin with, school systems in the main are not organized in a manner which facilitates *institutional* collaboration in the teacher-education enterprise. Consequently, an examination of large-city school system organizational structures will reveal notable differences which, in many cases, will inhibit such collaboration. In such instances it will be necessary to install costly coordinating mechanisms to cut across bureaucratic lines of authority and ensure easier access to an appropriate locus of decision making where cooperative teacher education is concerned.

Furthermore, no two large cities are alike in the nature of the school system's relationships with its teacher organization or organizations. Despite the militant adversary posture assumed by most big-city bargaining units, the underlying nature of the relationships varies from a city in which the teacher organization insists on being involved in planning and implementation *as an organizational entity* to one in which the teacher organization views itself *as a part* of the school system and expects to be involved as such by means of appropriate *intra-school system* coordinating mechanisms.

Similarly, few if any large cities are at the same point in the transfer of power from the tightly controlled central administrative bureaucracies to some type of wider community base. Even in cities that have attained some measure of "decentralization" there remain important differences regarding both the nature and extent of real power dispersion. This reality has implications for the teacher education coordination function within a large school system. It also, together with some of the factors mentioned above, emphasizes the need to rethink the concept of "parity" and the means by which to make that concept an actual force in cooperative teacher-education ventures.

The term "parity" is not perceived to mean the same thing from city-to-city, depending largely upon where the same city is in its progress towards the decentralization of power. In most communities, parity is looked upon as an opportunity for community representatives to review a plan of action before implementation. But there are some communities in which parity means participation in the writing of the plan, with total disregard for built-in constraints such as negotiated personnel policies and categorical funding directives, as well as payment for participation in the process.

Obviously Federal guidelines are essential if there is to be federal leadership in a clear-cut, well-coordinated thrust for improvement in teacher education. It seems equally obvious that organizationally negotiated school system policies cannot be dealt with in a capricious fashion by a group planning for a specific program or plan of action, particularly when the consequences may affect other school, community, or university personnel not involved in the program. The latter point is partly illustrated by the fate of a school-university collaborative effort in one city where the demand by the community to "screen and select" university faculty participants resulted in no faculty participants.

Most of the foregoing discussion argues for a flexibility which would: (1) permit a more productive consideration of local needs and realities in program planning and implementation; and (2) allocate federal resources in a manner which would provide greater assistance in gearing up for programs which properly take into account those local needs and realities. But much of what has been said here suggests also that, while there is need to work on strategies and arrangements for more effective institutional partnerships, there is an accompanying need to improve the coordination and integration of the various federally funded "programs" which now serve as "delivery systems" for new ideas in education. It would appear from experience that the notion of a *consortium of programs* is as valid as that of a consortium of institutions for program implementation.

Programs such as COP, Teacher Corps, TTT, and the like have demonstrated a certain effectiveness as agents for desirable change in teacher education *despite* the fact they have often operated as autonomous, self-contained, and controlled units. Each has its own administrative apparatus with the one hand little knowing, or understanding—or caring—what the other is up to. Each has its own university affiliation in which the university project leadership usually enjoys no better internal communication than is the case in the school system.

Each delivery system has its own liaison officer in the federal regime with whom relationships are zealously and jealously guarded by the local administrators. This is not, of itself, bad and is mentioned here only as a further illustration of the separatism which inhibits efforts to effect a coordinated thrust at the local level.

Finally, each funded project has its own community participation machinery ranging in one city from a rather elaborate COP Advisory Council which serves without pay—and at some cost to community participants least able to afford it—to a paid "community representative" plus unpaid local school advisory councils serving the Teacher Corps project. Again these variations are not cited as necessarily damaging effects of program autonomy; however, they do not appear to be planned variations to test several approaches. Rather, the variations seem to exist without a reason in most instances.

In summary, it is the intent of these comments to focus on some problems confronted by local education agencies as they attempt to engage in cooperative teacher education improvements efforts. Some, such as the hidden cost of after-school building use for "on-site" classes and seminars, appear minor, but they add up over time to a considerable local expense. Others, such as the factors of program coordination and integration, are more obvious but no less troublesome. Together with the varying interpretations of the concept of parity, these problems give rise to a serious need for more flexibility for local planning and, at the same time, more leadership from the federal education agency.

Greater flexibility might well result from federal guidelines which would recognize local differences and encourage and support the reflection of those differences in sharply varying program approaches within a given framework. Increased federal leadership might well take the form of support for an integrated "national" program thrust based upon accepted "essential elements," such as those recommended by experts inside and outside the federal agency, and a coordination of federal liaison functions so as to facilitate program integration at the implementation level.

CHAPTER 8

Relationships Between *Teachers for the Real World* and the Elementary Models, Programmatic Themes and Mechanisms, Payoffs, Mechanisms, and Costs

Richard L. Turner

The three papers which follow were selected from among the six somewhat specialized papers written by the author for the committee. The three deleted papers were addressed to very specific problems faced by the committee at particular points in its progress and are considered too specialized to be included here although certain concepts from them appear in the final recommendations of the committee. The three papers selected for inclusion, although specialized, are more closely tied to the original charge of the committee: (1) to articulate and integrate the five thrusts (Protocol Materials, Training Materials, Training Complexes, Performance-Based Teacher Certification, and the Elementary Models) examined by Task Force '72, and (2) to examine the feasibility (cost/payoff) of these thrusts.

In general accord with this charge, the first paper provides one articulation of the relationship among the five thrusts as evidenced in *Teachers for the Real World* and the Elementary Models. The second paper provides one way to integrate these five thrusts into broader themes and programs, while the third establishes a set of critical payoffs, then suggests programs and mechanisms which might be considered feasible from the standpoint of costs while at the same time remaining targeted on the payoff. Considerable disjunction occurs between the second paper and the third. A careful examination of the payoffs suggested that several of the mechanisms proposed in the second paper and, indeed, proposed by other authors were expensive and poorly targeted on payoffs, thus requiring a substantial modification of the mechanisms to bring them within the range of cost feasibility.

RELATIONSHIPS BETWEEN *TEACHERS FOR THE REAL WORLD* AND THE ELEMENTARY MODELS

The problem addressed in this paper is to explore the relationships among the five thrusts in teacher education currently under consideration by BEPD. Of the five thrusts, three are drawn from *Teachers for the Real World* (5): (1) the development of Protocol Materials, (2) the development of Training Materials, and (3) the creation of Training complexes. The remaining two thrusts, (1) the actual models for the in-service and preservice education of elementary teachers and (2) the use of performance criteria, are drawn centrally from the final reports attendant to NCERD's Comprehensive Elementary Teacher-Education Models (3).

The overall position taken in this paper is that the five thrusts broadly overlay and intersect; indeed, that they are, when properly arranged, responses to different aspects of a single question.

What is the question?

What should a teacher-education curriculum, preservice and in-service, be like? Although this question can be phrased in a great many different ways, the point in phrasing it as it is phrased above is to make the basic issues clear. They are *curricular* issues; issues about the sets of experience that preparatory and in-service teachers might have under tutelage, and especially about the range, content, and sequence of these experiences. The precise nature of the curricular issues and the way in which the thrusts drawn from *Teachers . . .* and from the Models bear on them may be most easily identified if one draws out of the preliminary question those subordinate questions intrinsic to it. These questions are:

1. What should the goals of the curriculum (or curricula) be?
2. How will you know (verify or confirm) that the goals of the curriculum have been met?
3. What will the students experience in the curriculum?—
4. What will be the bases of these experiences?
5. Do the experiences have to come in a particular order?
6. How will you know that a particular order of experiences is a good order?

7. How will you know (verify or confirm) that the experiences lead to the goals of the curriculum?

The way in which an individual or a group will respond to these questions, indeed, the questions to which they will respond, depends on the stance or orientation of the group. With respect to the groups involved in the five thrusts, two different stances may be identified. First, the Models group, on the whole, takes a "knowledge," "confirmation," or "research" stance. This group is willing to address all the above questions, but in addressing them it is always concerned with nagging underlying questions: "How will we know?" "How will we conform?" Because of the latter question, this group tends to be criterion or performance-criterion oriented. One cannot verify or confirm his hypotheses or speculations about curriculum components unless he specifies the criteria against which he will make the terminal or confirmatory judgments.

Second, the *Teachers . . .* group takes an "action," "mechanism," or "development" stance. The underlying question is: "What do we need to invent to improve the teacher-education curriculum?" On the whole, this group emphasizes questions involving curricular goals, student experience, and the curricular treatments or mechanisms through which these experiences are delivered. It does not emphasize the procedures or criteria for confirming that the student experiences, their order or the curricular treatments or mechanisms do pecisely what they are supposed to do. Hence, this group responds obliquely, if at all, to questions of confirmation.

Some resolutions of subordinate questions

Q. 1. What should the goals of the curriculum (a) be?

One of the two noticeable differences in curricular goals between *Teachers for the Real World* and most of the Models is that the curricular aims in *Teachers . . .* are predominantly bound to the preparation of teachers who will be successful in teaching disadvantaged groups, especially those in the inner city, while the curricular aims of many, but not all, of the Models are successful performances of teaching roles. This difference undoubtedly arose in a quite logical way. The initiators of the Models are college and university groups. These institutions prepare teachers for a broad spectrum of teaching contexts, hence cannot logically address themselves to preparation for success in a particular context. What they can prepare for is success in performing teaching roles, since roles presumably transcend particular teaching contexts. One broad thesis in the Models seems to be that, if one learns to perform his various roles as a teacher very well, he can easily adapt his performance to a particular teaching situation or context. *Teachers for the Real World* does not deny the relevance of teacher role performance; indeed, various roles are discussed in it, and skillful performance of them is emphasized. What it appears to challenge, however, is the concept that role performance can be easily adapted from one context to another, for example, from a middle-class school to a ghetto school. Indeed, much of the thrust of the early chapters in *Teachers* . . . is that the teacher must understand the context in which he is to teach if he is to be successful in that context.

The product of the differences between the curricular aim of contextually adaptive or successful behavior, as suggested by *Teachers for the Real World*, the aim of successful role performance, as suggested by the Models, seems to the author to be an expansion of the Models toward the inclusion of role performance in a spectrum of particular contexts, including disadvantaged urban and disadvantaged rural, as well as suburban middle class and small-town, mixed socioeconomic contexts. Expansion toward this contextual aim vastly complicates one of the five major BEPD thrusts, as will later be noted.

A second noticeable difference in the curricular aims between *Teachers for the Real World* and the Models lies in the sharp distinction between theory and practice in *Teachers* . . . and the relative absence of this distinction in most of the Models. Perhaps because the Models are highly performance oriented, a holistic or integrated view of the relationship of theory to practice is implied, if not openly espoused. There is, for example, virtually no distinction between concepts and skills, although there are distinctions between liberal or general education and professional education. That latter distinction is not, however, germane to the point at issue. In *Teachers* . . ., on the other hand, the aims of the professional curriculum are split, one part dealing with the interpretive use of concepts (theoretical) and the other with skills (practical). This split is a fundamental one, since the theoretical aims ultimately give rise to Protocol Materials as an instructional mechanism, while the practical aims give rise to Training Materials. The welding of these two to the contextual aims of the curriculum is partly accomplished through the use of reality-based materials (Protocol and Training both), but the chief mechanism for welding theory, practice, and context is the Training Comlex.

A reconciliation of the differences in expressed curriculum aims between *Teachers* . . . and the Models is perhaps easier than one might anticipate. The question is largely one of how to group the behavioral outcomes or competencies. Theory-practice is one kind of grouping, separation of competencies by roles is another, and delineation of integrated concept-skill sequence is a third. A precise reconciliation does, however, present a substantial practical problem.

To show the interrelations among the groupings, one would have to start with a pool of competencies or behavioral objectives, then sort them into the cells of a two, or possibly three, dimensional matrix, with each dimension of the matrix representing the different ways of expressing curricular aims, e.g., understanding teaching contexts, theory-practice, roles, or integrated concept-skill sequences.

Q. 2. *How will you know (verify or confirm) that the goals of the curriculum have been met?*

This question is an extremely difficult one because the answer to it has two parts, one apparent and one hidden. The apparent part of the answer lies in establishing performance criteria which, in sum or in toto, are taken to be equivalent to the goals of the curriculum. In the Georgia and Michigan State Models, these criteria are specified in great detail, and coded and stored on computer tapes. Verification that these criteria have been met, hence, verification that the goals of the curriculum have been accomplished, requires a set of procedures, and measurement and observation of teacher behavior, through which one certifies that the teacher does in actuality perform to the criteria. These processes seem sound, yet the hidden problem is partially revealed by the ComField Model, which requires not that the teacher demonstrate that he has particular behaviors, but that he demonstrate that he can bring about a specific type and level of learning in students. The ComField Model thus suggests that the validity criterion for the teacher-education curriculum lies in the performance of the students of teachers trained in the curriculum. Under the ComField Model, then, student learning is revealed as the hidden performance criterion for teachers.

Unfortunately, there is also a hidden issue in the ComField Model. If one is to rest his case on student learning, he must be able to implement this criterion first by acquiring the relevant measures of student learning, second by showing that the teacher is the factor responsible for whatever learning takes place, and third by showing that the teacher can replicate his performance in a variety of situations, i.e., that ability to bring about student learning is not merely a one-shot affair on the part of the teacher. Although it is not logically impossible to implement these procedures, within current resources constraints and know-how, it is probably impossible to implement them on a practical basis. The objective is sound, but reaching it seems unlikely in the foreseeable future.

Teachers for the Real World does not deal in any systematic way with the question of confirming that the goals of the teacher-education curriculum have been met. Insofar as performance criteria appear at all in *Teachers . . .*, they appear by implication from the nature of the teaching complex, since performance with students is intrinsic to the complex.

The issues which surround verification that the goals of a teacher-education curriculum have been met are of course the very same issues which surround Performance-Based Certification. From the viewpoint of the author, Task Force '72 should recognize from the outset that the basic question involved is the degree of confidence that one is willing to place in the procedures by which attainment of the goals of the curriculum is defined or by which the meaning of Performance-Based Certification is specified or operationalized. Different procedures will yield different levels of confidence. Moreover, it is quite possible to scale the degree of confidence one has in a given set of procedures. For example, student teaching supervisors now judge the performance of student teachers, either against criteria specified by the training institution or by criteria generated by the supervisor himself. The question is how much confidence is produced by this procedure. Would judgments by multiple supervising teachers as might occur in a Training Complex increase confidence? Would judgments of performance by panels of experts still further increase confidence? Would demonstration that the teacher brings about student learning increase confidence still further?

As one may observe in the above progression, as confidence in the procedures for appraising performance increases, the complexity of the procedures for making the appraisal also increases. Indeed, at the more advanced levels of appraisal, very substantial sophistication in research and evaluation methodology is required. For the latter reason, the author believes that resolution of questions surrounding the verification of curricular goals or the utilization of Performance-Based Certification will require substantial long-range support from NCERD as well as from BEPD if the answers to them are to be scientifically justifiable and defensible in the public eye. Almost any teachers' organization, any educational research organization, and many lay groups have the capability to destroy the concept of Performance-Based Certification if the procedures by which it is operationally defined are in any way unsound and, by implication, unfair.

Q. 3. *What will the students experience in the curriculum? What will be the bases of these experiences?*

The responses to these questions in the Models and in *Teachers . . .* might be interpreted as being in agreement on the first question and as different, but complementary, on the second. Both are in broad agreement on the first question in that both view the teacher as experiencing both general or liberal education in the academic disciplines and professional education. With respect to the education of elementary teachers, both also recognize the possibility of specialization in a particular discipline or in an area or at a grade level hence skills in teaching several subject areas and typically a range of grade levels. Both are in agreement that the curriculum provides for direct experience with pupils in school.

The responses of the Models and *Teachers . . .* to the question, "What will be the bases of these (curricular) experiences?" are of three different types. These types arise because there are different ways of construing what the "significant bases" of curricular experiences are.

In *Teachers . . .* the significant bases of curricular experiences are interpreted to be the *materials* encountered by the student. There are probably several reasons for this choice of interpretation. First, an emphasis on materials, and especially on Protocol and Training Materials, intrinsically permits one to represent different kinds of teaching contexts while at the same time teaching particular concepts or skills by means of the materials. Second, the use of carefully constructed materials yields an extremely high level of control over the nature and efficiency of student learning. In one sense, "curriculum" means a set of controlled experiences for the student, and the method of control in most curricula lies in the material which one chooses to have the student study or learn. For example, Protocol Materials permit one to take a controlled slice of a particular kind of experience, say in a classroom, and utilize it to help a student acquire specific concepts, enrich concepts which he already has by showing instances of them in contexts not before experienced, and help him gain functional interpretive uses of the concepts. The use of a controlled slice of experience in this way may generally be interpreted to be more efficient than exposing a student to a very broad and complex experience, since the number of elements to be interpreted in a complex experience, say working in a classroom full time, are too confusing to enable him to sort out and deal with what is going on in an analytic manner. Similarly, skill learning can be made more efficient by controlling the Training Material encountered.

A third reason for emphasizing the development of materials as the basis for curricular experience is that they are exportable or diffusable. They therefore potentially provide a basis for the curricular experiences of a wide range of students in a variety of institutions. Moreover, to the extent that the materials enhance the learning concepts and skills relevant to teaching and facilitate the understanding of teaching contexts, the total impact of carefully developed materials is probably greater than could be realized from any other single instructional mechanism.

In the Models, the significant basis of the curriculum is not explicitly interpreted to mean materials, although materials development may be implicit to several of the Models. Rather, the significant bases are, first, how the experiences are organized and, second, how the student is to make his way through the organization. One type of curricular organization in the Models deals with the way in which the curricular content is grouped. On the professional training side of the curriculum, this grouping is typically by the anticipated roles and functions of the teacher, as noted earlier. More importantly for this section of the paper, however, is the fact that many, if not most, of the Models attempt to reorganize standard college curricular structure by doing away with the "course" and substituting some other type of curricular unit, for example, modules, phases, subcomponents, and activities. The intent of this type of reorganization is undoubtedly to increase the flexibility of the curriculm so that a wider and more diverse set of experiences can be incorporated into it over a particular period of time. There is little question that such flexibility is desirable. Certainly there is little reason other than the traditions of colleges and professors for perpetuating the "course" as the principal curricular unit.

How a student negotiates or makes his way through a curriculum is not a material or content basis for a curriculum, but it is an extremely important basis for curriculum organization. Most of the Models take the stance that the preservice teacher should be able to negotiate his way through the curriculum on a personalized or individualized basis. Moreover, in many of the Models the curricular structure is laid out in such a way that the major points for students are readily apparent. The student can know beforehand what his potential experiences might be and can to a degree choose which experiences he will have contingent on his capabilities, interests, and objectives. Again, there seems to be little question that a curriculum which offers distinct choices within a well-defined structure and can be individually negotiated by a student is desirable when judged against the apparent values current in American society.

By almost any measure, the interpretations of the significant bases of the curriculum in *Teachers . . .* and in the Models are complementary. *Teachers . . .* addresses the specific kinds of experience which teachers should encounter in their curricula in the form of the materials with which they are to interact. The Models, on the other hand, are addressed to the way in which the curricular units might desirably be organized and how students might negotiate their way through these curricular organizations and thus determine in part the content of their own educations. In an innovative curriculum, Protocol and Training Materials might indeed be used as the most important materials in a modular curriculum individually negotiated by students.

Q. 4. Do the (curricula) experiences have to come in any particular order?

With respect to this question, *Teachers for the Real World* seems to the writer to be an implicitly theoretical document. The order of experiences implied by *Teachers . . .* is that theoretical knowledge is antecedent to the acquisition of teaching skills and that, in the final round, theoretical knowledge and teaching skills must be webbed together in an actual teaching context. Thus, the use of Protocol Materials and the attendant concept learning is generally antecedent to the use of Training Materials and the attendant learning of skills. The final integration of concepts, skills, and the understanding of teaching contexts occurs last, in the Training Complex, which is, for preservice teachers, a kind of specialized finishing school. It is important to recognize, however, that for in-service teachers the Training Complex is more nearly a "refinishing" school, a place where the in-service teacher may expand his skills, retool, and up-grade.

Inherent to the general sequence of professional development which appears to characterize *Teachers . . .* is also an implicit notion about successive levels of concept and skill development and the understanding of teaching contexts. Protocol Materials may not be anticipated to perfectly develop all needed concepts; Training Materials will not produce the ultimate or finished form of a skill; neither will it produce final understanding of a teaching context. It is in part because the total task to be accomplished by the curriculum cannot be completely accomplished by the use of Protocol and Training Materials that the Training Complex is needed. In the main, there are sound psychological reasons for this view. Conceptual interpretations of behavior and skill sequences must be "cued off" by the appropriate environmental stimuli if they are to be effective. The problem is one of both appropriateness and timing. Quite typically these cues cannot be made fully available through either Protocol or Training Materials; thus, neophyte teachers must spend considerable time "learning their cues," so to speak, by being engaged in actual teaching situations. The purpose of direct classroom experience is *not* to learn the skills, but rather to finish them. If the neophyte teacher simply lacks certain concepts or skills, one purpose of having a Training Complex is to enable her to return to the Protocol and Training Materials through which the basic components of the concepts or skills, or both, may be acquired.

Like *Teachers . . .* most of the Models have an order or sequence to the curricular experiences. It is for this reason that students reach successive choice points in negotiating the curriculum. Elaboration of the precise type of sequence for each Model goes beyond the bounds of this paper, but they may be observed in the original documents and certain summaries (3) of the Models.

Perhaps an important point to keep in mind in differences in sequences between particular Models and *Teachers . . .* is that the Models are virtually all university-based, and the feasible sequences are in some degree bound by this fact. *Teachers . . .*, on the other hand, makes some distinction between the work most appropriate to the university, that which is theoretical, and orders to the Training Complex many, if not most, of the training tasks.

Q. 5. *How will you know that a particular order of experiences is a good order?*

Teachers for the Real World does not deal with this question in any systematic way, probably because the order of experiences implicit to its theoretical position is very general. Most of the Models also do not deal with this question in a very direct way, i.e., they do not state specifically how the goodness of a proposed order will be ascertained. Nearly all of them do deal with this problem indirectly, however, by creating some kind of evaluation mechanism, which, presumably, has within its capabilities the securing of the information necessary to make decisions about the effectiveness of the proposed order of experiences.

Q. 6. *How will you know that the (curricular) experiences lead to the goals of the curriculum?*

In one sense, the answers to this question are precisely the same as the answers to Question 2 above, i.e., one will know whether experiences lead to the goal when he examines the products of the curriculum, the teachers prepared, against the performance criteria which are equated to the goals of the curriculum. Certain of the Models—including Georgia, MSU, and Syracuse—have, however, a slightly different way to answer the question. These Models include explicit sequences of performance objectives. These objectives in turn make possible an appraisal of the extent to which any particular set of experiences do in fact bring about a particular level of performance. Thus some formative appraisal is possible. They do not, however, completely answer the question since it is always possible that meeting the intermediate performance objectives does not predict how one will perform in the end when the actual classroom performance of the teacher is used as the criterion against which the ultimate utility of the curriculum must be appraised.

PROGRAMMATIC THEMES AND MECHANISMS

The contention in this paper is that to lead a successful reform movement in teacher education BEPD-NCERD should (1) focus on two programmatic themes and the policy positions attendant to them, and (2) fund selected mechanisms drawn from the classes of implementing mechanisms coordinate to these themes. The two programmatic themes may be expressed as follows:

1. The development of a nationwide system for the confirmation of the outcomes of teacher education.
2. The development of curriculum intervention strategies to increase the power of teacher-education programs.

These themes are implicit to *Teachers for the Real World* and the *Models for Preparing Elementary Teachers*, although they are not explicit in these documents. The explicit components of *Teachers . . .* and the Models are more nearly implementing mechanisms than themes. These components suggest particular devices and organizational structures which might be used in the reform of teacher education. Viewed together, *Teachers . . .* and the Models may be seen as presenting several instances of mechanisms which may be divided into classes with each class of mechanisms coordinate to a theme.

Theme 1: The development of a nationwide system for the confirmation of the outcomes of teacher education

The possibility that the nationwide system for the confirmation of the outcomes of teacher education could be established as a theme arises from two sources. First, of the five thrusts initially proposed by BEPD, Performance-Based Certification may be recognized as a potential policy position rather than as a mechanism. This position involves a clear intervention in the criterion which might be employed for teacher licensure or certification. The criterion implied is that certification is to be based on the observed and measured capabilities of the teacher, not on inferences about capabilities based on courses taken and credits received.

A second source from which the possibility of a nationwide confirmatory system arises is the Models. A key feature of all the Models is the espousal of a "systems" approach. Although a major selling point for the systems approach is that all the components of the system are integrated or coordinated, the critical feature of this approach is the confirmatory feedback mechanism. As the Wisconsin Model suggests, it is this feature of the system which makes it correctable, self-renewing, and capable of reform. Moreover, as suggested in the first paper by the writer, it is the Confirmatory Mechanism which permits one to know (verify or confirm) the extent to which the experiences within a teacher-education curriculum are valid when appraised against the criteria, goals, or ends for which these experiences were designed.

Development of a policy position

The development of a policy position bearing on a nation-wide confirmatory system involves at least three steps.

Step 1. The first step entails creation of a value-laden proposition. This proposition might be cast in the following way:

> The reform of teacher education requires the development of a confirmatory feedback system by means of which (1) changes in teacher-education programs may be appraised for their efficacy, (2) teachers may be certified, and (3) both public and professional confidence in the professional qualifications of teachers for their work may be assured.

The intellectual burdens of this proposition are very great. The immediate intent of the proposition, however, is to demonstrate recognition at the national level that an overarching, confidence inspiring system for quality control in the preparation of teachers and for entry into the teaching profession is an unconditional requirement for intelligent reform.

Step 2. The second step entails coping with the intellectual burdens generated in the first step. Although these burdens may be dealt with from several different perspectives, the writer believes that the key point to be examined is the development of several levels of criteria. These levels should make clear the points at which feedback to teacher-education programs could be generated and the points at which Performance-Based Certification could occur. In addition, they should, as a group, increase confidence in the quality controls exercised in teacher education. The several levels of criteria are suggested below.

Criterion Level 1. At the highest level, the criterion against which teachers (or teaching) might be appraised consists of two parts. The first part is observation of the acts or behaviors in which the teacher engages in the classroom. The observations must be conducted with a set of instruments which permit classification of teacher behaviors in both the cognitive and affective domains. The second part is systematic analysis of the level of outcomes achieved by the teacher with the pupils he teaches. Outcomes in both the cognitive and affective domains must be included. Because of variation in the entry behaviors of students and variations in teaching contexts, the residual outcomes in pupil behavior (the terminal behaviors corrected for entry behaviors and moderating variables) should be used as the criterion measures. To be placed at Criterion Level 1, the above two-part appraisal of teacher performance must be conducted over a relatively long period of time, probably at least two years (on a time-sampling basis), with both the observational and residual pupil behavior components assessed during each of the years. The reason for the two-year period is that both teacher and pupil behavior are open to some random fluctuation and care must be taken to obtain a sufficient sample of behavior from both sources to assure fair conclusions.

There are two principal uses to be made of the data obtained at Criterion Level 1. First, if the data are obtained during the teacher's first three years of teaching experience, they might be used to certify that the performance of the teacher is at a level to warrant relatively permanent certification. How permanent the certification might be depends on whether a cyclical pattern of certification (e.g., recertification once every ten years) becomes a socially acceptable policy, or whether life certification remains as the socially acceptable policy. Second, if observational data on teacher as well as pupil performance data are included in the criterion, the *relationships* between the observed behavior of teachers and pupil performance can be utilized as general feedback to teacher-education programs. These relationships will indicate which types of teacher behavior are most likely to be influential in bringing about particular changes in pupil behavior. Teacher-education programs would thus be able to increase the amount of confidence they have in intermediate performance criteria which involve only the actions of the teacher.

Criterion Level 2. Criterion Level 2 is identical to Criterion Level 1 except that a shorter performance period is involved. Current thinking about Performance-Based Certification, such as that in the ComField Model, appears to assume a teacher performance period of one year or less, after which certification might be awarded. Although a performance criterion involving the latter period of time is at a high criterial level, it is sufficiently open to error attributable to fluctuations in teacher behavior, pupil behavior, and the teaching context that it inspires considerably less confidence than does criterion performance based on wider sampling over a longer period of time. One may also note in this context that the ComField Model focuses almost wholly on pupil outcomes and largely eliminates observation of teacher classroom behavior. It therefore is of very limited utility in providing relevant feedback to teacher preparation programs.

Criterion Level 3. Criterion Level 3 differs from Criterion Levels 1 and 2 in that pupil performance data are eliminated from the criterion. Judgments about competence or proficiency are thus based on the observable behaviors of the teacher rather than on the pupil outcomes associated with these behaviors. Nonetheless, this Criterion Level is still performance-based in the sense that the teacher actually does engage in teaching and is gauged on the quality of his professional actions. How "good" or valid this Criterion Level is depends almost wholly on whether empirical relationships between teacher actions and pupil performance have been established through research or through data obtained by use of Criterion Levels 1 and 2.

The degree of confidence in Criterion Level 3 lies in the upper-intermediate range. In the judgment of the writer, this criterion yields sufficient confidence to be useful in the provisional certification of teachers. It is also highly useful in teacher-education programs since one may observe teachers to explicitly determine whether they evidence the behaviors which a particular teacher preparatory program claims to be producing, and by means of this observation it may provide the basis of feedback about efficacy to the program.

Criterion Level 4. Criterion Level 4 differs from Criterion Level 3 in that both the teaching context and the range of teacher behavior observed are restricted. The context might be a typical microteaching context involving a few pupils or even peers acting as students. The teacher behavior observed would be restricted to a few categories in the cognitive or in the affective domain.

This criterion lies in the intermediate range, but it inspires very modest confidence and cannot be construed as an adequate basis for Performance-Based Certification. Rather, its utility lies in providing feedback about the efficacy of particular segments of the teacher-education program and in providing diagnostic feedback to students about their own progress. It tells whether a student has acquired certain behaviors or skills and whether he can integrate these skills under specially arranged teaching conditions.

Criterion Level 5. Criterion Level 5 differs from Criterion Level 4 in that the teacher need not perform before live students (simulated students would be satisfactory). He must, however, be able to produce or show in his behavior at least one teaching skill, e.g., probing.

This criterion inspires virtually no confidence as a criterion for Performance-Based Certification, but it is very useful for providing feedback about the efficacy of targeted Training Materials or subcomponents of instructional modules or of courses. Its "goodness" as a criterion depends in substantial part on the extent to which the skill being assessed can be shown to be a skill associated with pupil performance outcomes as established either by research or by use of data obtained in using the higher order criteria noted above.

Criterion Level 6. Criterion Level 6 differs from Criterion Level 5 in that the teacher need not engage in producing a performance, but, rather, only show that he understands some behavior, concept, or principle germane to teaching. Within this criterion several levels of "understanding" can undoubtedly be identified. These levels of understanding can be operationalized by varying the kinds of problems the teacher is asked to respond to in accord with some type of taxonomy, such as Bloom's. Like Criterion Level 5, the utility of this criterion is primarily to provide feedback about the efficacy of particular program components within teacher education. Similarly, its "goodness" as a Criterion Level depends largely on the extent to which knowledge of particular behaviors, concepts, or principles may ultimately be shown to be useful in predicting attainment of one or more of the higher Criterion Levels.

Step 3. The third step in the development of a policy position requires a careful distinction between types of mechanisms relevant to a Confirmatory System. At the present time, at least two types of mechanisms can be identified. First, because the development of sequential Criterion Levels for assessing the outcomes of teacher education, as elaborated in the preceding step, one set of mechanisms must deal with the operationalization of these criteria. If one is to talk about performance criteria at any level, he must ultimately specify the permissible range of devices and instruments by which the actual assessment might occur. He must, moreover, produce the actual devices and instruments; otherwise, the actions suggested by the policy will remain theoretical, and practice will remain unaffected. In addition, if the use of such instruments and devices is to result in renewal and change, some system for reporting the results of their use must be established. For example, Protocol Materials may be used, if properly designed, for testing concept mastery. The results of using them in this way must, however, be fed back into the system if one is to learn about the efficacy of their use for this purpose, the efficacy of the components of teacher-education programs in which they are used as tests, and, ultimately, their efficacy in eliciting behavior which may be used to predict other, subsequently employed criteria.

Second, the various Criterion Levels previously noted cannot be brought into being without creating some kind of institutional or organizational vehicles to provide a context in which they can exist. For example, it is virtually impossible to imagine Performance-Based Certification of the ComField type (level 2 criterion) without simultaneously imagining the institutional structure or mechanism which can manage the procedures required to actually implement the criterion. The teacher seeking certification must be placed in a classroom, his pupils must be tested for entry behaviors, some observation of the classroom surely must occur, terminal tests must be given, and an analysis must be made. A certification decision must be delivered. Who will do all of this work? Who will support him? What will his career line be like? The answers to such questions lie in some kind of institutional mechanism which is designed to carry on the needed work functions.

Implementing mechanisms

Of the two types of implementing mechanisms described in the immediately preceding section, creation of the institutional structure through which the Confirmatory System can operate should be given the higher priority. There are a number of reasons for assigning top priority to these structures. First, a nationwide Confirmatory System must be composed of a decentralized, regionally distributed network of centers, complexes, institutes, or cooperatives. Although such centers or cooperatives must be coordinated by a central agency, the actual operations which comprise confirming the outcomes of teacher-education programs, giving feedback to these programs and, potentially, offering Performance-Based Certification must occur at a local level. Second, the creation of institutional structures should facilitate the more rapid development and adoption of devices, instruments, and procedures necessary to implement the various Criterion Levels described earlier, hence, the implementation of the processes by which Performance-Based Certification and feedback systems actually come into being.

The Class of Institutional Structures. Members of the class of institutional structures which might be used to implement a nationwide Confirmatory System must have certain characteristics in common, but the members of the class need not, and probably should not, be identical. Those characteristics which these structures should have in common are as follows:

1. Each should be connected to one or more institutions of higher education. All of these institutions must prepare teachers, but some must, in addition, have distinct R and D capabilities. Connection to teacher preparation institutions will help ensure a functioning feedback system and ease certification problems. Connection to R and D sources will greatly facilitate the development of functional devices, instruments, and analytic procedures necessary for accurate feedback and for the confirmation of outcomes.
2. Each should be connected to a diverse group of schools and their attendant communities. These schools should not only be diverse in setting, but highly diverse in their practices and in the types of teaching roles functioning within them.
3. Each must agree to return to the nationwide system the results of its confirmatory and feedback findings and practices and must develop a mechanism for assuring that this return occurs on a regular basis.

Aside from these few characteristics, each institutional structure should be permitted wide latitude to experiment with its own organization and functions.

Theme 2: The development of curriculum intervention strategies to increase the power of teacher-education programs

Unlike theme 1, theme 2 is quite explicit in *Teachers for the Real World* and in the Models. These documents are clearly aimed at developing interventions which increase the power of teacher-education programs and thus serve as the principal sources undergirding this section of the paper.

Development of a policy position

The development of a policy position for the development of curriculum intervention strategies involves at least three steps.

Step 1. As under theme 1, the first step is to assert a value-laden proposition; it might be cast as follows:

> The reform of teacher education requires vastly increasing the power of teacher-education programs by means of: (1) the development of instructional materials which increase the scope of concepts and skills acquired, the depth in which they are acquired, and the speed with which they are acquired; (2) the development of indepth professional experiences for the functional consolidation of these concepts and skills; (3) the development of accommodating curricular organizations; and (4) the development of intervention strategies which facilitate the installation of the materials, the experience, and accommodating curricular organizations.

BEPD has quite obviously already accepted and begun to implement the first two components of this policy position. In the opinion of the writer, these implementing moves are in precisely the right direction, and only increased refinement and targeting of the Protocol and Training Materials thrust and the accommodation of the Training Complex thrust to the confirmation-feedback system suggested in theme 1 are needed.

The immediate difficulty with the policy position already developed in BEPD is that it does not reach far enough to provide reasonable assurance that the power of the teacher-education programs will actually be increased. To give greater assurance, component three and especially component four of the above proposition need substantial development as policy positions. These components are therefore those focally addressed in step 2 below.

Step 2. One of the major difficulties with teacher-education programs in the nation is that their curricular organization is designed as if education is a discipline in the social sciences and has as its aim the production of social scientists rather than as if its aim is to produce practicing educators. This point is recognized not only in *Teachers* . . . . but also in many of the Models. The response to the point in *Teachers* . . . was to shift a major portion of the basis of instruction to Protocol and Training Materials and to the Training Complex. The response in the Models is more diverse. Most of the Models appear to have responded to the general point by moving toward a modular curricular organization and the possibility of a substantial amount of individualized instruction. Some, such as Columbia and Michigan State, seem also to have incorporated in their designs the concept that a teacher-education curriculum is a distinctly laboratory-based curriculum.

If the responses of *Teachers* . . . and the Models are combined to produce a more general policy position, something like the following emerges:

> The teacher-education curriculum should be developed around instructional modules and should incorporate two types of laboratory instruction. The instructional modules should be constructed around those families of concepts and skills which are on the one hand germane to the interpretation of human behavior and on the other germane to engaging in actions which maintain behavior or bring about changes in it, whichever is dictated by the goals of instruction and the interpretations of the teacher. The conceptual content and objectives of some of the modules suggest that they can most successfully be utilized under conditions of group or classroom instruction under laboratory conditions. Typically, these modules would be those which require the student to examine a performance, produce a performance, or acquire or exhibit a skill, and those which require the student to invent or develop some form of instructional material or aid.
>
> To maximize the impact of instructional modules and to increase the flexibility of the earlier portions of the curriculum toward greater individualization of instruction, each teacher-education program should be characterized by a large, in-house component of laboratory-based instruction in which problems in the interpretation of behavior are solved and in which teaching skills are practiced. In the later portions of the curriculum, the student should move from the in-house laboratory to an external laboratory which, for all practical purposes, is identical to the Training Complex.

From a policy viewpoint, the aim of the foregoing prescription is that BEPD–NCERD should incorporate among its reform efforts a thrust toward reorganization of the teacher-education curriculum. The central components of this thrust would be (1) curriculum organization by modules, with the modules tied to the Protocol and Training Materials thrusts, and (2) the development of college- and university-based laboratories in which the modules formed the foundation of instruction.

Step 3. The third step in the development of a policy position to facilitate the installation of curricular reforms in teacher-education programs requires the development of one or more installation strategies. Neither *Teachers . . .* nor the Models cope in any adequate way with installation strategies. Nonetheless, two general strategies may be recognized as having developed within BEPD–NCERD. One of these strategies may be identified as the dissemination strategy; the other, the concentration strategy.

A dissemination strategy is typically based on the assumption that the provision of information about new developments, together with some advisory help concerning how to take advantage of the developments, will gradually bring about acceptance and use by groups and organizations functioning in the areas in which the developments occur. The ERIC system functions on this premise, the Elementary Models were diffused on this premise, and the R and D Centers and regional labs operate predominantly on this premise. Although a dissemination strategy may be useful for the diffusion of R & D findings, that it leads to the installation of new developments or the institutionalization of major reforms seems to the author to be doubtful. It is indeed difficult to think of instances of major change in education which seem to have come about as a consequent of a dissemination strategy. Why a dissemination strategy does not rapidly lead to change, reform, or installation is an open question. One may only hypothesize that the possession of new information does not add sufficient incentive for change to overcome the barriers which militate against change.

A concentration strategy rests on the premise that a major barrier to change lies in trying to divert a finite set of resources from an established use to a new use. To remove this barrier, sufficient new resources must be made available to establish the new use (typically a program, device, or curriculum), which then competes effectively with the old use of resources and drains the resources from the old to the new use. One example of this type of strategy may be found in the support of computers and their utilization on college campuses during the late 1950s and all of the 1960s by NSF. By 1970, computer utilization was sufficiently established to eliminate external support, and the NSF program has consequently recently been phased out. The Elementary Models would themselves have been an example of a concentration strategy had the development phase been followed, as presumably planned, by an installation phase.

In the opinion of the writer, the development of a policy position to facilitate the installation of curricular reforms in teacher education should be based on a concentration strategy. Under this strategy, sufficient funds would be made available to selected institutions to permit them to reorganize their curriculum to incorporate *all* the developments (modular construction, Protocol and Training Materials, laboratory-based instruction, and participation in a Training Complex) proposed by BEPD-NCERD as an alternative to the former curriculum. Once the reorganized curriculum is fully functioning, external funds can be withdrawn and placed elsewhere. Subsequent changes in the new curriculum could then be introduced on a more modest basis as a consequent of the feedback returning to the institution through the nationwide confirmation-feedback system.

Implementing mechanisms

The question of the implementing mechanism for the policy position described above is largely an after-the-fact question. Protocol and Training Materials and Training Complexes are already under development. Various models of curriculum reorganization are available from the Elementary Models. The issue is basically not one of the development of mechanisms but, rather, one of timing the concentration of resources for the reform of particular teacher-education curricula. A key part of this issue is whether selected ones of the institutions which originally developed the Models have arrived at a point at which a concentration of resources would permit a powerful teacher-education program, limited though it may be to elementary teachers, to emerge.

PAYOFFS, MECHANISMS, AND COSTS

Unlike preceding papers by the author, this paper begins not with potential themes and mechanisms for BEPD programs, but with an examination of types of payoffs which must be achieved by these programs if they are to be considered successful, especially when gauged against the needs of the poverty community. These payoffs are separated into three levels: those related to pupils or students, those related to professional personnel in schools, and those related to colleges and universities. The nature of the payoff at each level is examined, and the priorities within and between levels are rationalized. Subsequently, the mechanisms believed most likely to bring about these payoffs are differentiated and examined in some detail. In this examination, the feasibility of previously suggested themes and mechanisms is tested. Finally, the costs attendant to the various mechanisms or interventions are examined relative to projected payoffs, and suggestions for funding are made. Broadly, the objective of the paper is to suggest ways in which the payoffs might be optimized, relative to costs, when the central control over inputs lies in the mechanisms to be created.

Levels of payoff

First-level payoffs

The first level of payoffs may be viewed as those criteria which must be achieved if federal programs are to have relevant impact and are to be described as successful. All such criteria lie in the behavior of preschool, primary and middle school pupils, and secondary school students from the poverty community.

Beginning with secondary school students, at least four types of payoff may be viewed as criterial:

1. Retention of students for a steadily increasing number of years of schooling, with the ultimate criterion being high school graduation for virtually all students. This criterion is drawn centrally from the report by Levin et al. (4) who suggest that number of years of schooling completed is the best single predictor of subsequent economic success.
2. Increased growth in general information (in the development of concepts and vocabulary) as evidenced especially in increased reading comprehension across a range of applied content areas. This criterion is also drawn from Levin et al., but it is redefined from general achievement into general information and reading comprehension so that the emphasis is on coping behaviors and on potential for continued growth by means of reading. This criterion overlaps the first criterion in that retention both reflects and is reflected in increases in conceptual development.
3. Growth in citizenship. On the negative side, this criterion is evidenced in decreased rates of crime, delinquency, vandalism, and drug abuse by high school students and increased feelings of political and economic potency and involvement (or decreased feelings of alienation and political and economic apathy).
4. Increased opportunity to learn. This criterion is indexed by the range of alternative education programs of high quality available, including not only vocation education programs but also general education programs which increase the coping behaviors of students in poor social environments.

For preschool, primary and middle school pupils, the payoffs are coordinate to those for secondary school students. In addition, part of the status of these payoffs may be viewed as lying in the predictive relationships they hold to payoffs at the secondary level. These payoffs are as follows:

1. At the preschool, primary and middle school levels, increases in general information, i.e., in the development of concepts and the attendant vocabulary by which concepts are communicated.
2. Expression of satisfaction with the schools by the community, in conjunction with (1) decreased pupil absenteeism from school (a predictor of secondary school retention), and (2) expression of satisfaction or happiness with school by pupils.
3. At the preschool level, increased oral language facility and increased facility with the fractional components of language and perception linked to reading readiness; at the primary level, increased attainment of reading and arithmetic skills; at the middle school level, increased attainment in reading comprehension and vocabulary, especially as related to the content areas or areas useful to increasing real-life coping behaviors.

Second-level payoffs

When instructional personnel are considered the central variable in influencing pupil outcomes (first-level payoffs), the second-level payoffs are those which bear on the careers and behaviors of these personnel. The payoffs relative to instructional personnel are as follows:

1. Placement in school practice according to training and specialization. As in any manpower training program, investment in specialized training, but a failure to place the trainee in a position relevant to his skills severely damages the payoff possibilities attendant to training. Collaterally, placement of inappropriately trained personnel in positions demanding skills these personnel do not possess also decreases payoff, not only by damaging the probability of better first-level payoff, but also by displacing appropriately trained personnel, thereby damaging second-level payoff.
2. Retention of personnel. High attrition of trained personnel immediately following training or during the first year or two of practice increases training costs relative to payoff, since the cost of training many persons must be distributed over the productivity of the few who remain in practice. In addition, supervisor costs attendant to beginning teacher personnel, as well as turnover costs, must be defrayed against fewer and fewer productive personnel if the attrition rate for beginning personnel is high during the first two years of practice.
3. Performance. The direct connection between first-level and second-level payoffs lies in teacher performance. Placement and retention are the conditions or precursors of performance. As

noted in the preceding paper, the ultimate criteria for the measurement of teacher performance are pupil outcomes. Pupil outcome criteria are difficult to employ fairly and accurately, however. An intermediate set of criteria, those based on the observation and appraisal of teacher skills and personality variables, are consequently important intermediate criteria in the payoff matrix, as suggested in the preceding paper.

Third-level payoffs

Third-level payoffs are those that meet two criteria. First, they must be a direct consequence of personnel training and/or selection. Second, because of the sequential nature of the levels of payoff, third-level payoffs must be predictors of second- and third-level payoffs. The direct consequences of personnel training must be expressed in what teachers know and can do, i.e., in performance. The precise predictive relationships between particular performances, as level three payoffs, and the various payoffs at the second and the first levels are, however, not known in any detail. What is known are the general areas or domains within which the predictive variables fall. These domains thus constitute the areas within which the third-level payoffs fall; discussion of the domains may be found in the chapters by Turner and by Rosenshine and Furst in a book edited by Smith (6) and in the Elementary Models.

1. Increased knowledge of the substantive areas in which the teacher is to offer instruction; increased comprehension of the structural relationships within these substantive areas; increased ability to identify where a pupil stands in his knowledge of a substantive area; and increased ability to designate where he should next move in his knowledge of a substantive area.
2. Increased skill to perform teaching tasks in at least four domains as follows:
   a. The diagnosis of pupil status and pupil learning difficulties.
   b. The development of learning treatments to move pupils forward in their attainments.
   c. The appraisal or evaluation of the efficacy of learning treatments, especially on the criterion of pupil performance.
   d. Instructional support tasks, including classroom management.
3. Increased ability to perform over a range of instructional styles, i.e., didactic and heuristic, and within a variety of settings, i.e., individualized, small group and large group.
4. Increased skill in controlling and monitoring the affective consequences of one's own classroom behavior, hence increased control over one's own affective behavior and interpersonal sensitivity.

Optimizing short-range and long-range payoffs

Although several sequential levels of payoffs have been described above, no attempt has been made to organize them so that a coherent funding pattern could be generated. To generate such a pattern, some particular first-level payoff must be established as the criterion payoff or the thing one is trying to optimize. The assumption made here is that *increased retention of secondary school students up to the limit that all students entering secondary school also graduate from it* is the payoff to be optimized. It is to be understood that this retention would not be gratuitous, but that it would reflect increased intellectual and skill attainments among the students retained. Retention is taken to be the criterial payoff because, together with achievement, it is the best predictor of economic success, which is in turn taken to be the central and necessary factor in getting members of the poverty community out of their condition of poverty.

The most obvious funding strategy for optimizing retention in secondary school would be to place the most resources on the development of the quality in secondary school personnel. This move, while good in the short run, would be a poor long-range strategy because of certain well-known empirical relationships.

As Bloom (2) has amply shown, and as is otherwise well understood, the behavior of pupils, and especially the intellectual or "achievement" behavior of students, is remarkably stable. The achievements of a child in any one year can be reliably predicted from his achievement in the preceding year. It follows that a child who enters primary school with poor achievement, relative to his peers, will in all probability continue in this condition until high school, at which time he has a high probability of dropping out. For such children, an extremely powerful intervention must occur relatively early if the probability of retention in secondary school is to be increased.

Although there is no point in arguing that a massive upgrading of the quality of preschool, primary, and middle school personnel will alone produce an intervention of sufficient power to massively affect the probability of retention of students in secondary school, it is also true that any intervention which does not update the quality of these personnel is unlikely to be at all powerful. In short, the argument is that the upgrading of preschool, primary, and middle school personnel is a necessary but not sufficient condition of increasing secondary school retention and, moreover, that such upgrading is the key or crucial factor in any strategy to optimize long-range payoff.

If the argument presented above is followed to its logical conclusion, the optimum long-range funding pattern would be one following an inverse relationship between magnitude of resource allocation and the grade level at which teachers teach (or for which preparatory teachers are planning to teach). Under this pattern, the greater resources would be placed on the training of preschool and primary teachers, somewhat fewer resources on the training of teachers of middle schools or of the intermediate grades and junior high school, and still fewer resources on the training of secondary school personnel. One must be careful under this pattern not to construe "still fewer resources" to mean virtually no resources or very minimal resources. If too few resources are devoted to upgrading secondary school personnel, short-range payoffs, as well as the optimization of long-range payoffs, will clearly be threatened. One may note that this pattern is essentially the reverse of the allocation of state and local tax dollars by grade levels, since per pupil costs in high school typically substantially exceed per pupil costs in elementary school.

If short- and long-range payoffs are to be optimized, a second major factor to be considered is the distribution of resources to upgrading personnel already in practice as opposed to those preparing to practice. Again, certain empirical evidence is germane to the way in which these resources should be distributed to obtain maximum payoff. First, a very large proportion (approximately 50 percent) of practicing elementary teachers have five or fewer years of experience. This fact is probably attributable to the extremely high attrition rate for teachers entering the elementary school. Second, there is some evidence that teacher skills remain relatively stable between the fifth year of experience and approximately the fifteenth year, with a gradual deterioration setting in (on the average) as experience increases. This pattern of deterioration is a relatively common one in the professions and should not be viewed as peculiar to teaching. Third, there is some evidence that teachers who remain in a school district for five years are very likely to remain as the stable core of teachers in the district (Turner, 1968).

Together, these factors suggest that the target population for in-service training are those teachers who have from five to fifteen or twenty years of experience. This group is most likely to remain in the school district and is perhaps most likely to benefit from upgrading. Moreover, new leadership in school districts is most likely to emerge from teachers in this population. To obtain the best short-range payoff, the greater resources should probably be allocated to the upgrading of this population. To obtain long-range payoff, however, several other factors must be considered.

As noted earlier, a central difficulty in obtaining payoff from training preparatory teachers, and in upgrading teaching as a profession, lies in the high attrition rate during the first five years of experience. Because of this attrition rate, further upgrading of this group is profitable only if it is conducted on an accurate, self-selection basis, i.e., those who intend to remain in the profession begin to upgrade themselves because of some foreseeable payoff (salary increases, prestige, advancement) from doing so. In point of fact, such self-selection already occurs and is almost universally tied to reentering the university to seek a Master's degree. This fact is important because it means that this population can be upgraded in a university setting where preparatory teachers are already present, thus creating the possibility of a concentrated pool of resources which can be effectively used to upgrade not only preparatory teachers, but also a self-selected portion of the teacher group having from one to five years of experience.

To obtain maximum long-range payoff, not only must resources be concentrated where they will affect both preparatory teachers and teachers with one to five years of experience, but they must also be concentrated in locations in which the greatest numbers of preparatory teachers and early career teachers appear. Hence, they must be concentrated in the major teacher preparation institutions. Concentration in these institutions will not only increase the probability that any beginning teacher entering the poverty community will be appropriately trained, but also make possible better cost/benefit ratios by effecting economies of scale.

So that the pattern of funding suggested up to this point may be viewed quite clearly, the intersection of the funding pattern by grade levels of school, by in-service and preservice teacher personnel and according to short and long payoff is shown in Table 8–1. Written in the cells of the table are the suggested priority ranks for funding, *considering only the factors taken into account up to this point.*

TABLE 8–1.

		Preschool and Primary	*Middle School*	*Secondary School*
IN-SERVICE	Short range	third	second	first
	Long range	first	third	fifth
PRESERVICE	Short range	fourth	sixth	fifth
	Long range	second	fourth	sixth

A major point to be considered in the priority rankings for funding, shown in Table 8–1, is that they were generated by trying to optimize payoff without regard to the particular mechanisms through which the payoff is to be achieved. The consideration of mechanisms is of course a critical factor in arriving at final rankings. For example, although maximum short-range payoff might be achieved by investing the most funds in in-service work for secondary school teachers, unless a mechanism is found by means of which payoff can actually be achieved, there is no point in expending the funds. "In-service work" is not a mechanism, but a theme within which mechanisms might be constructed.

Mechanisms

The criterion against which all mechanisms must be judged is workability. While the workability of a mechanism is always contingent upon specific (and frequently unforeseen) factors, a central consideration in workability is always the cost of creating and maintaining the mechanism. Thus, any mechanism which is not cost-feasible may be regarded as unworkable. In creating educational mechanisms, at least three assumptions about costs should be made.

1. Initial creation and maintenance costs must be within the reach of federal spending combined with some (usually minimal) state and local contribution.
2. Federal support will gradually be phased out, thus, throwing total costs on state and local support and possibly on individuals.
3. State and local tax elasticity in combination with multiagency competition for resources will permit relatively little increase in cost for educational services in the foreseeable future.

A second criterion against which workability must be judged is, of course, whether the mechanism is targeted to and achieves one or more payoffs. Considered in relation to the levels of payoff outlined in the preceding section, two types of mechanisms may be recognized as potentially profitable. The first type should have immediate impact on the retention of students from the poverty community in secondary schools; the second type should upgrade the quality of teachers in the poverty community, and indeed of all teachers, over the long run.

Mechanism 1: Alternative secondary schools

Alternative schools for secondary school students for whom withdrawal is imminent or who have already dropped out of school already exist in several school districts and are supported by state and local tax funds. One may recognize that OEO supported Job Corps Training Centers are also a functioning form of alternative schools. The clientele of such schools is relatively predictable. As a recent paper by Bachman (1) suggests, the intellectual abilities related to success in traditional schools are primarily sex-linked (girls do much better than boys) and to a lesser degree race linked (whites do slightly better than blacks). Thus alternative schools are much more likely to have a large male population than a large female population, and somewhat more likely to have black males than white males. To put the matter a bit differently, an alternative school would in all likelihood have the greatest impact if it were targeted on the education of males, and especially on the education of black males. The least likely clientele is the population of white girls, followed by the population of black girls.

The creation of alternative schools under (or in conjunction with) existing BEPD programs is less difficult than one might expect. Five existing programs seem clearly relevant; other programs may be relevant in ways not immediately apparent to the writer. The five programs are Teacher Corps, Urban-rural, Career Opportunities, School Personnel Utilization, and Pupil Personnel Services.

Grants to create one or more alternative schools should be made directly to school districts, preferably acting with liaison arrangements to universities. The easiest vehicle would probably be the Urban-rural Program. The initial staff of the school would undoubtedly have to be drawn in substantial part from existing school system personnel. Working with this staff should be three types of persons: (1) Teacher Corps trainees; (2) paraprofessionals, especially black males, and COP trainees; and (3) trainees from the Pupil Personnel Services Program.

In addition to the creation of alternative schools, an Alternative Schools LTI and a consortium of directors of alternative schools should be established. The leadership and consortium groups are critical in this instance since neither the types of curricula, the personnel roles, nor the personnel training relevant to such schools is well understood.

The alternative schools mechanism should be recognized to be in reverse of the mechanisms subsequently to be suggested in this paper. It targets on first-level payoff and moves downward toward the second- and third-level payoffs, rather than focusing on second- and third-level payoffs, as is characteristic of the remaining mechanisms.

Mechanism 2: Teacher education as laboratory-based education

The intent in developing this mechanism is to find a way to achieve second and third level payoffs in the long run while at the same time keeping all submechanisms within the feasible range and remaining congruent with the themes and mechanisms proposed in the preceding paper.

The first step in developing this mechanism is to recognize that *the Training Complex as an intermediate institution between the schools and the universities is not a feasible mechanism on the criterion of cost.* As presently conceptualized, the Training Complex would require the input of substantial new resources from school districts and universities, and probably also from general state funds, at the very time when each of these institutions is desperately short of resources. Elimination of the Training Complex as a mechanism requires that the functions which might have been discharged by it be covered by another set of mechanisms.

A second step in developing the mechanism is to observe that Performance-Based Certification for all entering teachers is not now feasible if the criterion for certification is set at either Criterion Level 1 or 2, i.e., demonstration of ability to bring about pre-specified changes in pupil behavior by either specified or unspecified means. At the present time, there are no acceptable procedures by means of which one could fairly and equitably show the behavior of the teacher. This does not mean that the development of such procedures should be eliminated, but only that certification should not be predicated on currently available procedures.

The procedures which probably are sufficiently developed to consider as a potential basis for certification are those that focus on the skills of the teacher as evidenced in classroom settings. In essence, such procedures would be used to certify that the teacher engages in "good practice," i.e., professionally acceptable practice. Operationally, certification that a teacher engages in good practice would mean that the teacher had achieved the "performance" criterion previously designated as the target criterion among the second level payoffs. It is specifically to this criterion that Laboratory-Based Teacher Education is directed.

Laboratory-Based Teacher Education should rest on two different laboratories, one based in the training institution, a college or university, and the second based in the field. This division in laboratory sites follows a separation in the level of skills to be attained by the trainee. The separation is marked by the attainment of Criterion Level 4 (demonstration of a single skill under microteaching or simulated conditions) in the university-based laboratory, while Criterion Level 3 (demonstration of integrated skills over a period of time in a classroom setting) is to be attained in the field laboratory.

The university-based laboratory. To convert teacher education at the undergraduate level to a laboratory base, each course would be accompanied by a regular lab. For example, a three-semester-hour course in reading would be accompanied by a two-hour laboratory. The materials used in this laboratory would in all likelihood be both

Protocol and Training Materials since virtually all preparatory courses seek both concept development and skill development among their objectives. In many instances, combined sequences of Protocol and Training Materials would be necessary since some concepts lead directly into skill training.

The precise organization of both course laboratories should be left to the preparatory institution. The only restriction is that students emerging from the sequence would have to be capable of functioning at Criterion Level 3. Operationally, this means that at the minimum a student would have to be capable of demonstrating a set of skills. He would be permitted to demonstrate these skills one at a time or in related sets. He would not be required to demonstrate his skills in an integrated fashion before a regular classroom group. The areas in which these skills would presumably fall are those noted in the description of third-level payoffs in the first section of this paper.

The field-based laboratory. The notion of field-based laboratories differs from the notion of a Training Complex in several ways. First, the laboratory would represent a joint arrangement among universities and colleges, state departments of education, and individual teachers, with school systems involved at a policy (or giving permission) level, but not at a financial level. Second, the laboratories would be extensions of the university-based laboratories, not a separate institution. Third, certification would remain the joint venture of universities and state departments without the direct participation of school districts as units. To create such laboratories, a reasonably radical series of steps needs to be taken.

1. *Performance-based certification for master-supervisory teachers.* A major problem with both the Training Complex and the field laboratory is that both depend on highly skilled personnel to be drawn from a population subset of unknown magnitude. The general population of teachers from which the highly skilled group might be drawn is the stable core of teachers with roughly five to twenty years of experience. To determine which members of this pool are highly skilled, a separate, performance-based, state certification must be awarded. The group attempting to achieve this certificate is to be a self-selected group.

2. *Salary incentive for master-supervisory teachers.* Few teachers will opt for a certificate which does not bear a salary differential. Thus, the certificate in question must bear a differential, and the differential must be an adjusted one. In operation, two adjustments would be necessary. First the state, not the local school district, would adjust the salary of each Master proportionate to his base salary (salary schedule salary) directly from state funds. To be feasible, this proportion should probably be about 5 percent. Second,

Master Teachers in low-income schools in poverty communities should receive a second adjustment of approximately 5 percent awarded through federal subsidies to state. These two adjustments should create a differential of about 10 percent for Master Teachers in the poverty community and should be sufficient to encourage some migration of high quality teachers to these areas as well as retention of teachers already located in these communities.

3. *Certification by observation.* If Performance-Based Certification at Criterion Level 3 is to have meaning, award of this certificate could be made only after a systematic time-sampling of the classroom behavior of the teacher. This sampling could be done by video-tape, or it could be taken on a "live" basis. In either instance, judgments about the performance of the teacher must be based on standard instruments used by trained judges, probably university personnel.

Preservice field laboratory. Two uses should be made of the Master Teacher in the field laboratory at the undergraduate or Preliminary Certificate level.

1. *Pretraining and diagnostic semester.* The first contact between the Master Teacher and an undergraduate trainee should occur during either the first or second semester of the junior year in college. At this time the trainee should leave the college and enter the classroom of the Master Teacher to which he or she has been assigned. The role of the trainee would be essentially that of a paraprofessional. The role of the Master Teacher during this period would be (1) to acquaint the trainee with the range of tasks performed by the teacher, and (2) to identify those areas in which the trainee would clearly benefit from additional substantive knowledge, better development of concepts, and skill training; in short, to diagnose the areas to which the trainee should give attention. If the Master believed the trainee to be inadequate to the tasks of teaching, a recommendation for termination in the teacher-education curriculum should be made. Following this semester, the trainee, if continued, should return to the college or university and continue study, with continued skill and concept development in the university-based laboratory.

2. *Preliminary certification semester.* At the end of the fourth year of training or during the fifth year of training, the trainee should again enter the classroom of a Master Teacher for one semester. The role of the trainee at this time would be to assume the duties of a regular teacher, with the meaning of "regular" to be determined according to the type of instructional organization used by the Master Teacher. The role of the Master during this period would be to aid the training in finishing or integrating the skills at Criterion Level 3

and to certify whether or not the trainee had been successful in operating at this Criterion Level. Although certification would remain in the hands of the state and the colleges and universities, the recommendation of the Master Teacher would be required to issue the Preliminary Certificate.

In-service field laboratory. The development of the field laboratory at this level requires certain organizations and policies.

1. *Advanced skills summer training schools.* Most teachers cannot both devote adequate time to their teaching and effectively upgrade their skills. For practicing teachers, the summer should be used for advanced skill training.

For the development of advanced teaching skills, instruction in graduate education courses is not an adequate device. Such skills are highly complex and probably must be acquired through practice in actual school settings. Included among the skills might be those involved in flexible grouping, managing individualized instruction, utilizing an heuristic approach to teacher, conducting an "open" classroom effectively, diagnosing learning difficulties, and the like.

So that these skills can be acquired in school settings, summer training schools, centered primarily in schools serving low-income groups, should be organized. These schools should be staffed by Master Teachers, with an advisory board of college and university personnel specializing in the development of particular skills and financed directly by state funds with federal subsidization. The children in the schools should be drawn from low-income families.

2. *Restriction of population.* Because many teachers leave teaching during the first three years, only teachers with three or more years of experience would be permitted to enter the summer training school. This restriction is probably essential to obtain a favorable cost-benefit relationship.

3. *Focus on the master-supervisory certificate.* Although all qualified teachers who wish to enter the summer training school should be able to do so for purposes of improving their skills, the focus of this school should be on training teachers who aspire toward the Master-Supervisory Certificate. The school should not award this certificate, but it should train for it.

4. *Relationship of advanced skill training to graduate degree.* There should be no formal relationship between the Master-Supervisory Certificate and a Master's degree or other advanced degree. Nonetheless, teachers who wish to obtain the Master's degree should be encouraged to take an advanced skills practicum and might be required to do so in certain university programs. The university would continue to be the source of work in the subject fields and in conceptual or foundational areas of professional training. It would not

participate directly in the advanced skill training, however. This function would be left to the summer training school as the field laboratory at the graduate level.

Support mechanisms

One set of major support mechanisms necessary to the field-based laboratory and Performance-Based Certification are the instruments by means of which performance is judged at the Preliminary Certificate and at the Master-Supervisory Certificate levels. The development of quality instruments requires the participation of personnel on a nation-wide basis and should be nationally supported. Development of such instruments should be on a project basis.

The development of a national confirmatory feedback system, as proposed in the preceding paper, is probably not a necessary system and probably would have a poorer cost-benefit ratio than locally controlled systems based on nationally developed instruments. Research relating teacher performance to pupil performance, and the development of procedures useful at some future time for certifying teachers on the basis of pupil performance, should be placed on a project basis.

A second set of support mechanisms for the field-based laboratory are Protocol and Training Materials. For the immediate future, the development of prototypic materials, and the development of guidelines for developing and field-testing such materials should continue on a nationwide basis. In three to five years, however, serious consideration should be given to (1) shifting materials development to local laboratories or (2) the preparation of completely packaged laboratory units for use in colleges and universities or (3) both.

Funding patterns and speculation on costs

Beginning with the funding pattern suggested earlier in Table 8–1, the resolution of a final (suggested) funding pattern requires taking the mechanisms suggested in the preceding section, and the time required for their development, into account. These mechanisms are summarized below. Subsequently they are placed in a second table (Table 8–2) and speculations about costs made. The cost speculations are based on the assumption that from $10 million to $20 million per year would be available.

Alternative secondary schools

The assumption is that such schools would be funded from state and local tax dollars, but that federal support would be offered for the training of personnel to staff the schools.

TABLE 8–2.

Year	*Preschool, Primary*	*Middle School*	*Secondary School*	*Support Systems*	*Certification and Salary Subsidy*
1972–73	Lab.-based curriculum 2.0 mil.	Lab.-based curriculum 1.0 mil.	Training alt. schools 2.0 mil.	Protocol and Training Mat. 4.0 mil. Instrument development 1.0 mil.	0.5 mil.
1973–74	Lab.-based curriculum 3.0 mil.	Lab.-based curriculum 1.5 mil.	Training alt. schools 3.0 mil.	Protocol and Training Mat. 4.0 mil. Instrument development 2.0 mil.	0.5 mil.
1974–75	Lab.-based curriculum 3.0 mil.	Lab.-based curriculum 2.0 mil.	Training alt. schools 4.0 mil. Lab.-based curriculum 1.0 mil.	Protocol and Training Mat. 1.0 mil. Lab. packages 2.0 mil. Instructional development 1.0 mil.	2.0 mil.

TABLE 8–2 (Cont.)

Year	*Preschool, Primary*	*Middle School*	*Secondary School*	*Support Systems*	*Certification and Salary Subsidy*
1975–76	Lab.-based curriculum 3.5 mil.	Lab.-based curriculum 3.0 mil.	Training alt. schools 3.0 mil.	Lab. packages 3.0 mil.	4.0 mil.
			Lab.-based curriculum 2.0 mil.	Training school feasibility 0.5 mil.	
1976–77	Lab.-based curriculum 2.5 mil.	Lab.-based curriculum 2.0 mil.	Training alt. schools 2.0 mil.	Lab. packages 3.0 mil.	6.0 mil.
			Lab.-based curriculum 3.0 mil.	Training school feasibility 0.5 mil.	

University-based laboratory

The assumption is that the preservice curriculum in teacher-education institutions would be converted to a laboratory base.

Field based laboratory

From the viewpoint of federal funding, the field-based laboratory has three potential costs.

1. Certification costs attendant to the Master-Supervisory Certificate. Instrument development, observer training, and the actual procedures for certifying in specific states must be included in these costs.
2. Salary subsidy. The salaries of Master Teachers in low-income schools would be subsidized. Probably not more than 20 percent of the population of teachers would hold the Master Certificate. About half of these would be expected to be in low-income areas.
3. Summer Training School. This mechanism should become operational only if the Master Certificate becomes operational. It is a very long-range mechanism.

Protocol and Training Materials

These Materials are viewed as the supporting materials for the university-based labs. In the long run they would be converted into a more nearly integrated set of materials labeled the *laboratory package*.

REFERENCES

1. BACKMAN, MARGARET E. "Patterns of Mental Abilities: Ethnic, Socioeconomic, and Sex Differences." *American Educational Research Journal* 9 (Winter 1972): 1–12.
2. BLOOM, BENJAMIN. *Stability and Change in Human Characteristics.* New York: Wiley, 1964.
3. BURDIN, JOEL L., AND LANZILLOTI, KALIOPEE (eds.). *A Reader's Guide to the Comprehensive Models for Preparing Elementary Teachers.* Washington, D.C.: ERIC Clearinghouse on Teacher Education and AACTE, 1969.
4. LEVIN, HENRY M. et al. "School Achievement and Post-school Success: A Review." *Review of Educational Research* 41 (February 1971):1–16.
5. SMITH, B. O., in collaboration with Saul B. Cohen and Arthur Pearl. *Teachers for the Real World.* Washington, D.C.: AACTE, 1969.

6. Smith, B. O. *Research in Teacher Education: A Symposium.* Englewood Cliffs, N.J.: Prentice Hall, 1971.

7. Turner, R. I. *Differential Association of Elementary School Teacher Characteristics with School System Types.* Final Report, USOE, CRP No. 2579, 1968.

APPENDIX A

Description of the Five Programs[1]

Training complex

The Training Complex is an institution to facilitate cooperation between schools, other human service agencies, universities and colleges, and communities in improving the preservice and in-service training of education and other human services personnel. The Training Complex has a clearly defined training mission. This training is aimed at the development of complex integrated skills appropriate for teaching and other human services in education and other social service settings. The function of the Training Complex is to provide an opportunity for preservice and in-service teacher training to be conducted in a variety of settings. Another function is the training of individuals for a new or second career, in education or other human services, building upon or extending competencies and skills individuals already have. Features which distinguish the Training Complex from other institutions include:

1. Establishment of training as the primary mission of the Training Complex.
2. Provision for the active participation by all those concerned in decision making regarding the training of educational personnel, at a policy level.
3. Access to the resources of the school, university, and community agencies to facilitate the efforts of the Training Complex.
4. Greater flexibility in employing and utilizing personnel from a variety of backgrounds, with or without the credentials applicable to specific institutions.

[1] These descriptions were prepared as working definitions by the Committee in April, 1971.

The Training Complex will be flexible in developing needed training services, varying in specific character according to the region and educational environment in which it exists. It could be established on "neutral ground" or at one of the cooperating institutions. The Training Complex could be funded federally, by drawing on the funds of the cooperating institutions, or both.

Models for Elementary Teacher-Education Programs

The Models for Elementary Teacher-Education Programs are descriptions of teacher-education programs which have been developed in considerable detail. They are an attempt to approach the description of teacher education from a logical, systematic analysis of the total program.

Ten "Models" or descriptions of elementary teacher-education programs have been developed. While the Models differ in various approaches to the problems of setting instructional goals, overall program organization, curriculum design, institutional relationships, and specific innovations, they share some common features. The features which distinguish the Models from other descriptions or definitions of teacher-education programs include:

1. Greater individualization and personalization of the teacher-education curriculum.
2. Orientation toward confirmation—teacher-education programs are designed against a clear statement of goals or performance.
3. Decision making on the basis of data—once a program is established, data is collected and used for decisions on revision and improvement.
4. Monitoring of human and other instructional resources so that thay are available to students as required—management and scheduling of resources.
5. Provision for breaking down the current course structure of teacher-education programs, and placing teacher education on a noncourse, e.g., module, basis.

An essential aspect of the systems approach is considering the teacher-education program as in a continual state of development—as a process—with provisions being made for the cycle of: decision—feedback from data collected on the program—revision of the program. The cycle for decision making also means that the Models are "data-based"—data must be collected in sufficient detail for decisions to be made. This includes data on the students as they progress through the instructional units of the program, characteristics of students on entering and leaving the program, and data to manage the scheduling of students as they go through the program. The emphasis on data collection also points to the potential of the Model Programs for answering questions about the education of teachers. The Models are researchable programs.

Performance-Based Certification

Performance-Based Certification is intended to make explicit what teachers know and can do (their skills) or achieve when they leave a program of teacher training. It has been argued that the adoption of a performance base for teacher certification would enhance the credibility of the certification process, strengthen teaching as a profession, and improve the quality of education in the schools. The performance-based approach also would make explicit to the public the skills and knowledge which teachers are expected to possess. Two features of the Performance-Based Certification approach seem to stand out. Performance-Based Certification would require the certification agency:

1. To ensure the explication of the nature of the performance standards which must be met for each type of certificate.
2. To ensure the setting forth of the mechanisms or procedures by which specific performance standards will be established and judged (assessed).

The explication of the nature of the performance standards means that what might be called the *level* of performance standards has to be decided. The level of performance standard required might vary with different certification agencies, from *knowledge* of concepts or specific practices, to demonstration of *skills* in laboratory or practice settings, to *demonstrated effectiveness* in a classroom, i.e., producing stated changes in pupil behavior. Different levels of inference to the ultimate setting of teaching in a particular school context with specific children are apparent in these of performance standards. The inference to on-the-job effetciveness is greatest from the *knowledge* level; somewhat less from the *skill* level; and perhaps least from the *demonstrated effectiveness* level.

The decision about the level of performance standards is a critical one and has implications for the second feature, setting the procedures to establish specific performance standards and the methods of assessment. Setting the specific performance standards would force the criteria for certification to be made public and would also have considerable impact on teacher-education programs. The requirement of setting specific standards would encourage the teacher-education institutions to train teachers to pass these performance standards, and would be a mechanism to effect change in teacher education. The training institution would have to be explicit, also, about the knowledge and skills that it has in its curriculum for preparing teachers.

Protocol Materials

Protocol Materials are instructional materials that lead to efficient mastery of concepts. The basis of the instructional materials are "Protocols," which are reproductions (audiovisual) of behavior that provide the means of learning concepts important in teaching and learning. The Protocol Materials enable the preservice in-service teacher to study concepts that are educationally significant. Mastery of the concepts in the Protocol Materials means development of the ability to identify the concept in simulated or real-life settings. The Protocols and accompanying instructional materials are developed to be widely distributed and used in any program of teacher education. The features which appear to distinguish protocol instructional materials from other instructional materials are that they enable the student:

1. To identify the concept in simulated or real-life settings.
2. To relate the concept to other concepts.
3. To use the concept in interpreting behavior in teaching/learning contexts.

An important aspect of the protocol instructional materials is that they emphasize that those concepts acquired have real-life reference. In this sense they are analogous to "Protocols" as used in clinical settings: transcripts or reproductions of actual behaviors are studied to understand behavior.

The ultimate purpose of Protocol Materials is to facilitate interpretive competencies in teachers. The concepts which may facilitate interpretation of classroom behavior will be drawn from disciplines related to problems of understanding behavior, such as psychology, anthropology, sociology, and philosophy. Terms such as *self-concept, aggression, reinforcement, culture, role,* and so on designate concepts that teachers can use to interpret behavior. To interpret, however, is not to treat. The development of skills to deal with behavior in given contexts is the function of Training Materials.

Training materials

Training Materials are instructional materials which lead to the efficient mastery of skills. They provide for the identification of skills, description of situations in which they are to be practiced, description of the performance the skills entail, and ways of giving feedback to the student on his performance. The Materials help the student identify his mistakes and see how to correct them. The fundamental purpose is the development of skills through practice and feedback. The features which appear to distinguish training instructional materials from other instructional materials are that they enable the student:

1. To identify the skill in use.
2. To perform the component parts of the skill.
3. To exercise the skill under laboratory or simulated conditions.

Skill in the performance of such abilities as questioning, probing, performing reinforcement operations, performing in and with small and large groups, evaluating student achievement, and so on would be developed through Training Materials. In training, it is the student's behavior that will be observed, analyzed, and modified. Elements essential to the Training Materials include specification of the behavior, performance, feedback, and modification of performance in a continual process until successful performance is attained.

APPENDIX B

Educational Specialty Boards

Myron Lieberman

This memorandum proposes the establishment of a system of extra-legal teacher certification tentatively entitled "Educational Specialty Boards." These boards, broadly based in governance, would certify teachers as possessing a superior level of professional skill and competence. Although such boards would be valuable for many reasons, they will be discussed here largely in terms of their potential for advancing the concept of Performance-Based Certification and for improving the quality of teacher education generally.

First, it should be noted that extralegal certification is a common practice outside the field of education. For example, in the field of medicine there are about twenty medical specialty boards. These medical specialty boards certify physicians in such fields as surgery, internal medicine, radiology, and dermatology to cite just a few. The diplomat of the American Psychological Association reflects the concept of extra-legal certification in the field of psychology. The distinction between CPAs and accountants is also suggestive, although CPA examinations are administered through state agencies.

In education, certification by an Educational Specialty Board would not be required for a regular teaching certificate. Specialty board certification should be accepted automatically as meeting the requirements for a regular certificate in any state, but this will require understanding and cooperation of the state certification agencies. Presumably, they would not want to be in the potentially embarrassing position of denying a regular teaching certificate to someone designated as a superior teacher by an agency under the auspices of leading national educational organizations.

In any case, one advantage of Educational Specialty Boards is that they would not require any change in state certification procedures. This is extremely important. The movement toward Performance-Based Certification involves many difficult problems. Before such a drastic change is applied to the regular certificates, it would be extremely helpful to have some broad, firsthand experience with the process of Performance-Based Certification. Extralegal certification can provide that experience in a meaningful way while avoiding controversy over existing certification requirements.

Another advantage of utilizing extralegal certification as an alternative route toward Performance-Based Certification is that the number of teachers involved would be manageable. For this reason, the Performance-Based Criteria could be more intensively applied and evaluated. This memorandum does not take a position with respect to the proportion of teachers in any given field who should be board certified after the boards are fully operational. This is a policy issue to be resolved initially with representatives of appropriate organizations in the development process.

Moreover, the subject-matter specialists will have to develop the standards for superior skill and knowledge in the subject-matter fields. A third advantage, therefore, is that extralegal certification would clearly constitute a unique opportunity for experts in arts and sciences and in pedagogy to work together to improve teacher education. Furthermore, experience in other fields suggests that representation from employer groups is helpful to prevent the lowering of standards of board certification, as it is extended to new fields of specialization. For this reason, it would be desirable to have representation from such organizations as the National Boards Association on the advisory group responsible for the development of the various Specialty Boards. It would also be desirable to have representation from agencies or organizations involved in civil rights and equal opportunity to keep the focus of the Specialty Boards on public rather than professional interests and to encourage the acceptance of board certificates by the community at large. At the present time, certification and licensing procedures are under widespread legal attack for their tendency to reflect the interests of the occupational group rather than the public. The introduction of new certification procedures should take careful account of the valid criticisms of existing certification procedures.

Ideally, professors of methods and materials and supervisors in the public schools would be "board certified." It may be feasible to think of two levels, as in the field of medicine. Physicians are first required to pass an examination procedure which renders them "board eligible"; then, upon completion of all the requirements, they become "board certified." Regardless of whether there are one or two levels, however, the fact that the procedures are under the auspices of national organizations is extremely significant. For one thing, it means that the successful applicant (that is, the board-certified teacher) will be able to get additional compensation wherever he goes. This is a very important inducement for teachers to apply for and prepare themselves for the board examinations. In this connection, it is expected that teachers will pay for their board examinations inasmuch as the rewards for becoming board certified will make such payment worthwhile. The same practical logic underlies the willingness of accountants to become CPA's or of physicians to become board certified in the various medical fields. The basic issue is public and professional confidence that the designation "board certified" actually reflects a superior level of professional skill and competence.

The value of such board certification to institutions of higher education and to school districts should also be noted. Instead of relying upon letters of recommendation, often from unknown sources with varying standards, institutions and school systems would now have a reliable way of identifying superior individuals who can work with new and inexperienced teachers, or with student teachers. For example, a high school science department which finds itself without a strong, experienced teacher or supervisor would be in a much better position to employ one if board certification were in operation. By the same token, a college of education looking for outstanding individuals to teach the methods and materials courses could also look for board-certified professionals to meet their needs.

Note also that Educational Specialty Boards would avoid the historic objections to merit pay by teacher organizations. Under Educational Specialty Boards, the designation of who is board certified would not be made locally; the local employer would not be involved in board certification procedures. For this reason, there would be no employer favoritism or subjectivity involved. Another important point is that the national organization of teachers (NEA and AFT) would be deeply involved in the research and development effort to establish various Specialty Boards. These organizations should have representation on the national advisory bodies and would be in a good position to monitor the development of the boards. At the local level, the teacher organizations could bargain for the differentials for board-certified teachers in the same way that they now bargain for differentials for advanced degrees.

The crucial point for teacher education is that the highest levels of skill and knowledge about teaching could be built into the board examination. Significant research carrying implications for teacher training could be incorporated immediately into the Specialty Board examinations. This flexibility provides enormous leverage in upgrading the quality of teacher education. If, for example, a superior elementary teacher should know how to diagnose and prescribe for certain reading difficulties, the board examinations can test the teacher's ability to make the diagnosis and prescribe for it—not on paper with pencil, but with actual students. If a research study justifies a change in what a superior teacher should know, or be able to do, there is no need to wait upon the legal machinery of state certification to give force and effect to the change.

It is crucially important to recognize the potential value of Educational Specialty Boards to state certification agencies. The boards would provide valuable feedback on all aspects of teacher education and certification. For example, they would provide data on the costs and technical feasibility of various Performance-Based Criteria for certification. They would develop a pool of examiners capable of implementing Performance-Based Certification for the regular certificate. They would or could provide valuable data on levels of subject-matter competence and of competence in dealing with guidance agencies, parents, and so on.

How could Educational Specialty Boards be initiated? Funds from OE and/or private foundations would have to be made available to an appropriate agency tentatively labeled the Educational Specialty Board Commission. The commission would develop board procedures and examinations for a new fields. Position papers would be drafted on eligibility requirements, the content of examinations, cutoff points, costs, opportunities to retake the examinations, the duration of certificates, the location of the examinations, and so on. These position papers should be reviewed and discussed by the commission with the persons who prepared the papers. Unquestionably, some attention should be given to the problems of extralegal certification, especially of evaluating professional performance, in other fields. As various issues are discussed, analyzed, and tentatively resolved, an outline of board procedures in a few prototype fields should emerge. It would probably then be necessary to field test the tentative board procedures, perhaps several times under various conditions. After such field testing, the first few boards should be ready to operate, with meetings and conferences scheduled to generate interest and support. Initially, financial incentives might be needed to encourage applicants and establish the board certificates.

Perhaps the single most important point is that these boards offer a way to move ahead quickly on a national front to implement Performance-Based Certification. The research and demonstration value and leverage of this approach should be enormous and should permeate all teacher education within a relatively short time.

APPENDIX C

The Role of the Disciplines in the Training of Teachers in the 1970s

Alan C. Purves

This paper comments on the role of the subject-matter disciplines in the training of teachers in the 1970s, with particular emphasis on the development of five activities: Protocol Materials, Training Materials, Teacher Training Complexes, the Models for the Training of Elementary School Teachers, and Performance-Based Criteria for the certification of teachers.

It might be said that in the 1960s two strong impulses governed the training of teachers. The first, in part resulting from the writings of Conant, who decried a lack of subject matter in the schools, and Bruner, who set forth the idea that the methodology of a discipline could be taught at any level in the development of a child, led to increased attention to subject matter both in curriculum development and in teacher training. There was a burgeoning of curricula in mathematics, the sciences, English and the arts and humanities, and social studies. There was a spate of summer institutes, experienced-teacher fellowship programs, and preservice training programs, all of which focused on the subject matter of the disciplines. Concurrently as a result of the work of such men as Smith, Bellack, and Gage there came to be a great deal of research and curriculum development related to the science of teaching. The thrust of this work was curiously abetted by the writings of the "romantic critics" of education—Kohl, Kozol, and others—who saw the importance of teacher attitude and student-teacher relationships in promoting learning, and who preached an "art" of teaching.

Toward the end of the 1960s these two thrusts could well have produced a wider gap between the subject-matter disciplines and the schools of pedagogy than had existed before the beginning of the decade, were it not for the emergence of some programs like that for the training of teacher-trainers (TTT), a program specifically designed to bring subject matter and pedagogy together. In many of the projects sponsored under TTT, the fusion of subject matter and pedagogy has had enormous effect on the university departments involved and, even more spectacularly, on the students in the schools.

The effect of the TTT program has yet to be fully felt, however, and, as those responsible for teacher education plan ahead, it would seem important for that effect not to be lost. While the titles of the five activities might indicate that each could be entirely pedagogically oriented, the contribution of the disciplines is crucial to the success of the activities in achieving their goals. Each of the five activities is addressed separately below.

Protocol Materials

Protocol Materials are intended to be examples of "real" behavior of people in the various roles they play in education (as student, teacher, administrator, parent, citizen, and so forth), presented to allow prospective teachers to see operating in that behavior certain specified concepts. The concepts might be related to pedagogy, social psychology, various subject matters, or other ways of perceiving and thinking about the education complex. Materials related to the various subject matters have existed for a long time; they are the base from which the disciplines have emerged. The concepts of language have emerged from analysis and interpretation of what people have said or written; those of literature from examination of literary texts; those of physics from examination of certain natural phenomena; and those of history from examination of the actions of individuals and of nations. The need for new Protocol Materials in the disciplines is limited save in a few areas. There needs to be some material which allows prospective teachers to develop the ability to analyze and interpret the behaviors that we have come to call "critical" or "scientific" or "historical" or the like as those behaviors are manifested in children. Prospective teachers see adults–their teachers–behaving like physicists, but they seldom see when children are behaving similarly. They need to learn how to do so.

This role of subject matter in the development of Protocol Materials is important but less crucial than the role subject matter can play in the development of Protocol Materials in pedagogy and the social sciences related to pedagogy. In those materials, the behavior manifested is usually that of a teacher teaching students. More often than not, there is a lesson in some content area (for example, reading, mathematics, or social studies). Since these materials present the behavior through film or video-tape, there is a high degree of verisimilitude that engages the attention of the viewer. The viewer is asked not to react emotionally or evaluatively, but analytically and dispassionately; and he is asked to focus his attention on the form, that is to say the teaching behavior, in the material. By consciously paying little attention to the *content* of the teaching, the viewer may well tend to assume that the content is acceptable. In many Protocol Materials such may not be the case. Similarly, in those Protocol Materials that seek to provide data for analysis of behavior in the content areas, the teaching strategy may be unacceptable and neglected in the analysis.

If this is the case, it is crucial that any Protocol Material be rigidly scrutinized for the conceptual adequacy of the *content* of the lesson by a subject-matter specialist, and the *form and technique* of the lesson by a specialist in psychology and pedagogy. Not to do so is to run the risk that the Materials intended for analysis may inadvertently act as the wrong model for future behavior.

Training Materials

What has been said above applies even more importantly to those materials that are specifically designed to show students what to do when they teach. Teaching should not be analyzed and defined in a fashion that abstracts teaching from the thing taught. Even Training Material that isolates a particular form of teacher-student interaction will show a teacher and a student interacting *about* some content. The presentation of that content must be intellectually sound according to the best thinking of the discipline that treats it as subject matter. A training film may portray a beautiful relationship between student and teacher, one that seems to illustrate the best facilitation of learning. The whole thrust of the training film is vitiated if one sees the student learning that there was no black culture before 1954. Such an example is blatant, of course, but subtler errors, misapplications of theory, or discarded notions are even more pernicious than such a blatant falsehood. It is to prevent those subtle errors that provision for subject-matter specialists to help conceive and review the Training Materials seems hardly a luxury, but a necessity.

Teacher-Training Complexes

As the term *complex* implies, these new institutions would bring together the schools, the colleges of education, the communities, and the subject-matter discipline in a new confederation in order to make the training of prospective teachers more adequate to the situations they will face once they are actively engaged in their profession. It goes without saying that there is an important place for the disciplines in these Complexes, but to let the matter drop there is to perpetuate a problem that has long plagued the teacher trainer. It is true that there is subject matter in the schools and in the arts and sciences colleges of the universities. However, to infer that the two aspects of subject matter are the same can be risky. Literature in the schools might be said to be the object of critical attention; in the universities, of historical attention. Or to take grammar as an example, an important function of the schools is to insure that children employ the grammatical richness of the language in communicating in speech or in writing with other people. In the university the emphasis might better be placed on the analysis of grammar and language systems as a disciplined form of inquiry. The function of that analysis might well be to enable the teacher in the school to understand better what his students are doing.

The difference in function and approach to subject matter that separates general from special education may also separate scholarly from pedagogical education. It may be useful for certain kinds of students to be able to perform the functions of the textual editor or the descriptive bibliographer; it would seem more useful for the prospective teacher to be able to perform a content analysis of textbooks in order to discern critical biases.

All the disciplines are so wide and complexly structured that it is necessary for the establishers of a Training Complex to determine what aspects of each discipline are most useful to the prospective teacher. In English, for example, it would seem that psycholinguistics and sociolinguistics are more useful than is philology. Further, it would seem that courses dealing in analysis of the concepts and procedures of the disciplines are of greater use to the prospective teacher than are courses which simply present the results of those procedures and the scattered details with which those concepts deal. To this end the disciplines must contribute in the planning of the program of the Complex, but must, in turn, be required to examine their premises, procedures, and conceptual bases.

As a result of such examination, there should emerge a program for prospective teachers which will provide a sense of the conceptual bases of the discipline, the power and limitation of that discipline as a means of knowing, the basic procedures of that discipline, and, finally, how that discipline might be made available to children of various ages. In literature, for example, we might say that three of the basic concepts of the literary work are voice, metaphor, and form. These concepts tell a great deal about the aesthetics of a work, but little about the human significance of the work. Critics operate through language to lay forth these three concepts as they operate in specific literary works. These concepts may be made apparent to young children through such devices as role playing, word games, and examination of the formal elements of comic strips and children's stories.

It is essential, therefore, that scholars in the disciplines, particularly those scholars who have a commitment to general education and therefore to teacher training, be a part of the curriculum planning process in a Training Complex. These scholars must, however, be asked to confront people from the pedagogical fields and from the schools, and particularly people from the community, in order to assure that their conceptions will meet the read needs of school children and society. They must be asked to justify the discipline and the selection of concepts in the discipline in terms of the real world. Once they have held themselves accountable in this way, then, and only then, should they proceed to planning the training of teachers.

Elementary Models

The Elementary Models proposed seek to create a structure for the total education of elementary school teachers. From the summaries[1] it would seem that the Models are formal arrangements of the components of a teacher-education program and are concerned with the relationships of the various parts of a program to each other, whether those relationships be structural or sequential. An obvious feature of these Models is the specification of goals of the program and clarification of the roles of the various decision-making groups.

As a member of one of these decision-making groups, one is impressed by the artfulness and clarity of many of the Models, but remains wary of the series of empty boxes on the various organizational charts, boxes labelled "subject-matter instruction," or "educational objectives." The Models are beautiful buildings, but at this point no one seems to inhabit them. As they become inhabited, there must be close scrutiny of the content to insure conceptual adequacy and efficacy. As with the Teacher Training Complexes, these Models must be scrutinized not only for the interrelation of structural components but also the content that is being taught. In the basic subjects—language arts, mathematics, social sciences, natural sciences, and arts—the elementary years are crucial to the future development of the individual. The teachers that these Models produce must know what they are doing in each of those basic subjects when they are presenting them to children or facilitating the development of the chil-

[1] J. Klatt and W. LeBaron, *A Short Summary of Ten Model Teacher Education Programs.* (Washington: National Center for Educational Research and Development, Office of Education, 1969); and the articles comprising Volume 3, Number 3 (Spring, 1970), *Journal of Research and Development in Education.*

dren's skills in each of the areas. It is urgent that the content of these models be as elaborately worked out as the organization.

Performance-based certification of teachers

This last activity seems to be the one that sums up the other four activities. It represents a call to make professional training of teachers comparable to the professional training of doctors, dentists, and architects. The qualifications of an individual will depend upon what he does as judged by other members of his profession, not simply upon whether or not he has been in a certain number of classrooms. The Elementary Models, Training Complex, and Protocol and Training Materials all provide ways to enable prospective teachers to gain and demonstrate their professional competence.

The import of this activity is to force the teacher trainer, whether in the traditional disciplines or in the pedagogical fields, to think—or rather to rethink—what it is that he has been doing. It forces him to focus not merely on the history or taxonomy of his field, but also on the skills, concepts, and procedures a person must master if he is to be certified as a teacher. This is a radical rethinking of the disciplines and a rethinking that is long overdue.

To say this is not to overlook the many pitfalls that await the person who devises performance criteria. To think of a discipline in terms of performance is to relate behaviors to specific aspects of the subject matter, aspects which occur in a context. "A student demonstrates his understanding *of* irony *in* a column by Art Buchwald." Such a statement forms an infinitesimal part of the language arts, and one could generate objectives like this in the billions. There must be both a grouping of these objectives into some conceptual scheme, and a selecting of those groups that are most pertinent to the teaching situation and most respectful of the conceptual framework of the discipline.

In English, such action has already been undertaken by the Illinois Statewide Curriculum for the Preparation of English Teachers (ISCPET). The performance objectives in the report of that project are a base for the development of any Performance-Based Criteria for the certification of secondary English teachers. It may be that they should be modified; certainly they need to be expanded and made more specific, but they represent an important start, one undertaken by the joint efforts of those in English and those in pedagogy. It would seem important that similar steps be undertaken in other disciplines.

The second major pitfall is that related to evaluation. Just as the selection of objectives runs the risk of trivialization of the discipline, the demand for certain kinds of qualification can reduce the evaluators to thinking only in terms of standard test scores and the like. In setting forth criteria, the representatives of the disciplines and the evaluation staffs must strain their imaginations to the utmost to develop observational techniques, questionnaires, attitude scales, and other measures perhaps not yet conceived to certify that the objectives have been met. The recent trends in evaluation give hope that such can be done; there must be full partnership between the disciplines and the evaluation staffs.

Summary

Two threads are apparent throughout all these comments: partnership and performance. There must, it seems, be a partnership of the subject-matter disciplines and the pedagogical disciplines; neither can effect the training of teachers alone. Such a partnership means that the subject-matter component and the pedagogical component cannot be related to consecutive parts of the students' training (e.g., a fifth year in pedagogy or a fifth year in subect matter). There must be integration throughout the whole of preprofessional training. Whether it be in the planning of models of training, setting forth of criteria, or development of materials for analysis or training, the two components must inform, test, and harmonize with each other.

To do this, both must look at what they do and what they want the trainee to do. They must examine the performance of professionals and determine the concepts underlying that performance. They must look at the behavior of people in the real world so as to influence the training of teachers for the real world. Performance has a form, how one does things, and a content, what one does. For a purpose of analysis form and content can be separated, but in performance they cannot. Performance must be analyzed so that the performer can be trained, and the performer must learn about both form and content. Performance in education deals with people teaching or learning something. The disciplines tell us about the something; pedagogy and psychology tell us about teaching and learning; both must help the student become a performing teacher.

APPENDIX D

Summary of the Review of Committee Papers

Carol K. Tittle

Additional perspective on the program proposals developed by committee members was provided by a group of external reviewers. Abstracts of the proposed programs were sent on May 20, 1971, to a number of individuals knowledgeable about and concerned with the problems of teacher education. A copy of the abstracts is presented at the end of this summary section (see pages 238–248).

The group of reviewers was assembled from names suggested by committee members, as well as by staff of the Bureau of Educational Personnel Development. The group of reviewers represented community groups, school administrators and teachers, critics of teacher education, associations for professional groups in education, and university faculty and administrators—both in education and the liberal arts. The distribution in Table D–1 shows the groups repre-

TABLE D–1. Distribution of external reviewers

Group	*Mailed Number*	*Returned Number*
Institutions of Higher Education		
Education Deans/Faculty	27	14
Liberal Arts	7	1
State Education Departments	3	3
School Superintendents	10	7
Teachers/Professional Associations	4	2
Teacher Education Associations	6	4
Community Organizations/Critics	8	2
Other Education Groups (R&D Centers, Regional Laboratories)	5	5
Total	70	38

sented. A total of seventy abstracts were mailed, and thirty-eight individuals responded (54 percent returned comments).

Three sets of comments were received: (1) ratings of a number of ideas in the committee papers; (2) comments on the most useful and least useful aspects of each proposed program; and (3) suggestions for ideas which reviewers felt were overlooked in the committee's papers. It should be noted that these comments were based on *abstracts* of the papers as they had been developed by the middle of May. Individual committee members have revised or developed new papers since that date. The comments served, therefore, to guide the revisions of preliminary papers and to provide a partial framework by which to assess the recommendations contained in the final report.

The summary below takes into account the revisions, or new papers, prepared by committee members and is intended to represent the pros and cons of the main ideas reflected in the papers which are presented in the appendixes to the final report.

Ratings of major ideas

A number of items were rated for their potential utility in the redesign of teacher-education programs. The raters were to take into account the usefulness of the items as they related to a major goal of the Office of Education: to improve the quality of education for disadvantaged minority, racial, and ethnic groups. Items were rated on a scale from *one* (critical item; must be taken into account in designing teacher-education programs) to *five* (of little or no interest for redesigning teacher education). The ratings for each item are given in Table D–2.

Items which were rated as critical (given a rating of *one* or *two* by 80 percent of the group responding were:

#3 Establish Performance-Based Teacher-Education Programs.
#9 Develop measuring "instruments"—knowledge/skills/observation of teaching behavior.
#23 Personalize or individualize teacher training program.

The high ratings for two of the items, performance-based teacher education and development of measuring "instruments," are emphasized in the committee recommendations for a program of Competency-Based Teacher Education and a project proposed to develop instruments for Competency-Based Teacher Education and Certification. The emphasis on personalization/individualization is a general goal for education, and is well discussed in two committee papers. (See Chapters 4 and 6 by M. Vere DeVault and Mary Golladay, and H. Del Schalock.)

A second group of items were rated as critical by at least 60 percent of the individuals responding:

#1 Establish a parity group for policy making.
#5 Use Training Materials.
#8 Develop a data-based feedback system for performance following training.
#10 Establish Training Complexes, consortium training centers, parity-based teacher centers.
#22 Recruit students and adults from minority groups.

Two of these items are reflected specifically in the committee recommendations: Training Materials and organizational structures for teacher training. A third, the data-based feedback system, is encompassed in the provision for recording trainee performance and evaluation by teacher trainers, in the development of instruments for use in classroom and simulated practice settings, and in the evaluation program for the centers for teacher training. The concept of a parity group for policy making is not specifically mentioned in committee recommendations, but is discussed in the chapters by Benjamin Rosner and H. Del Schalock. "Parity" is a policy issue which could be included in guidelines for project funding. Recruitment from minority groups is not discussed directly, but it is also a general policy which could be given priority in most in-service or preservice teacher-education programs and implemented through project guidelines.

The remainder of the items were given ratings of *one* or *two* by fewer than 60 percent of the group. One item, "Establish extralegal certification systems," was rated as critical by less than 40 percent of the group, and yet is one of the committee recommendations. The rationale for extending the career line of teachers through Educational Specialty Boards, working outside a state framework, is given in the text of the final report and in the paper by Myron Lieberman (Appendix B).

Comments on proposals

Reviewers were asked to comment on the aspects of each proposal which they thought most useful for reform and on the elements in each which they found less desirable. The main points mentioned for each abstract are summarized below.

A five-year goal for Training Complexes

A major feature of this proposal was the use of the concept of "neutral ground" to mean interdependence; reviewers favored the concept of essentially "forcing" the necessary partnership or closer integration of schools and universities and the involvement of community and industry. When narrowly interpreted as building new institutions, many reviewers were skeptical of the possibility and preferred to change the present institutions involved in teacher education. The sequential exposure of students to the education professions and the gradual induction to teaching were considered strong features.

Another set of comments considered the separation of the theoretical (university) and practical learning experiences of students to be a weakness. The concept of the Educational Service District was considered premature, in view of the present stage of knowledge in teacher training, and the ESD was seen as potentially bureaucratic in character. The number of Training Complexes proposed for development in a five-year period was seen as unrealistic; competent personnel would not be available to staff the Training Complexes.

A master program for reform in teacher education

Strong features of the program were the emphasis on teacher competencies and the development of Protocol and Training Materials. The capacity for schools to identify the performance they seek in teachers and the option for students in the program to identify the types of competency they wanted to develop were considered positive features of the program. The research potentiality of the system and the idea of a dynamic, continuously evolving, and evaluated model were also identified as strong features of the program.

The reliance on a systems approach was received positively by some reviewers and less favorably by others. Some reviewers questioned the suggestion of a central policy committee and suggested a stronger emphasis on local needs. A weakness of committees was noted as the amount of time members would have, and a strong staff was suggested as a necessary condition for program development.

Levers for change in teacher education

The description of sources of power for improvement of teacher education was seen as a valuable analysis. Cooperation between school and university staff in training and curriculum efforts, the concept of parity-based governance, and transcripts with competency profiles were seen as useful aspects of the proposal. There was considerable agreement that changes in teacher education must be accompanied by other changes, such as curricula in the schools.

The proposed split of university faculty into two groups—foundations at the university and clinical in training schools—was regarded as undesirable by a number of reviewers. It was suggested that the two groups must work together throughout the teacher-education program. The idea of two entry points into the profession—paraprofessional and undergraduate—was considered unnecessarily restrictive. The extralegal certification of teachers trainers to extend the career line for teachers received both positive and negative comments. Several reviewers suggested that this certification should be done within the "legal" (state) framework. Some reviewers commented that the proposed rotation of faculty to develop training schools was unrealistic.

BEPD, NCERD, and teacher education that makes a difference

The statement of basic guidelines for Educational Personnel Development Programs was endorsed by many reviewers. The statement included a field-centered, personalized, and Performance-Based Teacher-Education Program; a broad base for decision-making; evaluation data; and a research orientation. Some reviewers questioned certification at the "product" level, i.e., teacher behaviors must result in specified learning outcomes for children.

The idea of a statewide network of centers, established on a cost-sharing basis, received both positive and negative comments. Some reviewers noted that state boundaries were limiting, but others commented that the state was too large a unit with which to start. Centers for the Preparation of Educational Personnel (CPEP) integrated the Training Complex and Elementary Models ideas satisfactorily for some reviewers.

Programatic themes and mechanisms

Among the major ideas stated in this plan were levels of criteria, the levels at which Performance-Based Teacher-Education and Certification could occur. Reviewers found this a very useful clarification of the concept of "performance." The focus on the criterion levels as they related to various phases of preservice and in-service teacher-education programs and the idea of curricular intervention were identified as strong aspects of the paper. The criterion levels were seen as providing a strong emphasis on accountability, although the concept of a National Confirmatory System was considered unworkable and unnecessary by a number of reviewers.

Curricular intervention through instructional modules based on Protocol and Training Materials was endorsed by a number of reviewers, as was the idea of university- and field-based laboratory experiences. The funding plan (concentration in one site, then funds moved to a new site) was questioned; some reviewers indicated institutions might not be able to sustain programs under this type of funding plan.

Additional suggestions

This section summarizes many of the ideas which reviewers suggested were overlooked in the abstracts of committee papers. The decision to circulate abstracts rather than full papers was taken in view of the length of the original papers. The brief abstracts, however, could not adequately represent the more considered discussion given to a number of issues in the original papers. As a result, some of the ideas summarized below will have been discussed in individual papers, but are presented here to emphasize the suggestions of the reviewers. The suggestions have been grouped under headings for clarity of presentation.

Teacher education: general structure

Both school and university staffs should be effective teacher trainers.

School districts should be encouraged to see teacher education as an integral part of their responsibilities and programs.

A longer continuum is needed for teacher preparation, with guided, supervised induction.

One alternative is the use of the BA as the entry level for teachers, except for paraprofessionals, with all formal preservice teacher education placed in state supported units in existing school organizations, and provision for increased in-service and postgraduate training in the university.

Both the career concept for teachers and the schooling system are outdated; a human and social development model is needed, not a school context.

Teacher education: content

More attention should be given to the affective aspects of the teacher's behavior.

Teacher education needs to be less standardized and less traditional in emphasis.

Teacher training institutions as we know them should not have a monopoly on teacher training, and, similarly, teacher-education programs should be more open and outside existing structures.

A better integration of theory and practice is needed.

There should be more emphasis on differentiated staffing, and realistic levels of expectation for teacher performance roles.

Career factors

There should be some consideration of the problem of retraining those teachers who have left teaching and then want to return.

With high dropout rates for new teachers, perhaps there should be a briefer training for these teachers and more thorough training for career teachers.

The joint problems of recruitment and selection, in a society which gives few rewards to this profession, are not considered.

Performance based

The push to performance-based preparatory programs runs the danger of reinventing the two-year normal school to train teachers.

Lack of knowledge of the performance-based area should be fully recognized.

We do not have the know-how to prepare fully professionally trained people in performance-based settings.

It must be recognized that competence for teachers exists in a context.

There is the problem of context in developing the Performance-Based Certification at Criterion Levels 1, 2, and 3.

The role of the state department offices of teacher education and certification should be given more attention.

Accountability

A greater emphasis on accountability is needed so that teacher preparation institutions will validate their efforts.

The university faculty must be held accountable.

Teacher education is accountable to the universities and to the teaching profession, and, broadly, to the public. There is a distinction between accountability and responsiveness to other agencies (schools, etc.).

There appears to be a confusion between student performance objectives and teacher-education objectives (training in behavior shaping).

Other factors

Increased capital investment in instructional systems for schools is needed.

More attention should be given to strategies to improve the schools themselves.

Teacher education cannot be reformed without a direction for change in public education.

Training of administrators: A discussion is needed of the role, objectives, and evaluation of school administrators.

Increase research on the educative process.

Planning

Mechanisms are needed to establish community educational needs, then state, regional, and national goals, in terms of student performance objectives.

Any plan for teacher education should seek to encourage the development of the profession.

Teachers should share in decision making. Teachers should have a role in planning the teacher-education program and planning should be more open.

OE goals and sites for projects

There is a lack of attention to USOE goal of improving the quality of education for depressed and minority groups.

It seems that most funding will go to where salaries are already high and where there are good working conditions, rather than to core city areas.

Special attention should be given to problems of large urban school systems that are heavily black.

More emphasis is needed on pupil and societal priorities; priority in sites should be given for disadvantaged minority, social, and ethnic groups.

There is a problem in how to handle the poor, small teacher-education institutions which are continually left out of funding efforts.

Technical support and program development

Strong federal motivation is needed but also as much decentralization as possible.

Cooperative work should be done with NIE, NCERD, and NIH.

More attention should be given to diffusion and installation strategies.

Long-term funding should be used to develop self-supporting mechanisms.

Careful technical assistance should be lent to project sites before starting programs.

Realistic strategies for organizational development are needed.

Organizational and other models should be "tested" before implementing on a large scale.

The number of centers should be smaller in order to permit

careful data-dependent monitoring, and some training centers should train researchers.

More attention should be given to research and confirmation methods so that training centers and training procedures do not develop a "truth" of their own.

Training materials must be data-dependent for modification.

Successful practices should be collected and disseminated.

In summary, it can be noted that many of the comments made by reviewers suggest differences in the views of individuals concerned with teacher education. There appears to be considerable uncertainty about the appropriate criteria for accountability in teacher training. On the one hand, some reviewers would equate the accountability of the schools with accountability in teacher education, i.e., pupil growth is the only valid criterion for teacher education. On the other hand, some reviewers would limit the accountability of teacher education to the preparation of competent teachers, recognizing the criterion of pupil growth as a research variable to guide the selection of content for teacher training curricula.

More basic differences tend to center on a concern over the use of technology, more detailed definitions of skills and competencies, and possible standardization in teacher education, versus the concern that teacher education reflect a "humanistic" and open approach to the education of teachers and pupils. The reconciliation and accommodation of these basic views seem to be necessary conditions for the broad acceptance of any new program proposals and the improvement of teacher education.

TABLE D–2. Ratings of Items

After reading the program descriptions included in the set of materials, rate each of the following items for its potential utility in the redesign of teacher-education programs, in line with OE objectives, e.g., to improve the quality of education for disadvantaged minority, racial, and ethnic groups.

1—Critical item; must be taken into account in designing teacher-education programs
2—
3—*Important item,* but not as high in priority
4—
5—*Of little or no interest* for redesigning teacher education

Item	*Frequency of Ratings Given Each Item* 1	2	3	4	5	NR*
1. Establish a parity group for policy making	16	10	7	2	2	1
2. Apply systems design to teacher-education programs	15	7	12	4	—	—
3. Establish Performance-Based Teacher-Education Programs	23	8	4	—	1	2
4. Use Protocol Materials	7	13	12	4	1	1
5. Use Training Materials	10	14	9	3	2	—
6. Use the Models for Elementary Teacher Education	7	10	13	4	4	—
7. Develop Education Service Districts	4	4	15	8	4	3
8. Develop a data-based feed-back system for performance following training (Micro Confirmatory Systems)	9	14	8	5	2	—
9. Develop measuring "instruments"–knowledge/skills/observation of teaching behaviors	27	6	3	1	1	—
10. Establish Training Complexes, consortium training centers, Parity-based teacher centers	18	7	5	4	2	2
11. Establish extralegal certification systems	6	7	10	8	4	3

* No Response.

TABLE D–2 (*Cont.*)

Item	Frequency of Ratings Given Each Item 1	2	3	4	5	NR*
12. Develop standardized exercises to assess degree of skill in performing classroom tasks	12	6	9	5	5	1
13. Institute state regulated Performance-Based Certification	12	6	13	3	2	2
14. Integrate academic disciplines in teacher-education programs	10	6	12	4	5	1
15. Establish state networks of Centers for Preparation of Educational Personnel	7	7	8	11	2	3
16. Develop National Confirmatory Feedback System	6	10	5	12	4	1
17. Establish "facilitating groups" to provide direction/technical assistance for ideas such as Performance-Based Certification	8	14	10	2	2	2
18. Establish Institutional Training Centers	8	8	9	7	2	4
19. Establish Competency-Based Program Centers	8	9	11	5	3	2
20. Establish national committee for policy recommendations in training educational personnel	9	9	12	4	3	1
21. Modify college/university transcript to reflect profile of teacher competencies	10	12	5	6	3	2
22. Recruit students and adults from minority groups	17	7	7	3	3	1
23. Personalize or individualize teacher training program	26	5	4	1	1	1

Total Number of Responses = 38

SUPPLEMENT 1

ABSTRACTS CIRCULATED BY THE COMMITTEE ON NATIONAL PROGRAM PRIORITIES IN TEACHER EDUCATION MAY 1971

A five-year goal for Training Complexes: Proposal A

The concept of a Training Complex has for its objectives the development of an entity sufficiently independent of existing institutions to take responsibility for the training of the classroom teacher and also establish a system that will interact and be interrelated with those institutions that are concerned with teacher preparation on a continuing basis. The training regimen offered by the Training Complex follows the sequence of teacher preparation in higher education, either undergraduate or the combination of undergraduate and graduate, and precedes the in-service preparation that the schools continually provide the teacher. "Neutral ground," as a concept upon which the Training Complex is built, therefore, does not mean isolation but rather interdependence. "Neutral ground" is suggested as a functional technique for involving both higher education and the schools, and to a certain extent the community and industry, rather than as a means of ignoring them or allowing them to disengage from the teacher training process.

The Training Complex would be staffed by school teachers and college faculties, supplemented by part-time faculty from industry and from the community. The pupils would be youngsters from the schoolroom and school dropouts, adults without schooling, and others for specialized purposes. Starting with small groups, eventually, the trainee would take on full school classes. At the end of from half a year to a year in the Training Complex, the trainee would enter the school system as an intern, the internship to cover the first year as a teacher and under direct control of the school.

College teacher preparation would abandon student internship and would concentrate on the theoretical aspects of learning, on subject-matter specialization, and on career development. The Training Complex could perform a direct function in this preservice phase by conducting career interest workshops for college students interested in teaching. Starting at the freshman and sophomore years, these workshops could serve to identify those students most interested in and suited to teaching careers, then sequentially expose the student to elementary and secondary education, education of the handicapped, etc. In the junior and senior years, workshops could be developed along specialized interest lines and include work in the schools as teaching aides and tutors.

The Complex would also serve as the core for another kind of institutional framework, the Educational Service District.[1] Such Districts are conceived as comprehensive agencies which would include the country's more than 20,000 public school districts and 3,000 higher education institutions and link the schools, universities, community, and industry. The role of the Districts would include placement, paraprofessional recruitment and programing, diffusion of Protocol and Training Materials, curriculum innovation, serving as a locus for community social action programs, and research services.

The development schedule for Training Complexes over a five-year period calls for 100 Training Complexes in Year 1 to 3,000 in operation in Year 5. The cost per Training Complex is estimated at $1.5 million; total cost in Year 5 would be $4.5 billion, and annually thereafter.

A National Model for reform in teacher education: Proposal B

The central theme of the Model is the potential of systems design in education, and the National Model is based on a systems design. A system which establishes controls by providing knowledge about the nature of change and its impact on learners delivers a continual flow of information useful in determining the future course of the various alternatives. Through the operating systems design, the National Model for teacher education serves as a major research instrumentality—to direct continuing reform in teacher education. Reform in teacher education will result from the National Model through the dissemination of both its products and processes (use of systems management, procedures for faculty training, etc.).

Three specific types of activities are required if the National Model is to function effectively. These include: (1) policy making and coordination; (2) implementation of operating instructional programs; and (3) the development and regeneration of Protocol and Training Materials.

It is recommended that policy leadership be provided through

[1] See B. O. Smith, ed., *Teachers for the Real World* (Washington, D.C.: AACTE, 1968), p. 104.

a strong national committee in the area of Competency-Based Teacher Education. The Competency-Based Teacher Education is at the level of the assessment of the performance of the teacher, that the teacher can perform in stated and specified ways. The National Committee functions: to identify continuing national needs; to monitor and disseminate information concerning the effectiveness of Competency-Based Programs as they evolve; to coordinate, through subcommittees, local Competency-Based Program (CBP) Centers; and to make regular reports and recommendations to OE.

The operating instructional programs of the National Model take place within the CBP Centers (see Figure D–1). These Centers include the operating elements of both the Training Complex and the Experimental[2] Models Program. The Experimental Models Program functions within the Training Complex in that the latter is responsible for the interinstitutional cooperation which gives major impetus to operating instructional programs. The Training Complex assumes certain management functions, faculty training within the schools, and final certification of teachers. The option is presented to teachers in preparation to identify the sets of criteria by which their own performance is to be judged and ultimately certified. Schools will be in a position to identify the kinds of performance they want in the teacher they seek. Certification is then a verification of the fact that the teacher can perform as indicated in the records available—that the teacher can perform in stated and specified ways.

Within each CBP Center the Models Program assumes responsibility for teaching/learning activities, management of resources and learners, faculty training on campus, student recruitment and placement, and assessment and research activities.

Each of the CBP Centers is served by the National Program for Protocol and Training Materials. It is recommended that these instructional materials be developed with balance between the need for program variety among CBP Centers and the need to reduce to a minimum duplication of materials which could be equally effective for instructional programs in more than a single center.

Levers for change in teacher education: Proposal C

The levers or mechanisms by which reform in teacher education can be attained come from four sources of power: the school, the community, the university, and professional associations. Reform based solely on the power of any single source is inadequate. The identification of mechanisms which focus the power of all sources on a common objective will be most effective in institutionalizing change.

[2] The term *experimental* implies models in both elementary and secondary education.

Analysis of the policies and practices of the sources of power suggests that changes in teacher education must be accompanied by changes in governance, certification, school and university curricula, school and university curriculum evaluation, and university admissions and school employment practices. Specifically, the levers may be defined as: parity control (governance), legal and extralegal certification, Performance-Based Teacher Education (curricula), a

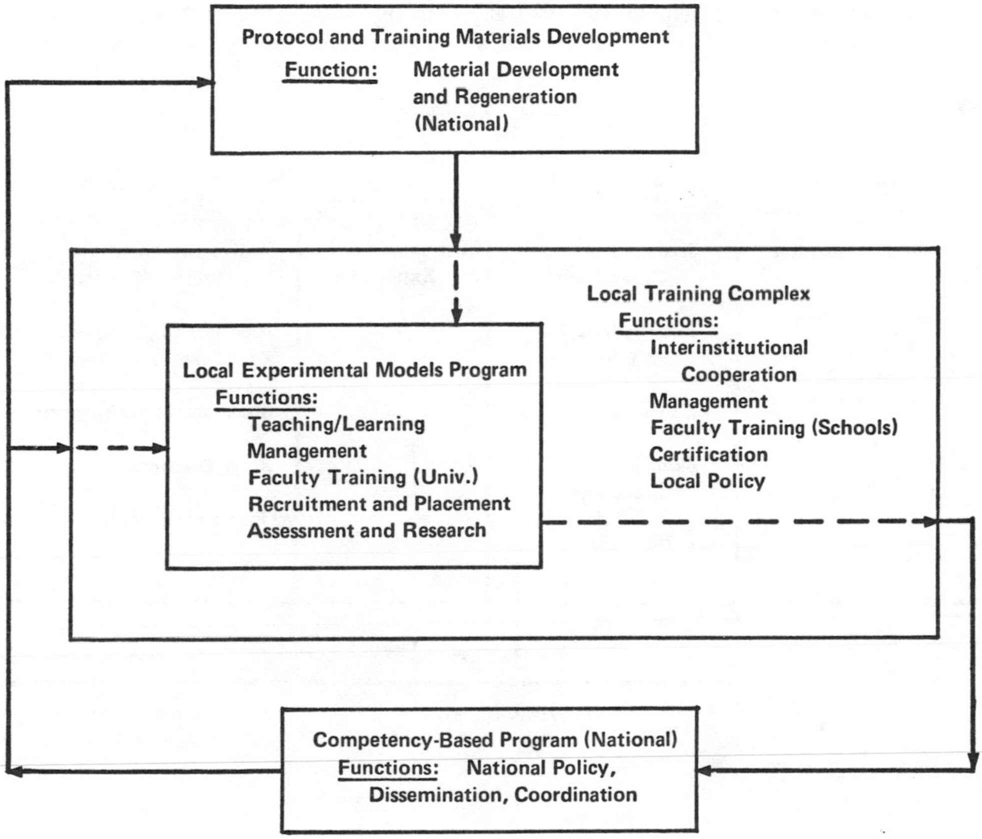

FIGURE D–1. ***Functions of the present BEPD programs within a Competency-Based Program Center.***

Confirmatory Mechanism (curriculum evaluation), and recruitment (admissions and employment). These levers are inserted in the Parity-Based Teacher-Education Program Model, although they could be employed in a variety of teacher training contexts.

The Parity-Based Teacher-Education Program is a school-university model. The governance of the teacher-education program, both the university and school components, is conducted by a parity group. Each aspect of the training program is involved in the Confirmatory System, as indicated in Figure D–2. The Model serves to prepare school personnel to assume the field-based training responsibilities typically associated with methods and curriculum faculty in the university. In addition to training personnel, the role of the education faculty includes that of change or dissemination agent.

The Model assumes that curriculum reform in the schools is an indispensable aspect of teacher training, since the training school must be an effective example of quality. The Model also assumes

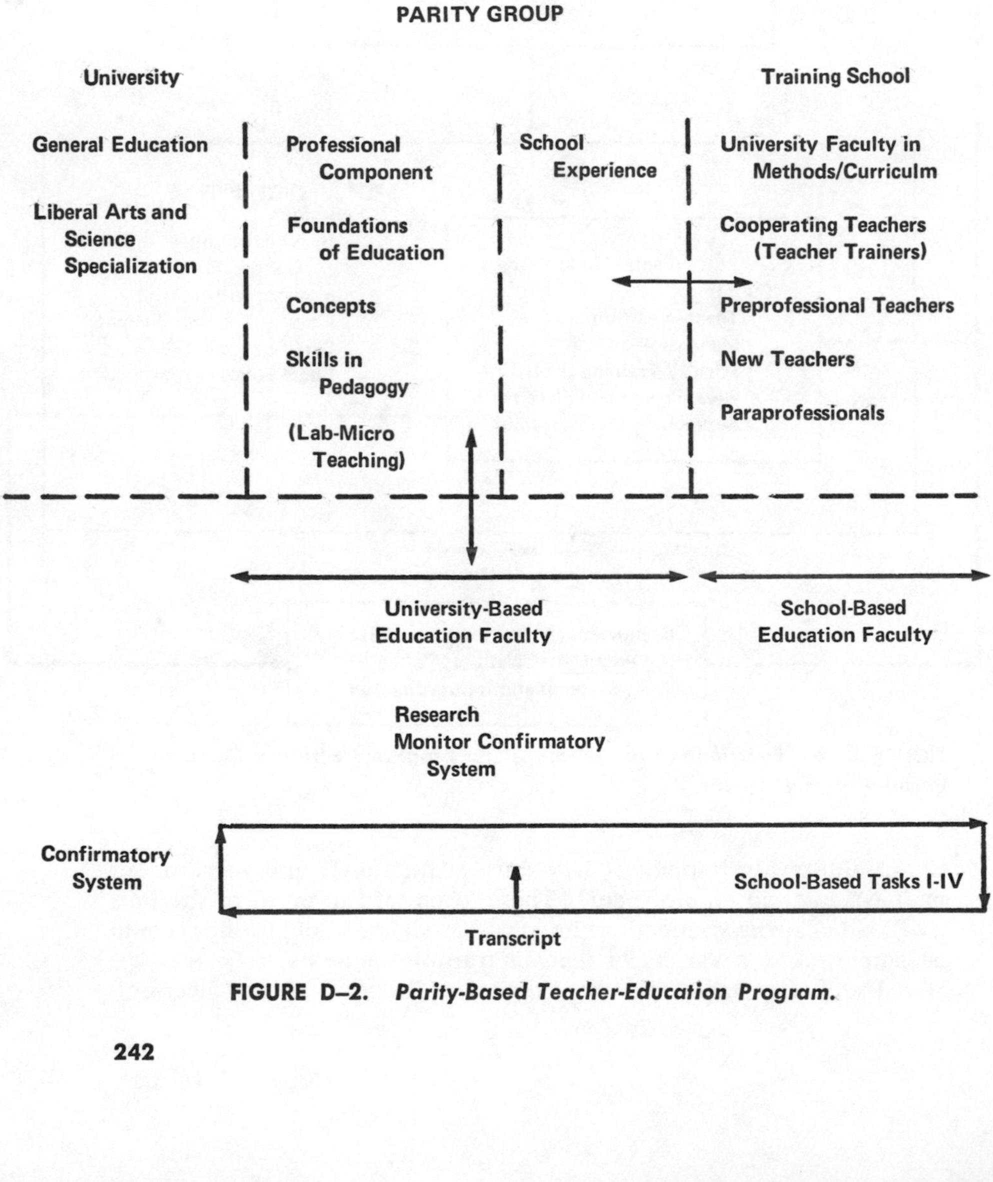

FIGURE D–2. ***Parity-Based Teacher-Education Program.***

that the school-based training component must be defined and concretized by specific, standardized exercises or School-Based Tasks. These Tasks form part of the Confirmatory Mechanism, along with a change in the university transcript to a profile of competencies (Figure D–3).

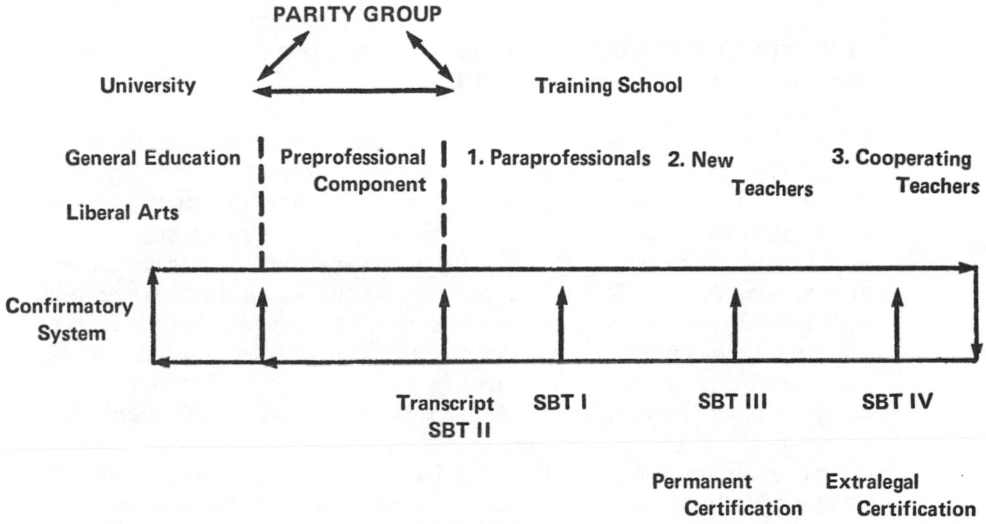

FIGURE D–3. ***Levers for reform.***

The Model assumes that there are two entry points for preparation as teachers: the school route appropriate to the paraprofessional and the university route appropriate to the high school graduate. The program attempts to design the preparation of school-based teacher trainers by using the lever of extralegal certification as a teacher trainer, extending the career line of teachers.

The university faculty would be divided into two groups: One group would be based primarily at the university and concerned with the foundations of education, research relevant to teaching and learning, and monitoring a Confirmatory System. The second group, concerned with methods of instruction and curriculum, would be reassigned and housed in specific schools designated as training schools. The major responsibility of this latter group would be the training of selected numbers of cooperating teachers to train preservice teachers and paraprofessionals, and induct new teachers over a two-to-three-year period. The cooperating teachers, or teacher trainers, would be expected to take over the training responsibility of the school within a three-to-four-year period. Then the education faculty would be transferred to a new school to be designated as a training school, but would provide continuing support and dissemination of new training and curricula materials to the teacher trainers in the developed training school. It is this rotation of education faculty which is the strategy for reforming schools on a systematic basis.

BEPD, NCERD, and teacher education that makes a demonstrable difference: Proposal D

To be effective instruments of educational reform, Educational Personnel Development Programs must do the following: (1) Shift from the current emphasis on providing opportunities to experience, to a performance base. The outcomes of the program must be specified in terms of knowledge, skills, attitudes, sensitivities, competencies, and so on. (2) Shift from a primary focus upon knowledge and skill mastery to one of product development. The production of tangible products involves, for example, the completion of instructional tasks resulting in specified learning outcomes in children and the completion of instructional support tasks resulting in products such as a "unit" of instruction, an examination, a curriculum guide, a course evaluation plan. (3) Shift from a Data-Free to a Data-Dependent Mode of Operation—the collection of data on teacher mastery of skills, knowledges, effectiveness, and relation of these data to the teacher preparation program. (4) Shift from a training function to a research, development, and training function. (5) Shift from an impersonal, instructor-oriented environment to one that is personalized and student oriented. (6) Shift from a college- or university-centered program to a field-centered program. (7) Shift from a narrow decision-making base to one that is broader—comprising schools, university, students, community, and professional groups.

The proposal would establish on a cost-sharing basis illustrative statewide networks (see Figure D–4) of Centers for the Preparation of Educational Personnel (CPEP). Each Center would have the organizational characteristics of a Training Complex and the operational characteristics of one or more of the Elementary Models. The Training Complex provides the context within which skills and competencies can be developed and demonstrated. The design of the CPEP should keep in mind that the Center is seen as an integral part of all teacher-education programs within a state and not simply a demonstration program; that it is a context within which only selected aspects of any given teacher-education program will be conducted; and that it will be developed around exemplary elementary-secondary programs. Centers would identify competencies to be demonstrated at the product level, carry out assessment techniques,

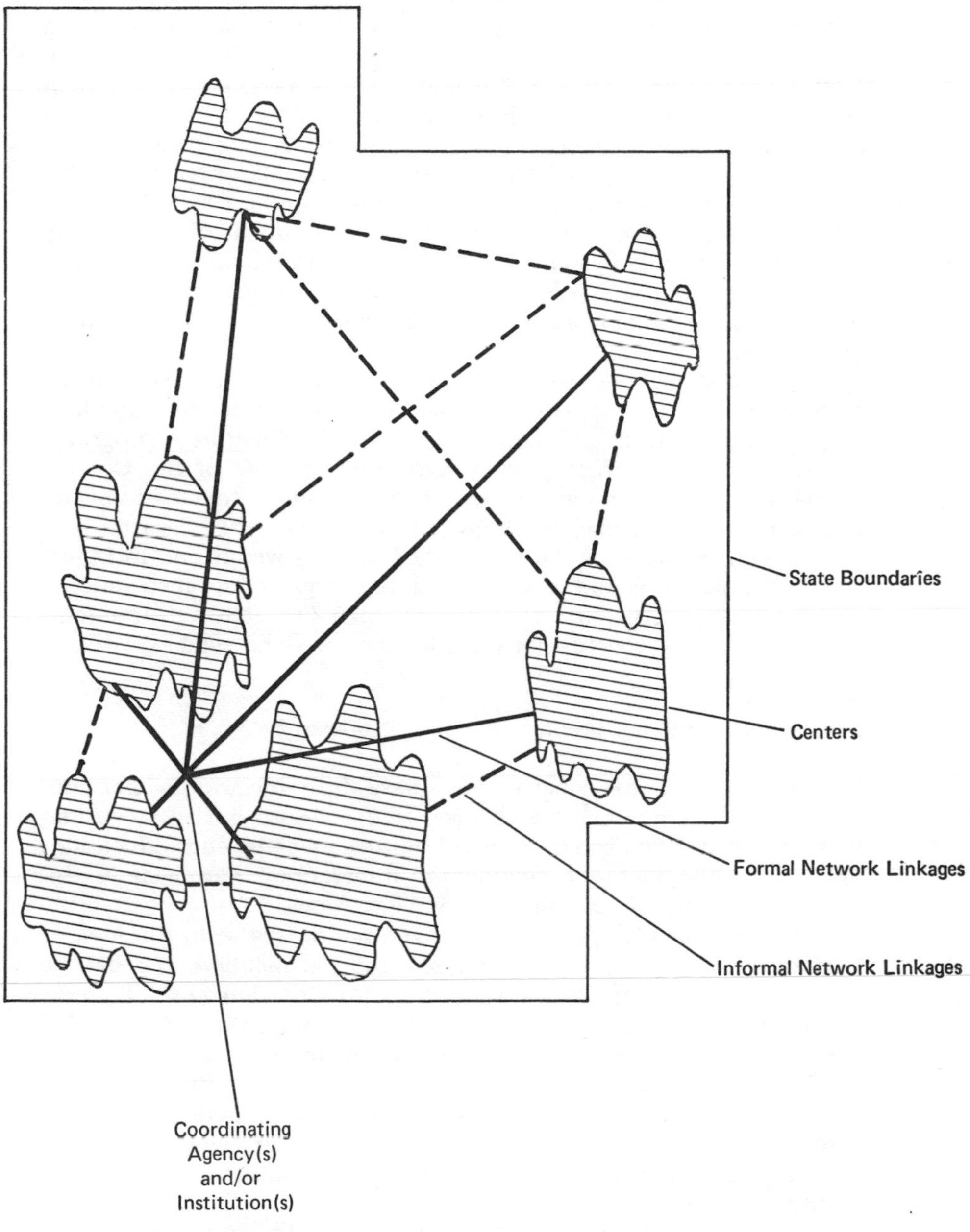

FIGURE D–4. ***A schematic illustration of a statewide network of Centers for the Preparation of Educational Personnel, and the formal and informal linkage mechanisms that would be necessary for it to function effectively.***

and provide training leading to the demonstration of specified competencies. The Center would use Protocol, Training, and Integrating Materials that are available and consonant with the program. It follows that in order for a state to adopt a competency-based plan of certification at the product level, the state must first establish a network of Centers where competency can be demonstrated.

The state is proposed as the primary unit of organization for the network, with regional linkages: certification is a state responsibility and legislation, funding sources, and many institutions may be primarily defined by state boundaries. The rationale for cost-sharing between state and federal governments rests on the importance of education nationally and a need to demonstrate commitment at both levels.

Each statewide network initially funded could serve as a "pilot" state in relation to a region, and assume responsibility for establishing regional linkages, and perhaps establish demonstration programs within other states. Within each state, one or more of the Centers would have the functions of research, development, evaluation, and diffusion. (Other branches of OE could support the research and evaluation functions.) Each network of Centers would link to industry for assistance in the design and development of its instructional and support systems so materials, etc., can be produced and marketed. It is also proposed that diffusion networks be established.

Programmatic themes and mechanisms: Proposal E

The contention in this paper is that successful reform in teacher education should focus on two themes: the development of a nationwide system for confirmation of the outcomes of teacher education; and the development of curriculum intervention strategies to increase the power of teacher-education programs.

The nationwide system for confirmation arises from the idea of Performance-Based Teacher Education and Certification, and can be clearly spelled out in six criterion levels. At Criterion Level 1 observation of teacher performance is linked to pupil outcomes, sampled over a two-year period; at the lowest level, teachers in preparation would demonstrate understanding of concepts and principles. It is proposed that for teacher-education programs Criterion Levels 6 through 3 be operationalized. For a Microconfirmatory Feedback System, the criterion levels can be related to training as shown in Figure D–5.

Figure D–5 shows "Payoff Categories—Skills" in the lower left-hand corner (increased skill in diagnosing pupil status and learning difficulties, giving learning treatments, evaluating, and the instructional support domain). Intersecting the training at various points

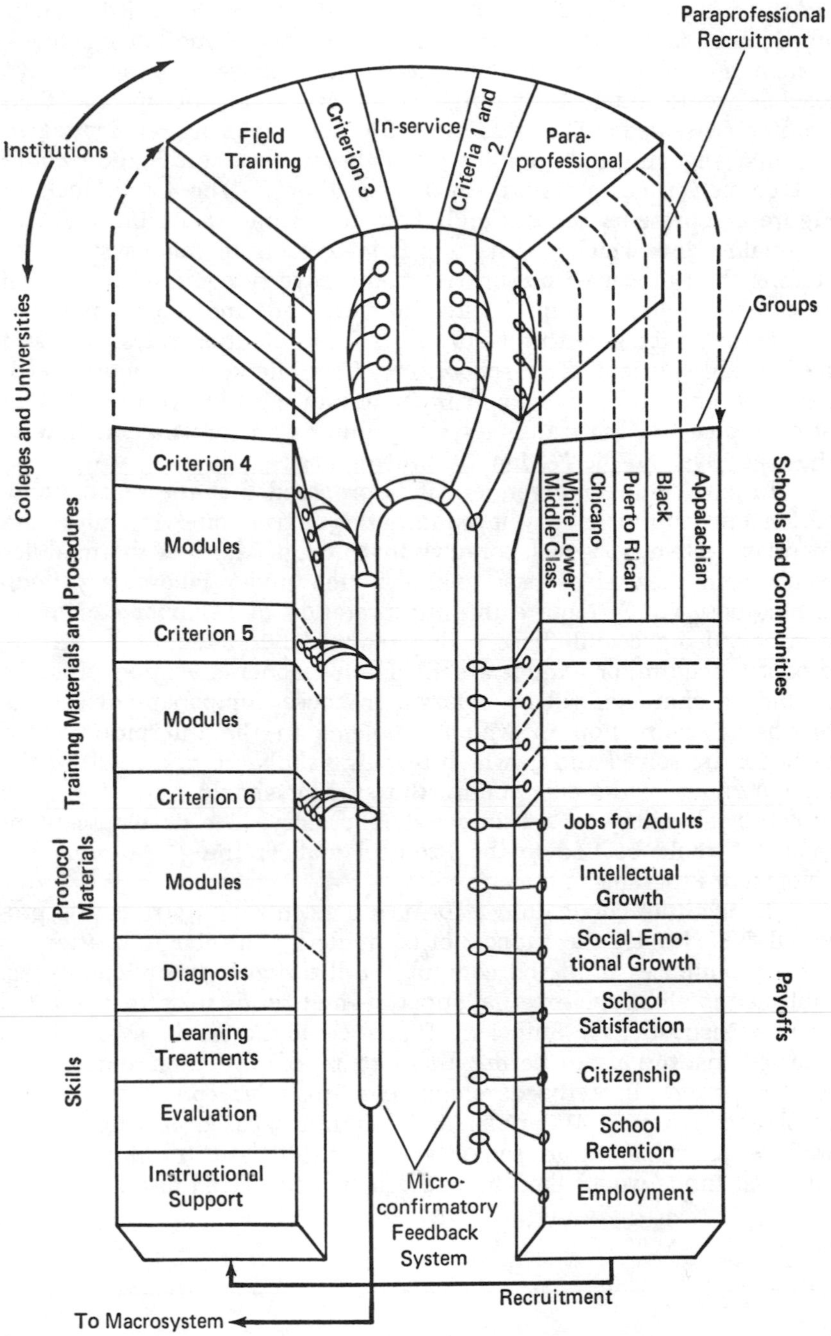

FIGURE D–5. ***Microconfirmatory Feedback System.***

are three levels of performance criteria—Levels 6, 5, and 4. Criterion data at each level are fed into the Microconfirmatory Feedback System. Following the teacher preparatory phase, the prospective teacher would enter a training school or center for specific field training (assessed at Criterion Level 3). After entering regular teaching, and engaging in in-service work, permanent certification could rest on performance criteria at Levels 1 or 2. The final block in Figure 5 represents schools and their communities. At the end are the main items which are payoffs from the entire microsystem, including the number of persons from the poverty community trained as paraprofessionals, pupils' school achievement and social-emotional growth, satisfaction with the schools, school retention rates, rate and type of employment after school, etc. The Microconfirmatory Feedback System functions to confirm performance, to return information at each phase of the training system, and as an information flow to the macrosystem, the National Confirmatory System.

In curriculum intervention, it is proposed that the teacher-education curriculum be developed around instructional modules and incorporate two types of laboratory instruction. Many of the modules would lend themselves best to instruction under laboratory conditions: those which require the interpretation of behavior shown on film or videotape and those which require the student to examine, produce, acquire, or exhibit a skill. Each teacher-education program should be characterized by a large, in-house component of laboratory-based instruction in which problems in the interpretation of behavior are solved and in which teaching skills are practiced. In the later portions of the curriculum, the student should move from the in-house laboratory to a field-based laboratory. The development of modules would be tied to the Protocol and Training Materials Development Programs.

To institute curriculum reform, a concentration strategy is proposed. NSF funded the support of computers and their utilization on college campuses until the computer utilization was sufficiently established to eliminate external support (and funds were then rotated to new institutions). Sufficient funds could be made available to selected institutions to permit them to reorganize their curriculum to incorporate all of the developments—modular construction, Protocol and Training Materials, and laboratory-based instruction, as well as participation in some type of field-based training center. External funds would then be withdrawn and placed elsewhere.

APPENDIX E

A Review of The Power of Competency-Based Teacher Education

Stephen M. Barro

The final report of the Committee on National Program Priorities in Teacher Education (CNPPTE) recommends that the U.S. Office of Education invest heavily in an array of teacher training activities linked by the common theme of "Competency-Based Teacher Education." The underlying premise is that if teachers are trained to exhibit certain specific behaviors ("competencies") in the classroom, they will be more effective in achieving desired educational outcomes (changes in pupil behavior) than teachers trained in the usual way. In order to provide the new form of training, the committee would have USOE support a network of teacher training laboratories, where new and experienced teachers would learn and practice presumably effective classroom behaviors. USOE is also urged to fund development of instructional materials (continuing and expanding programs supported by BEPD in the past) and efforts to construct competency-measuring instruments, both to be used in the training laboratories. In addition, support is requested for a scheme to certify teachers at the "master teacher" level based on demonstrated classroom competency.

My principal reactions to the rationale and program, which I elaborate on below, are as follows:

1. The idea of training teachers in specific classroom behaviors, using behavioral measurement instruments and extensive feedback, seems eminently reasonable and worth testing.
2. Federal funding for such a test would be appropriate since a finding in favor of Competency-Based Teacher Education (CBTE) could translate into higher quality schooling on a national scale.

3. The proposed program does not constitute such a test and, lacking any experimental design or evaluation components, could not possibly provide policy-makers or educators with information on whether Competency-Based Teacher Education "works."
4. Implementation of CBTE on the scale proposed here (100 laboratories, 20,000 teachers per year, etc.) would not be justified until *after* it has been shown that CBTE is (a) effective, and (b) cost-effective relative to other proposed educational reforms.
5. A program with a much more experimental flavor is needed to provide a real test of the power of CBTE. The essential feature of such a program is that it be conducted within the framework of an overall, *a priori* evaluation design. Such a test could be carried out for a fraction of the cost of the program proposed in the Report.
6. An appropriate format for a test of CBTE would be a major, planned-variation experiment in which CBTE and conventional teacher education would be compared and alternative versions of CBTE compared against each other. In particular, it would be desirable to compare versions that feature special training laboratories, audiovisual facilities, and instructional materials, as recommended in the Report, with versions that do not rely on these expensive features.
7. The proposal for Competency-Based Certification at the master-teacher level seems unwarranted given our limited knowledge of what works in the classroom. If adopted, it could undercut efforts to establish teacher accountability for results, to introduce more direct performance incentives for teachers, and to try out a number of other promising educational reforms. At the moment, payment for outcome (pupil performance) rather than for process seems to be a more legitimate way of rewarding teacher proficiency.
8. Both the training and certification parts of the program could lead to premature standardization and codification of "good professional practice" in education, unjustified by empirical research findings. This is just the opposite of what seems to be needed, namely, great diversity in both education and teacher education with major efforts to assess emerging alternatives.

The rationale for Competency-Based Teacher Education

The Report gets off to a strong start with the discussion of Professor Turner's six-level taxonomy of performance criteria. The key point, clearly, is that acceptance of any set of classroom behaviors ("competencies") as the basis for a teacher education curriculum must depend on a demonstration that those behaviors lead to improved educational outcomes. Until that demonstration is provided, as the Report acknowledges, the superiority of CBTE over other training methods remains conjectural—a hypothesis to be tested. Had the implications of this insight been carried to their logical conclusion, I believe that a program substantially different from the one outlined in the Report would have been proposed.

I would go somewhat further in defining the burden of proof to be borne by those who call for heavy public investment in a new form of teacher education. The case for Competency-Based Education, it seems to me, depends on the truth of all three of the following propositions:

A. Teacher behavior, in general, is a significant determinant of educational outcomes ("teaching makes a difference").
B. There are specific teacher behaviors that consistently have positive effects on pupils' learning.
C. Effective classroom behavior (assuming that some are discovered) can be taught to prospective teachers.

Proposition A must be an article of faith to many teacher trainers. But in the face of recent evidence that schooling itself—much less teaching—has not been effective, it can no longer be taken for granted.[1] Moreover, teaching may not provide the best leverage point for qualitative improvement compared, say, to such alternatives as restructured schools and school systems, new roles for parents and communities, and "relevant" curricula. The notion that changes in teacher training can have substantial effects on outcomes should not be taken for granted, but should be treated as something to be determined in the course of a test of CBTE.

Even if teaching does make a difference, it does not follow that there are specific teacher behaviors that are generally desirable. Appropriate teacher behavior may be highly contingent on circumstances, e.g., characteristics of the child, the school setting, the subject matter, and the personality and background of the teacher herself. If these interactions are as important as some researchers now suggest, proposition B may not hold and relatively few universal "competencies" may be discovered.

Finally, even if propositions A and B are both true, it must still be shown that effective classroom behaviors can be taught. It is conceivable, for example, that a teacher's ability to behave in certain desirable ways (e.g., to be accepting and positively reinforcing) depends so strongly on that teacher's own background that little can be done in the course of training to produce such behavior if it is not already compatible with the trainee's personality. If that is true, then much of the emphasis must be shifted from teacher training to teacher selection. If the interaction phenomenon is also important,

[1] See, for example, F. Mosteller and D. P. Moynihan (eds.), *On Equality of Educational Opportunity* (New York: Random House, 1972).

the question of matching teachers to pupils is likely to be as important as anything done in training.

The important thing, it seems to me, is to recognize that the "rationale" part of the report leaves us with a hypothesis to be tested, namely, that a program of Competency-Based Teacher Training will lead to improved educational outcomes for pupils. To make the case for CBTE, it is necessary to demonstrate effectiveness in terms of level one criteria. Then if one wants to go further and recommend *implementation* of operational Competency-Based Training Programs, it is necessary to show also that such programs are *cost-effective;* i.e., that it costs no more to obtain given increments in pupil performance by the teacher training route than it would cost to obtain equivalent gains by other means. A program billed as a "test" of Competency-Based Teacher Education should focus on these effectiveness and cost-effectiveness issues.

The proposed program

Viewed in this light, the most striking feature of the proposed five-year program is that it does not call for a major experiment or evaluation study, but for installation of Competency-Based Teacher Training Programs. The attributes that most clearly reveal the nature of the proposal are the following:

1. *Scale:* It is recommended that USOE fund 100 laboratories capable of training 20,000 teachers per year—much larger numbers than would be needed to determine the effectiveness and cost-effectiveness of Competency-Based Training.
2. *Permanence:* The concept appears to be that the laboratories will continue in operation indefinitely. That is, it has been taken for granted, before a test has been conducted, that they will be useful and successful.
3. *Lack of Experimental Design:* The program is not set up to permit comparisons of CBTE and conventional training or of alternative versions of CBTE. Nothing is said, for example, about experimental control (of programs, curricula, resources, etc.), selection of trainees for CBTE and conventional comparison groups, selection of pupils for practice classrooms, and so forth. These omissions would preclude *ex post* inferences about the impact of the new mode of training.
4. *Lack of Provision for Evaluation:* Nowhere in the proposal is anything said about finding out whether graduates of the CBTE program are, in fact, more effective in obtaining desired educational outcomes than other teachers. This is by far the most serious shortcoming of the recommendations, since without an evaluation very little is likely to be learned from the five-year

multimillion dollar effort about whether CBTE is effective and worth pursuing.[2]

Based on what is said in the Report and appendices, I feel that a properly designed major experiment or evaluation study of CBTE would merit USOE support, but that there is little justification for funding a large-scale operating program at this time. As the Report states repeatedly, little is known about the relationship between teacher behavior and school effectiveness, and there are no validated teacher competencies on which to base a CBTE curriculum. Moreover, no claim is made that CBTE has been tested or found promising even in small experimental settings, or that program developers have succeeded in identifying, operationalizing, and validating sets of desirable teacher behaviors.[3] Therefore, a reformulation of the program as a developmental effort, to be followed up by a serious field experiment or evaluation study, seems to me to be necessary to justify federal funding.

Materials, training labs, and teacher trainers

One characteristic of the proposed program is that it gives heavy emphasis to two elements of the teacher education system—instructional materials and training laboratories—but says little about some other elements that may be important, e.g., the teacher trainers themselves.

It is asserted that special instructional materials must be developed to facilitate "concept and skill attainment" in a Competency-Based Program and that new, specially staffed facilities (training laboratories) must be provided to create opportunities for trainees to practice under real and simulated instructional conditions. However, the logic of a Competency-Based Curriculum does not, in itself,

[2] The proposed program does include an evaluation component, but one aimed solely at assessing program performance at criterion level 3 (i.e., do trainees exhibit supposedly effective behaviors in the classroom?). What is needed is evaluation at criterion level 1—Does the CBTE program lead to improved educational outcomes? Much of the discussion in the Report of level 1 vs. level 3 criteria is confused because of a failure to distinguish between the type of quality control appropriate to an operating program and the type of evaluation needed in an experimental or developmental program where the validity of the basic approach is in doubt.

[3] While preparing this review, I learned that efforts have been underway for some time in a number of stages to develop Competency-Based Curricula and Certification Standards and to introduce competency-based instruction into teacher training programs. It is puzzling that such ongoing activities were not mentioned in the Report since that would have increased the realism of the discussion and given the recommendations greater credibility.

imply that either component is necessary. Since both components are expensive, their inclusion means that the CBTE Program will have to demonstrate considerably greater effectiveness advantages than would otherwise be needed to justify the program's cost.

It would be feasible and desirable as part of a CBTE experiment to assess the contributions of special training laboratories and special materials to the overall objective. That is, as part of the effort to find out whether CBTE is effective an attempt should also be made to find out the degree to which its effectiveness depends on inclusion of the two expensive program components. This implies that variant forms of CBTE should be tested and compared in the course of the program (see next section).

Another point about instructional materials, which relates to my concern about premature standardization, is that the Committee seems to be recommending development of one set of materials and one set of instruments to be used in all 100 training laboratories. This may not be the best strategy, since it rests the whole case for CBTE on a single unproven conception of teacher competencies. Here too, I think that multiple approaches and comparative evaluation are called for in the program design.

I was surprised that virtually nothing was said about teacher trainers in a Report that calls for major restructuring of teacher education. Apparently, the concept is that the same people who provide instruction to teachers now will continue to do so under the new system. Questions: Is there any reason to believe that teacher trainers will behave differently under the new system than they have in the past? Is it not possible that practicing teachers who display the desired competencies (master teachers) would make the best trainers? If nothing else, isn't there a need for some sort of retraining for the teacher educators who will operate the new system and should that not be part of the proposal? The faculties of teacher training institutions are probably the most important resources in the system. It does not seem satisfactory simply to assume that they will automatically adapt to a new way of doing business.

A planned-variation experiment

My own recommendation, based on the information contained in the "rationale" part of the Report and the appendices, would have been that USOE support (1) multiple, parallel efforts to develop Competency-Based Curricula and associated materials and instruments, and (2) a major planned-variation experiment to compare alternative forms of CBTE with conventional teacher training and with each other. What I mean by the latter is something along the lines of the current planned-variation study of Head Start[4] or the recently concluded OEO-sponsored experiment on performance contracting. The main features that would distinguish such a program from the one proposed in the CNPPTE Report are, first, that determination of the costs and effectiveness of CBTE would be the major objective of the effort; second, that alternative ways of providing Competency-Based Training would be compared (the only alternatives provided for in the Report are alternative organizational contexts for training laboratories); and third—and most important—that the entire program would be carried out according to a predetermined evaluation design.

The variations to be tested in such a study would include not only the organizational variations discussed in the committee Report, but also variations in curriculum/materials/instruments arising out of the parallel development projects. Hopefully, some of the variations would depend heavily on audiovisual and other laboratory facilities, as recommended in the Report, while others would not; some would use existing teacher education faculties, and others would use school district or private sector personnel; some would incorporate CBTE into the usual four-year college programs, and others would break away from that mode; and so forth. Thus, comparisons of a number of approaches would be possible.

The key element would be the evaluation design, which would specify how program effectiveness (at criterion level 1) would be determined, how costs would be measured and extrapolated to operating programs, how trainees would be selected for each CBTE program and for conventionally trained comparison groups, how pupils would be selected for the actual classrooms in which trainees would demonstrate effectiveness, and how implementation of specified alternatives during the course of the test would be monitored and ensured.

It should be possible to design a CBTE experiment that would provide information to federal and state policy-makers, school administrators, and teacher educators on the returns to be expected from investments in Competency-Based Teacher Education. Such a program would be much less costly than the 100-site, 20,000-teacher-per-year program called for in the Report. While it is not possible to estimate dollar costs, it seems likely that closer to 20 than 100 sites would be required; not all sites would need major equipment installations; and materials of the type suitable for large-scale distribution would not have to be prepared. The time required would depend on both the current state of the art, which I can not assess from information contained in the Report (e.g., do any fully devel-

[4] For a description, see J. S. Bissell, *Implementation of Planned Variation in Head Start* (report prepared for the Office of Child Development, HEW), National Institute of Child Health and Human Development, April 1971.

oped models already exist?) and on the duration of the training program itself (e.g., one year of CBTE following three years of college or a full four-year competency-oriented program). Once results were in, however, it would be possible to replicate the successful model(s) with minimal delay.

Some economic aspects

Costs

Setting aside other objections for the moment, the Report would benefit substantially from clarification of the cost estimates contained in Tables 2–1 and 2–2. At least the following additional information would be needed to permit an assessment of the estimates and to support any kind of cost-effectiveness analysis:

1. A description of how the proposed CBTE activities fit in with the overall teacher education system. If I understand correctly, the plan is to have trainees spend one year at the labs. But does this year replace a year of the conventional undergraduate program or is it an extra year? If the former, there will be a saving in college costs that should be deducted from the direct cost of CBTE to obtain the net, or incremental, increase in total system costs. Whatever the arrangement, a full system description is needed to facilitate assessments of the cost impact.
2. A description of specific resources requirements, e.g., staff, of program components. The only information I was able to find on the make-up of the training laboratories, for example, was in Professor Cohen's chapter (Chapter 3), where a trainer/trainee ratio of one to five was specified. Other details are lacking. The basic cost assumptions should be spelled out and explained in the body of the Report.
3. A set of year-by-year cost estimates broken down into (a) nonrecurring program development costs, (b) initial investment costs (e.g., nonrecurring costs of setting up training labs), and (c) recurring operating and support costs. Lacking such a breakdown, I was unable to determine such vital information as, for example, the annual operating cost per trainee or the incremental costs of setting up additional training sites. These figures would be essential for any cost-effectiveness analysis.

From a casual inspection of the cost figures, it does not appear that operating costs for the centers have been included; i.e., if 20,000 teachers per year are to be trained in years 4 and 5 of the program, and if the trainer/trainee ratio is 1:5, then a total staff of 4,000 would be required. Allowing only $25,000 per staff member (including overhead), this would come to $100 million per year just for operating costs, as compared with the $114 million estimated for the entire program. The whole question of costs and financing is much in need of clarification.

Cost effectiveness

Obviously, nothing quantitative can be said at this point about the cost-effectiveness of the proposed new mode of training, since its effectiveness has not been tested and an adequate cost analysis has not yet been performed. Nevertheless, it may be useful to say something about the appropriate cost-effectiveness criteria.

In my view, it would be appropriate to appraise the program as part of the entire elementary and secondary educational system. The teacher training component of that system, according to Professor Cohen, costs about $1.5 billion per year, as compared with roughly $45–50 billion for direct operation of the schools. The cost-effectiveness question, in its broadest sense, is what happens to the output of the whole $50 billion system when the cost of the relatively small teacher training component is increased sharply by a shift to CBTE. It is apparent from stating the question this way that there is great potential leverage in investment in teacher training. Since total teacher training costs are only about 3 percent of the total system cost, a very large increment in teacher training expenditures (doubling or tripling) could be justified by an improvement of, say, 5 to 10 percent in average pupil performance. Thus, if it were eventually shown that CBTE consistently produced improvements of that magnitude, a very strong case for the investment called for by the committee would have been made.

It follows from the same formulation that the appropriate alternatives to compare CBTE with are not necessarily teacher training alternatives, but other reforms also aimed at improving outcomes of elementary and secondary education. The question is, how can federal education dollars best be spent?—for Competency-Based Training, for paraprofessionals or specialized instructors, for instructional technology, to promote structural reform (community control, alternative schools, etc.), or what? Here too, however, teacher training enjoys the advantage of leverage, for there is very little that can be done directly in the classroom for the roughly $30 per pupil per year that would be required to double expenditures for teacher training. This, if nothing else, makes it worthwhile to search and to carry out experiments to discover a form of teacher training that translates into improved educational outcomes.

Certification

The proposed "career development" component would establish a number of "educational specialty boards" to certify experienced teachers at the "master teacher" or "teacher trainer" levels on the basis of certain behaviors exhibited in the classroom. The rationale is that this will provide incentives for "staff development" and, presumably, that there will be subsequent beneficial effects on the quality of schooling.

While I am very much in favor of trying out performance incentives for teachers, I would be strongly opposed to implementing this plan. I do not feel that certification on the basis of level 3 criteria (teacher behavior in the classroom) is warranted by current knowledge of relationships between teacher behavior and educational outcomes. More important, I see the possibility of a number of adverse consequences stemming from this type of certification, including interference with innovations and structural reforms that might help to raise the quality of schooling.

The most direct objection, of course, is that none of the teacher behaviors that might be selected as bases for certification have been scientifically shown to be useful or desirable. Therefore, by adopting the proposal, we would be rewarding teachers financially for behaving in ways that may or may not be beneficial to pupils. There is no evidence that the money expended for salary increments would buy better teaching or that teachers who really are effective (in terms of pupil performance) would receive the rewards.

An even worse effect of rewarding teachers for displaying "officially approved" behaviors would be to promote premature standardization of classroom practice. "Correct" behaviors, as defined by certification boards, would be rewarded; deviant approaches to teaching would be discouraged without regard to their actual effects on pupils. It would become that much more difficult to promote the diversity, willingness to experiment, and openness to reform that seem necessary if we are eventually to discover and perfect more effective approaches to schooling.

I am especially concerned that certain promising pathways to reform would be obstructed by the certification proposal. I refer here to the general concept of professional accountability for results and to such specific concomitants as incentive pay (for output), decentralization, community and parent participation in the instructional process, and various types of alternative schools. None of these is compatible with the notions of "good professional practice," educator-determined standards of quality, and insulation of teachers from client evaluation that seem embedded in this proposal.

Fortunately, the "career development" component is not an integral part of the larger proposal for Competency-Based Training. The overall package would be improved, in my opinion, if the certification element were dropped.

Recommendations

To sum up the above arguments, my major recommendations would be as follows:

1. The proposed program should be reformulated as a major planned-variation experiment to determine whether Competency-Based Teacher Education is cost-effective relative to current methods of teacher training and alternative approaches to educational reform.
2. As part of the experiment, the specific approach recommended in the CNPPTE Report, which features special training laboratories and specially developed instructional materials, should be compared with approaches that do not emphasize these features.
3. The proposal for Competency-Based Certification at the master-teacher level should be eliminated from the proposal and should not be adopted until adequate evidence on the relationship between teacher behavior and pupil performance has been obtained.

APPENDIX F

Comments on the Final Report

Ivar Berg

A sociologist whose explorations into the general realm of primary and secondary education have been modest and indirect may speak to the Committee on National Program Priorities in Teacher Education's Final Report only hesitantly. One does not question lightly the formulations and prescriptions of knowledgeable authorities, especially in such vexing areas, containing as many mettlesome problems, as those faced by the committee. There is, in short, a sound presumption that the committee's members, all of whom are experienced, able, and perceptive, know a good deal about the matters to which they address themselves. That they have spoken to these matters in a most authoritative manner is clear.

This "outsider" has an additional difficulty in that he has not read the major papers prepared for BEPD and USOE on each of five programs discussed on pages 102–103 of the Final Report, and upon which the authors of this Report have, in some measure, drawn. It is reasonable to assume that these reports, like the papers written by the committee's own members in earlier stages of the committee's work, contain a good deal of documentation that lends credibility to the Final Report's conclusions.

Having said as much, however, one hastens to add that the Final Report does not offer many hints as to the committee's thoughts about "contextually valid" structure. Much has been said in recent years about the need for systems and organizations to be situationally relevant, but not much by way of specifications appear in the literature on health, educational and political arrangements. There is a fair amount of material on business organizations and the degree to which market conditions, technology, labor market factors, legal requirements, and managerial discretion act as independent variables in determining innumerable organizational characteristics. If, on the one hand, the committee's conclusions are based on similar materials the analyses of which point to specific principles that will maximize the relevance as validity of particular clusters of structures that best serve particular clusters of local "situations" then these same suggestions need to be specified.

If, on the other hand, the committee expects to discover the types of structures best calculated to serve in these situations from the enterprises the Report is endorsing, then a more coherent research model needs to be described than that in the Report.

Furthermore, the implications of the recommendation regarding "contextually valid" structures need to be juxtaposed with the recommendation that "salary increments associated with postcertification training" be utilized in connection with incentives ". . . clearly necessary for those already certified." (p. 12) My data are limited, but they suggest that when salary increments are utilized as an inducement regarding certified teachers, these professionals tend to opt out of education altogether, out of feelings that their postcertification educational exposures qualify them for other jobs, or to opt out of teaching in favor of administrative and related work within the educational apparatus.

One disastrous byproduct of salary ties to postgraduate training is that teacher *training* institutions are thereby crowded with significant numbers of salary-conscious teachers. One serious consequence of such arrangements is that training institutions have no financial inducement to change curricula in accordance with pupil needs and to explore the conditions under which alternate structures, methods, and practices are most appropriate, relevant, and valid. Uncritical use of financial inducements do not reduce the risk that teacher training institutions can go their merry way nearly oblivious to needed reforms in training programs simply because the general demand for these programs' credentials exceeds supply by a wide margin. If postcertification training is limited to pupil performance and pupil performance to salary increments, we are likely to be far better off in straightforward economic terms. I am, in short, decidedly skeptical about the utility of establishing further linkages between salary and postcertification training than already exist in public primary and secondary education.

Although the committee may have addressed the issues, the program described by the Committee does not indicate how teacher training institutions will be encouraged to change those of their offerings that are not "modernized." One may enthusiastically approve of contextually relevant training without being optimistic that training *institutions* will be responsive to incentives offered their postgraduate *students!* Most of the inventive, new, and useful discoveries pertaining to the learning problems of particular pupil populations will not likely be introduced into training programs affecting pre- or postcertified teachers unless the incentives apply to the supplier rather than the school board and teacher "consumers" of postcertification training. It is, after all, teachers—school board employees—who would receive the training recommended in the committee's four-year program.

These points reflect not upon the competence of the Report nor upon its members. It simply highlights some interrelated problems, as do the next several points, that face all task forces obliged to provide guidance for policy makers and those responsible for making the shrewdest investments in the service of youths' needs. These task forces must attend, perforce, to the matter of making their arguments in support of their recommendations as persuasively as possible. The argument that incentives be allocated as suggested in the Report would be significantly reinforced by allusions to evidence showing that it is teachers rather than their training institutions who need remedial exposures. It would be interesting to know, for example, whether the skills and competencies of pupils in statistically matched groups of low-, medium-, and high-income area schools are appreciably different in school districts that *do* and do *not* pay salary increments to their teachers for various postcertification educational achievements. In the absence of such suggestive evidence, and in the face of minimal but suggestive contrary indicators, the argument is tenuously made.

The "master teacher" notion, linked with the use of career ladders for postcertification teachers, is also a most attractive idea, though thought possibly needs to be given to the mechanisms that protect such a ladder from becoming more nominal than real. It is a fact that in other work settings a significant number of job titles are in fact nominal. Over time, titles are simply added to salary increases as the logic of seniority ratings overtakes the original logic of meritocratic arrangements. What was originally intended to help avoid the pitfalls of strict seniority qualifications for promotion and salary tends to become perverted if the job titles do not have *intrinsic relevance to the statuses and obligations of those to whom they are assigned.* "Real" is as "real" does. Would master teachers have significantly different functions? Responsibilities? Obligations? The answer to this question will bear importantly on the "survival value" of the proposed new occupational category.

Discussions of the fruitful notion of career ladders suggests another point to which attention could well be given in the interest of enhancing the Report's persuasiveness. In at least two places references are made to teachers' unions in a manner that some readers could reasonably infer is pejorative. The committee might be better advised to specify the pros and cons of a point, insofar as the cooperation of teachers must be enlisted. Unions are not infrequently valuable allies in connection with changes affecting the work of members; they are never grateful for unilateral determinations of their members' interests or for unilateral determinations of the requirements that affect members. This is not to argue that they will favor *all* proposals, but to suggest that favorable responses to *some* proposals have been forthcoming. The fact is of interest and quite likely of importance *vis-à-vis* the Report's future prospects. Policymakers like to know such things.

In this connection one may reassert the need, mentioned earlier, for giving more careful thought to the matter of incentives and to the matter of career ladders. Both are of strategic interest to members of teacher groups and of great tactical importance to their leaders. Labor-management experience suggests that statements about unions that may be inferred to be negative, in reports calculated to help introduce innovations in an occupational setting, will serve to frustrate union cooperation. More seriously, it is of great importance that salary and career arrangements be worked out cooperatively between employee representatives and their counterparts lest the arrangements be even more easily subverted by time than earlier paragraphs have suggested.

The misgivings of the committee's members about unions, if there are any, ought not reduce a good program's prospects. The present text, in short, gives something of the impression that the various interests of union compel the inventive architect of social change to locate solutions that can best be implemented on a unilateral basis. One would be hard put to deny this inference or justify the assumptions underlying the implication.

Finally, the Report would be far more persuasive if it conveyed to a much greater degree than it now does, the sensitivities and competencies of its formidable members. A recommendation for the expenditure of $75 million for the development of Teacher Laboratories, for example, can only gain from a brief statement of the most proximally related types of ventures now underway in the nation's leading teacher training apparatuses. It is inconceivable that there are not now, in these settings, *some* version of the two or three most hopeful and suggestive clusters of techniques applicable to the solution to the problems that the Teaching Laboratories will be tailored to confront. The amount of the outlay in this particular part of the committee's proposal is of such a magnitude that the matter deserves attention.

If it is the case that *no* modest experimentation of the type implied will support the design, instrumentation, and practices in these laboratories, the thoughtful reader will question whether there is a sufficient base on which to build. If there is such an empirical base then the professionally competent reader will wonder about the committee. And professionals who have experimented with alternatives regarding educational techniques will question its competence.

Perhaps what is inconceivable is true. Intelligent minds have not infrequently been boggled by truths. If, indeed, there are *no* trials underway, no experiments in progress, and *no* lessons reasonably well learned that could underpin the workings of the laboratories recommended, then there is a need for far more attention to be given to the research design that will inform the parallel research efforts proposed in the Report. Having made that suggestion it follows logically that there needs to be some thoughtful consideration of the number of sites to be employed and to an outline of the alternative "variables" that would be manipulated, controlled, and the rest. If the number of sites presently proposed is based on nonscientific criteria, they will, by definition, serve scientific purposes only accidentally.

In the same way, and in conclusion, it is probably incumbent upon the Committee to address itself, if only in a general way, to questions that have been raised by such investigations as the "Coleman Report," on the one hand, and those that have sought to identify the "costs and benefits of educations," on the other.

Consider that many readers will wish to know the committee's assessment of the sources of problems addressed in the Report and its understanding of its recommendation's prospects in solving them. Thus it would be useful to stake out the "cans and can'ts" of successful efforts along the lines proposed by the committee. What evidence is there, stated in a very general sense, regarding the proportion of variance in a problem area to be explained in terms of the competency of teachers? In a society in which cost-effectiveness, as the Report recognizes, has become a watch word expression it is important to meet, if not resolve, the question of returns on the types of investments suggested. A few figures on the relative shares of teacher-related versus other types of problems will reassure sensible readers that thought has been given to what is an issue of growing moment. The committee will not serve its cause well if a friendly critic can point out that with only slightly larger investments in alternative programs one may have far larger effects of the types sought.

Again, one makes these comments "at the margins" in the hope that they may serve to enhance the value of a thoughtful enterprise. I am particularly impressed by the committee's sensitivity to the value of undertaking its proposals in ways that are compatible with research requirements. The return will be *far* greater if the results include detailed research findings regarding each of the parts of the contemplated program.

APPENDIX G

Some Remarks on the Report of the Committee on National Program Priorities in Teacher Education

Robert E. Herriott

In general, I found the Report entitled *The Power of Competency-Based Teacher Education* to be insightful into the limitations of present approaches to teacher education and certification and innovative in proposing a structure for the introduction of a Competency-Based Approach. The discussion that follows is designed to expand upon the Report by emphasizing a sociological perspective on teaching and teacher training. As such, it focuses largely upon the social contexts in which teaching takes place (environmental, organizational, and interorganizational) and on how these contexts can act either to facilitate or inhibit the development of the type of reform proposed in the Report. My remarks are addressed to four major questions that I would like to raise at our forthcoming conference: (1) What should be the relative emphasis upon preservice and in-service training? (2) How will the proposed training laboratories be insulated from domination by current structural arrangements in public education? (3) What are "contextually valid" training laboratories? and (4) Who will develop the knowledge base necessary for valid Competency-Based Certification?

1. *What should be the relative emphasis upon preservice and in-service training?*

Although it acknowledges the importance of Competency-Based Training for both preservice and in-service teachers, the Report concerns itself primarily with the matter of preservice training. If, as many observers predict, the demand for new teachers will decline markedly in the near future, it would seem that the major avenue for the improvement of practice in teaching lies with the two million teachers who are currently active as practitioners rather than with those few teacher-trainees who are likely to gain employment in the near future. But even if the present dire predictions are wrong, from a cost-effectiveness point of view resources spent on experienced teachers are much more likely to yield returns *in the classroom* than those spent on teachers in training, many of whom are likely never to become practitioners.

Although recent national longitudinal data about the subsequent careers of persons who have prepared to be teachers are not available, some picture of the inefficiency of present teacher education can be gleaned from earlier surveys. Charters, for example, has reported that 40 percent of a sample of 546 graduates of the University of Illinois between 1937 and 1947 who were qualified to teach never did.[1] Further, half of those who did teach left the occupation after only two years, and only about 10 percent taught continuously for at least ten years. If the proposed Competency-Based Approach to Teacher Education is to be cost-efficient, some method will be needed either to concentrate upon those persons who are already committed to careers in teaching or on teacher-trainees for whom there is a high probability for a teaching career of great duration.

2. *How will the proposed laboratories be insulated from domination by current structural arrangements in public education?*

As a sociologist I am impressed by the desire expressed in the Report to free teacher training from the constraints imposed by existing distinctions between the organizational settings in which teachers are currently trained (i.e., schools of education) and those in which they are later employed (i.e., public schools). One of the serious limitations of the traditional approach to teacher training has been the division of labor between schools of education and public school systems. As a result, teacher-trainees, after being extensively socialized to behave in ways consistent with the expectations of their trainers, are quickly resocialized (many would say desocialized) once they accept employment as full-time teachers. In general, it is then that the teacher learns the "realities" of teaching as they are revealed by their students, their fellow teachers, and school administrators. Here for the first time the teacher also is influenced by the organizational nature of teaching and learns about authority

[1] W. W. Charters, "Survival in the Profession: A Criterion for Selecting Teacher Trainees," *Journal of Teacher Education* 7 (1956): 253–55.

and reward structures, organizational prestige, career mobility, organizational morale, etc. It is here also that they learn to deal with the realities of sociocultural differences in pupils, and of the largely middle-class orientation of most instructional approaches and curricular materials. Thus, at the time when beginning teachers most need help in relating "theory to practice," they are wholly dependent upon practitioners.

Although the period of internship teaching required of all teacher-trainees has often been defended as a bridge between theory and practice, it is generally far too brief, far too unrealistic, and far too subject to co-optation by the host school to enable the teacher to develop effective strategies for coping with the organizational nature of public school teaching as it will be later encountered "on the job." Thus, it is most encouraging that implicit in at least three of the four new organizational forms proposed in the Report is the creation of an organizational setting distinct from existing structural arrangements in public education that can simulate the conditions of public school teaching and yet be free from the constraints of both traditional teacher education and traditional schooling. However, what is unclear in the Report is how this neutrality can be initiated, implemented, and routinized in such a way that the desired forms of organizational change will take place.

If the proposed laboratories are located on university campuses, staffed primarily by university-oriented personnel, and draw their "live students" primarily from the university community, they will contain few of the realities of public education with which teacher-trainees must later cope. On the other hand, if they are located within local public school systems, staffed primarily by experienced school system personnel, and draw their students primarily from the local community, they will most likely lack the essential conditions for innovativeness. Although neither of these extremes is likely to be proposed by those who respond to the call for training laboratories, forces clearly exist that will attempt to pull fledgling laboratories in both of these two directions, and structural arrangements are needed which will ensure their neutrality.

3. *What are "contextually valid" training laboratories?*

In developing the rationale for a program of Competency-Based Teacher Education, the Report discusses at length (pp. 14–19) the types of "contextually valid" organizational structures that will be necessary in order to link together the resources of universities, school systems, state departments of education, and other relevant agencies concerned with the training, certification, and employment of teachers. As it is used in the Report, the term *contextually valid* implies primarily a political consideration that the training laboratories be related to the needs of the sociocultural areas in which they are to be located.

But there is another definition of *contextually valid* that the Report seems largely to ignore. That is the extent to which the organizational contexts in which teachers are trained and certified are "comparable" to those in which they will later work. One of the limitations of both teacher training and teacher certification in the past has been its lack of differentiation of teachers on grounds other than level (elementary vs. secondary) and subject matter speciality, for there has been a need also to differentiate the training of teachers in terms of the settings in which they will work.

In analyzing the teacher's work setting, Dreeben has distinguished between *external* settings (e.g., the relationship of the school to the community and to the school system of which it is a part) and *internal* settings (e.g., the ecology of the school, the modes by which students, teachers, and administrators are affiliated with it, and the authority relationships that exist within it).[2] Schools vary greatly in terms of these dimensions of their settings. Thus, a fully rationalized approach to Competency-Based Teacher Education would need: (1) to specify in great detail the types of work settings for which it is preparing teachers, (2) to train and evaluate teachers in such settings, (3) to have the capability for placing teachers in such settings once they have been trained and provisionally certified, and (4) periodically review their competency in such settings.

Such a proposal goes far beyond simply differentiating teacher work settings in terms of the characteristics of the pupils to be taught (e.g., urban ghetto, rural poor, black, Spanish-surname, etc.), for it provides as well for such organizational properties of schools as their degree of complexity, centralization, formalization, specialization, etc. It will obviously not be easy to create training and certification contexts that reflect the full range of the organizational reality of American education, but until some effort is made in this direction there is little reason to expect that the behavior that teachers exhibit in meeting level 3 criteria *in their training laboratories* will subsequently be exhibited with regularity when they are employed full time *in real schools.*

4. *Who will develop the knowledge base necessary for valid Competency-Based Certification?*

One of the major contributions of the Report to the analysis of teacher competency is its identification of six distinct criterion levels. By distinguishing among teacher-produced changes in pupil

[2] Robert Dreeben, *The Nature of Teaching* (Glenview, Ill.: Scott, Foresman and Company, 1970).

behavior (levels 1 and 2), teacher behavior in teaching contexts (levels 3 and 4), and teacher behavior in nonteaching contexts (levels 5 and 6), the Report offers a badly needed clarification of a complex issue.

However, although the Report acknowledges the importance of research at levels 1 and 2 as a basis for validating criteria at the other levels, it offers no agenda for the authorization or funding of such research. This is a serious oversight, for, as Rosenshine has recently documented, we currently know almost nothing about those teacher behaviors that produce desirable changes in the behavior of pupils of various types.[3]

If the recent program plans for the various USOE-NCERD–supported R & D efforts in instructional personnel development are any indication of present thrusts in this area, there is little reason to expect that existing research activities will produce new knowledge at criterion levels 1 or 2 during the next few years. In spite of an overall budget in excess of $10 million per year, this area of research by the USOE-supported labs and centers has only two minor programs directed specifically at identifying teacher behaviors that produce desirable changes in pupil behavior. Given the apparent lack of commitment to this problem by USOE, it would seem most unwise for the designers of the training and certification program proposed in the Report to assume that others will develop the knowledge base at levels 1 and 2 essential to the validation of the criteria that they propose to develop and apply at levels 3, 4, 5, and 6.

[3] Barak Rosenshine, *Teaching Behaviours and Student Achievement* (London: National Foundation for Educational Research in England and Wales, 1971).

APPENDIX H

The Power of Competency-Based Teacher Education: A Critique

Michael W. Kirst

Although I am basically sympathetic to and enthusiastic about the concept of Competency-Based Teacher Education, I find my appointed role to be critical of a very bold proposal for its implementation through federal categorical aid. Many of my comments stem from my analyses of past federal programs. The same issues seem to reoccur, and this proposal is fraught with them. Many of the key points I made in a paper "Delivery Systems for Federal Aid to Disadvantaged: Problems and Prospects" I did for the U.S. Senate Select Committee on Equal Educational Opportunity (Volume 17) apply to the CBTE proposal.

The state of the art and federal programming

I reread Stanley Elam's (December, 1971) paper on the CBTE state of the art after reading the Committee's recommendations. I was struck by the many unanswered questions that still plague CBTE on the one hand, and the Committee's proposal for a massive federal program entailing over $114 million and 100 training laboratories, on the other hand. I am sure my old friends in the U.S. Budget Bureau would be skeptical of such a large-scale effort when such basic conceptual questions as these remain unresolved:

1. Who should assess performance or parity, etc.?
2. Are there valid and proven teaching procedures that can consistently change pupil performance?
3. Can performance in the affective domain be assessed as effectively as other domains or mechanical aspects; e.g., do we have

the measurement techniques and instruments to implement CBTE?

4. What criterion should be used—pupil attainment? Teaching skills?

In short, we are very much in a trial-and-error phase from the government's viewpoint, and the magnitude of the proposal could strike many people as grandiose. It might be better strategy to acknowledge frankly the state of the art and insert a greater "contingency" and trial-and-error tone to the document. The larger expenditures would be contingent on successful pilot efforts.

Along this same theme in the document is the complete lack of substantiation of available personnel to implement the proposed activities adequately. Do we have the clinicians to staff one hundred labs? Do we even have the personnel to train them? What about the supply (now and projected) of high-quality researchers to tackle the questions of criterion, assessment of competencies, and instructional material development? This reminds me of the 1965 situation under Title IV of ESEA. Someone made a decision to establish twenty R & D labs when we could barely staff five with high quality. I think a paper on availability of personnel and future training needs, including a subfield analysis of preservice, inservice, bilingual, English, etc., is badly needed.

Any large-scale federal program proposal also needs to acknowledge the complex political system that supports the present teacher training, certification, and in-service structure. We need strategies for getting political leverage to change each part of this system. How will the $114 million change the decision makers in the state departments and shake up the university and NCATE monopoly certification power? Or will the OE program for CBTE be confined to an ancillary supplemental apparatus that can never really challenge the existing interest group alignment? Teachers would still have to get university credits in order to be certified or receive salary increments.

Many jobs and careers are at stake in the present teacher certification and training system. Federal budget analysts need to be convinced of likely political impact on the mainstream of decisions. Very often federal programs become sideshows or showcases while the bulk of business continues on the usual basis. As I view most specific CBTE proposals one of the major losers of power will be the institutions of higher education. They are not likely to give up without a political struggle and this should be discussed in the document. The same can be said for harnessing the potential influence of teacher organizations.

Finally, with regard to the state of the art, is the issue of R & D to identify teacher competencies associated with the *attainment* of educational goals (p. 13)? The R & D need is mentioned but never linked explicitly with program planning (p. 24) or the labs and instruments. In fact, the whole R & D strategy is not coordinated with NIE or any current USOE research instrumentalities. This research need raises the issue of explicit program phasing: can you produce sound instructional materials before you have developed evaluation instruments? Or is evaluation an afterthought following the development of instructional modules? Perhaps the phasing of the five-part program should be elaborated in detail, building on the page 27 narrative. In short, what developments and research must come prior to a large-scale federal effort?

Issues relating to past federal programs

This proposal will confront the old "hard-money–soft-money" issue for the operational stability of the labs. After the federal money phases out, who is going to provide the long-term basic operating cash? I note on page 26 that $75,000,000 is allocated to operating laboratories and field testing. Is this a one-shot $75,000,000, and, if so, how is the lab to be financially sustained? My experience with consortiums of universities or schools (pp. 16–19) is that they are viewed as marginal by the established institutions and one of the first places to take budget cuts after the "soft money" is phased out.

This basic operating money also makes me believe the Specialty Boards are unrealistic. I doubt that the federal government will commit itself to underwriting *forever* $1,500 of a master teacher's salary. The Report is unclear as to whether the federal subsidy is for one year or longer. EPDA programs have a history of extreme instability—the OE cannot stick with any teacher training program more than two years. Will hard-pressed local districts experiencing rapid salary escalations be sympathetic to paying the extra $1,500 after OE changes its priorities or the U.S. Budget Bureau orders a cutback?

I would attempt to divorce the Specialty Board concept from a permanent federal underwrite of teacher salaries. But by doing this one confronts the local district's reluctance to inflate salary costs to a greater extent than they are now. In some differentiated staffing schemes there are some lower-paid staff used in addition to higher-paid master teachers. I note that the career development program and Specialty Boards could be vulnerable to criticism—that it will only drive salary costs up with no design for offsetting reductions.

On pages 11–12 it is stated that "new certification for master-level teachers is best introduced on a national scale outside the framework of state certification." This needs to be carefully worded in order to deflect charges of "federal control" and the political charges the National Teacher Corps encountered. Anything that implies cutting back state prerogatives in an area like teacher certification raises the specter of national standards and will engender opposition from Chief State School Officers and other lobbies to which USOE is particularly sensitive. Unless the state prerogatives are handled very carefully, even the Education Commission of the States could turn from a supporter to an antagonist.

Incentives and guidelines

Given the previously mentioned political problems with national awards or recognition as viable incentive devices, the incentives section on page 12 needs to be expanded. I am not certain what is meant by 6 (a) or (c). Most of the suggested incentives will cost money (particularly salary increments for postcertification training). In short, the incentives are not convincing. The major incentive must be the official sanction of the state government that CBTE is a preferred or sole method for obtaining certification and receiving salary increments. At this stage of our research knowledge on whether teachers make a difference, this is a risky policy.

A number of states will move to statewide bargaining and a statewide teacher salary schedule as the states assume a greater percentage of local school costs. The *Serrano* decision will hasten this trend. Some states already operate under a statewide teacher schedule. States' certification codes now have a large impact on what courses state colleges will offer. This relates to my earlier point that I see no linkage between a political strategy to institutionalize CBTE and the incentive structure. The state role is not explicitly defined anywhere in this report. One incentive system might involve states' paying for advanced training salary increments only if the "courses" have competency-based components. OE responds to state political pressure, particularly the CSSO's. A more explicit state role would strengthen the incentives section as well as neutralize the State Superintendents.

If teachers have a choice of getting salary increments for *either* the existing inservice college courses or competency-based experiences, they will probably most often choose the former because they are easier. The CBTE movement should use the states to abolish payment for the existing college courses or else reward competency-based in-service training at a higher rate. In short, I fear that until CBTE can get a political handle on what states will consider for certification and encourage state colleges to offer, it will remain a supplement to the existing system.

This raises the issue of whether the Report should not address itself to federal *conditions* and priorities for selecting grantees. You mention federal guidelines on page 15 in terms of making them "contextually valid." This is fine, but it provides very little explicit direction for defining federal priorities if more people apply than there are funds available for. Unless the nongovernment planners give some explicit recommendations on federal guidelines, their intent is often emasculated by the OE guideline writers. As you know, grantees react to the implications in the guidelines, not the planning documents. A consistent problem with federal guidelines (even where they encourage local variation) has been to include too many and conflicting objectives. Consequently, priorities do not emerge, or there are so many priorities that scarce resources are spread thin. In sum, the Report should be explicit on the standards for judging good local proposals and what is "contextually valid."

The Report could also be strengthened by some explicit linkage with current OE planning for coordinating and focusing their diverse array of categorical programs. In the past, each federal program has operated largely in isolation of others. The teacher center (or some similar comprehensive planning concept) is designed to concentrate programmatic approaches and overcome the fragmentation of teacher training efforts. There is no reason why a CBTE lab could not be an integral part of a renewal or teacher center. Indeed, the competency concept may provide some substance to the elusive and vague renewal concept. In short, CBTE can be easily integrated with ongoing (new careers, etc.) and planned variation efforts, like Follow Through. The Report shows that CBTE is congruent with general BEPD objectives, but it could also demonstrate linkages with specific BEPD program thrusts.

Parity and conflict

A final issue that could use some elaboration is the parity concept in planning and implementing the efforts. I noticed that Fantini in his 1972 report to the New York "Fleischmann Commission" proposed a year-long statewide discussion of the problem, involving all interested parties, before specific recommendations for CBTE emerged. He seems to assume that the basic value conflicts over CBTE can be resolved by extended deliberation. It is quite possible that no agreement can be reached among all the interested and relevant parties. Community control advocates will not be able to reconcile their views with teacher organizations. Institutions of higher education that have a lot invested in the present academic proficiency system will not be able to agree with competency adherents. Humanists and educational philosophers will be unable to compromise with the measurable skills emphasis of CBTE. Consequently, I can not agree with Fantini's optimistic assumption that:

> An enabling framework would allow the parties of interest in each locality of the state to engage in a cooperative process for problem solving.[1]

The outcome could be either stalemate or a series of compromises that dilute the competency concept beyond recognition. This concern relates to the Report's proposed program planning and coordination committee. This committee should be the body to resolve or rule on these inevitable conflicts. If they are all left to USOE, then the federal guidelines will reflect the conflicting viewpoints and objectives I mentioned earlier. In effect, OE will not choose one or the other conflicting viewpoint, but will incorporate them *all* in the same program—despite the obvious inconsistencies. One solution is an explicit, planned variation program design that would let a plurality of interests implement different forms of CBTE within an experimental framework.

Final observation

Overall, I think that the Report is a good start in urging and outlining a course of federal action. It shows the different components needed to implement CBTE. If we accept the Report's assumptions that teaching practices can make a difference, my problems are more with what is not mentioned. Fantini's proposal outlines the relationships and prerogatives between state policies, regional boards, institutions of higher education, local schools, and community groups. This is not done in this Report, nor are the potential political antagonists dealt with. Finally, the experimental and prototype language used on page 21 is somewhat contradicted by the proposal to spend $114 million and start 100 labs. That is a large-scale program for a concept that may not be amenable to large-scale implementation.

I am reminded of the crash program to install PPBS in the California schools. Now, even the adherents of the effort wonder if the basic conceptual framework is particularly useful in the local school situation. The local schools have reacted by implementing the accounting form of PPBS and not its decision-making substance. I would opt for a slower build-up and a flexible timetable for CBTE. The lead times for basic R & D (measurement, skill categories) and training of leadership personnel might be longer than we would hope.

[1] *Phi Delta Kappan,* April 1972, pp. 476–480.

APPENDIX I

The Power of Competency-Based Teacher Education: Views of a Civil Rights Lawyer

William L. Robinson

Over the years, civil rights organizations have issued many statements and litigated numerous law suits challenging the disparate racial impact resulting from policies adopted with respect to many aspects of the educational process including policies governing: the hiring, assignment, and pay rates of teachers and administrators; the assignments of students; the procedure for determining the amount of funds made available to a school district; and other practices which might determine the availability of equal educational opportunities. The Report discussed herein has some bearing on all of the areas mentioned above. However, the Report appears to have two primary thrusts. First, the Report discusses and recommends an analysis of teacher education for the purpose of determining the specific skills which a teacher must possess in order to affect student behavior in the desired manner. In short, the Report proposes that teacher education be subjected to a "validation study." (In this paper the term *validation* is used in the same sense as it is used by the Equal Employment Opportunity Commission, that is, the process of determining that the standard is effective in selecting persons who will be capable employees or teachers.) Secondly, the Report discusses and recommends that a number of specific steps be taken in order to create the "conditions" for competency based on "validated" teacher education. This paper will focus on the civil rights legal implications of the first principal thrust.

The validation of teacher education

Recent times have witnessed a striking and increasingly successful challenge by civil rights claimants and others against many formal job prerequisites or screening devices that (1) exclude a disproportionate number of minority applicants and (2) are not "job related" or "validated." In *Griggs* v. *Duke Power,* 401 U.S. 424 (1971), the Supreme Court ruled that a company's requirement that employees achieve a given score on one of two employment aptitude tests or possess a high school diploma were racially discriminatory in violation of Title VII of the 1964 Civil Rights Act, 42 U.S.C. §§2000e et seq. The Court essentially based its ruling on the grounds that the requirements had an adverse impact on black employees and had not been validated. Other courts have reached the same result with respect to various other employee screening devices, including requirements that excluded persons with arrest records, a history of wage garnishments, and minimum height and weight requirements. The Equal Employment Opportunity Commission has published a detailed set of *Guidelines on Employee Selection Procedures,* 29 C.F.R. §1607 et seq., which set forth in great detail the validation requirements which that agency will require to demonstrate compliance with Title VII. These guidelines were specifically approved "as expressing the will of Congress" by the Supreme Court in the *Griggs* case. And in the 1972 Civil Rights Act, Congress expanded the coverage of Title VII to include state and local government employees and eliminated the earlier exemption for educational institutions. Thus, it is particularly appropriate that educators now address themselves to the task of validating their educational and certification requirements.

While the civil rights lawyer must generally applaud all genuine efforts at validation such as the one involved in the present Report, the Report requires several words of caution with respect to the specific validation process proposed therein.

The EEOC Guidelines suggest that three kinds of validations might be permissible under Title VII: criterion-related validation, content validity, or construct validity. Criterion-related validation involves the development of the statistical relationship between test performance and work performance as measured by some performance "criterion." The data may be derived from a predictive study in which a sample group is first tested and then put to work for a period of time, or by a "concurrent" study in which present employees are tested. In either case, a statistical evaluation is then made of how well the test predicted actual or eventual work performance. Content validation relies on a subjective comparison between tests and job rather than the development of a statistical correlation. Content validation suffers from the obvious problem that a test may look similar to a job or have "facial validity," but in fact have no genuine validity. The more obscure technique of construct validity refers to the relationship between physical or mental traits, known as *constructs*, needed on the job and a test that measures the same physical or mental traits.

The EEOC and civil rights attorneys invariably prefer the more rigorous and the more reliable criterion-related validation. Content and construct validation should be used only when a statistical study is not possible. Therefore, the Report is commendable in that it seeks to develop a criterion-related validation for teacher education. At the same time the Report in several instances makes reference to techniques commonly associated with content or construct validation. It is imperative that the Report and all follow-up on it strictly maintain a requirement for criterion-related validation and consistently adhere to this single-validation strategy.

The development of performance criteria

The first requirement for criterion-related validation is, of course, the identification of criteria by which to assess the effectiveness of trainee and teacher training programs. The Report identifies six different criterion levels. The chief difference in the criterion levels appears to be in the degree to which the criterion is concerned with the effects of the training program on teacher knowledge and understanding, and the degree to which the criterion level is concerned with the effects of teacher behavior on changes in pupil achievement and well-being. In brief, the necessary criterion for assessing the effectiveness of teacher education programs must properly include both considerations. The Report simply does not measure up to the necessary standards to the extent that it emphasizes criterion number three, which addresses itself to the effects of training on teacher's behavior to the exclusion of a concurrent measurement of its effect on student behavior.

The important first step in developing performance criteria is to perform a proper job analysis by carefully reviewing the job and breaking it down into its component aspects, determining the relative importance of each aspect. In this regard it is important to note that the performance criteria must be developed without regard to the discriminatory attitudes of a union or parent group or other employees.

Sample of subjects

In choosing the sample group for a criterion-related study it is important that the group be "representative of the normal or typical candidate group for the job or jobs in question." However, any improprieties in the employers' recruitment procedures which unnecessarily decrease the numbers of minority applicants must be corrected by the inclusion of a representative group of minority applicants. The sample group should include a representative number of each minority group that constitutes an identifiable factor in the local labor market. It is perhaps permissible to base one's study on a composite sample drawn from several locations. However, it is important to note that teacher knowledge and skills and their effects on pupil behavior may differ substantially in an urban ghetto school with a large black student population as compared with a rural school with a large white Anglo-Saxon Protestant student population. It is imperative that the sample group or groups and the criterion take these possible differences into account.

Certification requirements

As noted in the Report, it is absolutely necessary to be able to measure or test the degree to which a teacher's ability to perform in the training program predicts or coincides with his or her ability to perform the competencies and thereby affect student behavior in an actual classroom situation. In other words, the test must have utility at a statistically relevant level; but this statistical measure alone is not sufficient. A validity study may show test scores to be significantly related to grades received in a training program; and the study may also show that eventual performance on the job bears no relationship to grades received in the training program. The Report recognizes the need for this correlation; however, it is perhaps appropriate to repeat the need to identify performance criteria that take into account the possible differences between necessary teacher competencies and their affect on student behavior in the black ghetto as opposed to a predominantly white rural school district. It should also be noted that the correlation between test score and performance on the job should be shown separately for each minority group included in the sample.

Assuming the correlation identified above, Competency-Based Teacher Education is the appropriate basis for teacher certification. Yet, the Report candidly acknowledges the virtual impossibility of applying the performance-based certification requirements to teachers who presently hold permanent certification. A requirement for "continuing" certification will also be difficult to establish. The basis for opposition to performance-based recertification or continuing certification will vary; but to the civil rights lawyer the problem is chiefly one of assuring that performance-based certification remains validated and is applied fairly to each individual teacher, who also must be guaranteed a meaningful opportunity to protect his rights. Many

Southern school districts, under court order to desegregate, discharged large numbers of long-tenured, well-educated, and "certified" black teachers on the grounds of incompetency. Civil rights groups and teacher associations have successfully challenged many of these firings through court action. However, the vast majority of the incidents went unchallenged. The litigation process is simply too expensive and time consuming to afford meaningful due process protection to the individual teacher.

The Report recognizes the need to ensure fairness in Performance-Based Certification, and the specialty boards are a good beginning. However, specific techniques must be developed that go further to ensure that individual teachers are guaranteed the fairest possible treatment and due process protection.

Conclusion

Validation is a highly technical, relatively uncharted process that is being increasingly required by various governmental agencies. The Report recognizes many of the difficulties in developing performance-based or validated teacher education procedures that must be utilized in order to determine the competencies necessary for performance-based education, and makes a number of specific recommendations which, at least to the layman, appear consistent with developing the conditions necessary for achieving and implementing it.